Serving the Claims of Justice: The Thoughts of Paul B. Henry

Serving the Claims of Justice: The Thoughts of Paul B. Henry

Douglas L. Koopman, ed.

The Paul B. Henry Institute
for the Study of Christianity and Politics

Paul B. Henry Institute, Grand Rapids, MI 49546

Printed in the United States of America

Library of Congress Cataloging-in-Publication Control No. 2001089437

Koopman, Douglas L.
Serving the claims of justice: The thoughts of Paul B. Henry

ISBN 0-9703693-4-4

Contents

Foreword

David S. Broder

Every time I walk from the Capitol South Metro station to the Capitol, I look for a moment at the memorial tree placed alongside the facade of the Cannon House Office Building as a tribute to Paul Henry. I remember the morning it was planted by members of the Michigan delegation, led by the dean of the House, John Dingell, with many others of Paul's admirers – members, staff and reporters – in attendance.

What was it that made this relatively junior member of what was then the minority party in the House so important to so many people? The one-word answer is character. The real explanation is a little more nuanced and complicated, but it does not take you far from the simplest explanation.

The first nuance is the historical context in which Paul Henry served. When he was elected to the House in 1984, Republicans had controlled the White House for twelve of the previous sixteen years. But Democrats had held the House majority for thirty years. Partisan tensions were high, both between the branches and within the House itself. After being intimidated for a time by the popularity of President Reagan, Democrats had found their voice – and their backbone – and were using their muscle in Congress to challenge the man who was now a lame-duck president. House Republicans complained, not without justification, that the rules and procedures were rigged against them, and they adopted guerilla tactics designed to make life as difficult as possible for the domineering Democrats.

The second nuance was institutional. Paul Henry's background as a college professor and scholar made it natural for him to seek a place on the Education and Labor Committee. But, as it happened, that committee was one of the most partisan cockpits in a partisan Congress. The

AFL-CIO had stacked the Democratic side of the committee with reliable friends and the teachers' unions had been particularly assiduous in seeing that allies filled the Democratic chairs. Almost reflexively, some of the most conservative Republicans in the House went onto the committee, in hopes of slowing or tempering its liberal impulses.

It was in this setting that Paul Henry chose to play the political role to which his principles and his personality impelled him – the reasonable man, searching for areas of agreement, rather than trying to score rhetorical or political points.

He was not naïve. He had cut his teeth in Michigan politics, leading the Republican Party in Kent County, a sophisticated constituency which set high standards for its elected officials. He had served in the Michigan house and the Michigan senate and had learned the arts of legislative compromise and craftsmanship.

But none of that fully prepared him for the animosities he found in his committee and on the floor of the House. His refusal to be intimidated by them was what first attracted me to him. Politicians are expected to be upbeat, but many of the Republicans who were Paul Henry's colleagues had had their hopes frustrated and their ideas rejected so many times that they had become embittered or, what was almost worse, indifferent to their legislative duties. Their unspoken attitude was: I'm going to worry about getting reelected, because these blankety-blank Democrats won't let me do anything else up here.

That was never Paul Henry's attitude. He came to Congress to accomplish things, for the people of his district and for the country. And even in that atmosphere of rancid partisanship, he communicated that intention so clearly that colleagues in both parties found themselves responding. He was so straightforward in his motivations and his purposes that others found it embarrassing to be cynical.

The authors in this volume – most of whom knew Paul Henry far longer and more intimately than I did – can explain the sources of his strength of character, and they can recount the many accomplishments of his too-brief career.

Let me offer just one thought. As a political reporter, nothing pains me more than hearing voters say, as many do, "Those politicians – they're all the same." It is not meant as a compliment, because the following sentences make clear that their concept of a politician is somebody who is in it for power, for money, for ego, for partisan advantage, or all of the above. I know that is a caricature, not a portrait, of what some journalists refer to demeaningly as "the political class." But that caricature cannot be effectively rebutted by any reporter's counterclaim. Disabusing that notion will require much greater public familiarity with men and women in public life whose actions and principles give a lie to the cynicism.

Paul Henry was such a man, and this book, I hope, will tell more Americans how fully one politician lived up to the highest standards of public service.

Acknowledgments

Publishing a book takes a great deal of effort by many people, especially an edited volume such as this with ten contributing essayists and more than a score of original sources. At the risk of offending anyone who might be left out, I wish to thank many people for their labors.

First, gratitude goes to the copyright holders of previously published materials, especially Judson Press, for generously allowing republication of many of the selections. Items not referenced as copyrighted were determined to be in the public domain. The Paul B. Henry Collection in the Heritage Hall Archives of the Hekman Library at Calvin College provided most of Henry's writings included herein.

Deep thanks go also to each of the ten individuals who contributed personal essays for their time and effort, and for the substance of what they wrote. These essays reveal important aspects of Paul that could be found in no other documents. Many of Paul's former constituents offered copies of letters he had written to them; thanks go to each one of them.

This project received major funding from the Calvin Center for Christian Scholarship at Calvin College. I want to thank the CCCS Governing Board for its advice and support, and Director James Bratt for his guidance and encouragement. Program Coordinators Donna Romanowski and Amy Bergsma were helpful in organizing many details of the project and keeping me on track. Henry Institute Director Corwin Smidt provided personal and Institute support, and often looked the other way when I was spending time on this project instead of on pressing Institute business. Amy DeVries, Assistant to Calvin's Dean for Instruction, tied up many loose ends as the project neared its completion.

Many people deserve credit for helping in the research and writing stages, particularly my student assistant Ryan Hunt who dedicated his summer of 2000 to this effort. The staff members of the Heritage Hall Archives, especially chief archivist Richard Harms, were a great help. My editor-wife Gayle Boss made my portions of the book read far better than when they left my hands. Jan Ortiz meticulously edited the entire manuscript. The folks at Calvin College Publishing Services, especially Bob Alderink, deserve credit for making the text visually inviting.

Most important, I give thanks to God for the privilege of working for Paul Henry and for the friendship he offered me, if but for too brief a time.

Contributors

David S. Broder David Broder is national political correspondent for The Washington Post. He has earned many journalistic honors, including the Pulitzer Prize in 1973 for distinguished commentary, the White Burkett Miller Presidential Award in 1989, and the prestigious 4th Estate Award from the National Press Foundation in 1990, which also honored him with the Distinguished Contributions to Journalism Award in 1993. He is author and co-author of seven books, including "The System: The American Way of Politics at the Breaking Point" with Washington Post alumnus Haynes Johnson (Little, Brown and Company, 1996) and "Democracy Derailed: Initiative Campaigns and the Power of Money" (Harcourt, 2000).

Mr. Broder received his bachelor's degree and an M.A. in political science from the University of Chicago. He has been a Fellow of the Institute of Politics of the John F. Kennedy School of Government at Harvard University and a Fellow of the Institute of Policy Sciences and Public Affairs at Duke University.

J. Dennis Hastert Elected to the United States House of Representatives in 1986, Speaker of the U.S. House of Representatives Dennis Hastert represents Illinois' 14th Congressional District, a suburban district west of Chicago. Prior to his election as Speaker, Mr. Hastert served as Chief Deputy Majority Whip and as Chairman of the House Government Reform and Oversight Committee's National Security, International Affairs and Criminal Justice Subcommittee.

Prior to his election to Congress, Mr. Hastert served three terms in the Illinois General Assembly. Born on January 2, 1942, Hastert is a 1964 graduate of Wheaton (IL) College and earned his master's degree from Northern Illinois University at DeKalb in 1967.

Mark O. Hatfield Over the course of a political career spanning five decades, Republican Senator Mark Hatfield has distinguished himself as a leading voice for human rights, nuclear disarmament, and the peaceful resolution of international conflicts. He has also been a powerful advocate for domestic social and health issues.

After serving in the Oregon state legislature, Mr. Hatfield became the youngest Secretary of State in Oregon history in 1956, at the age of 34. He was elected Governor of Oregon in 1958 and became the state's first two-term governor in the twentieth century when he was re-elected in 1962. In 1966 he was elected to the United States Senate as an outspoken critic of the war in Vietnam.

Hatfield retired from the Senate in January 1997. Along with service on a number of other boards and commissions, he was appointed by the President to the National Institutes of Health National Advisory Council on Aging, beginning in 1998.

Paul C. Hillegonds A friend and legislative colleague of Paul Henry, Paul Hillegonds served in the Michigan House of Representatives from 1979 to 1996, representing a portion of southwestern Michigan. Mr. Hillegonds served in several party leadership positions during his time in the Michigan legislature, including as Speaker of the Michigan House. Currently, Mr. Hillegonds is the president of Detroit Renaissance, a non-profit organization of business leaders focused on the economic revitalization of the city of Detroit.

Douglas L. Koopman Mr. Koopman is Associate Professor of Political Science at Calvin College and Program Director of the Paul B. Henry Institute for the Study of Christianity and Politics. He is the author of several articles and book chapters, and of "Hostile Takeover: The House Republican Party, 1980-1995" (Rowman and Littlefield, 1996).

Stephen V. Monsma Stephen Monsma holds the Blanche E. Seaver Chair in Social Science at Pepperdine University, Malibu, California. He taught political science at Calvin College from 1967 to 1974 and served in the Michigan legislature from 1974 to 1982. He was a colleague of Paul Henry in Calvin's Political Science Department from 1970 to 1974 and in the Michigan legislature from 1980 to 1982. He is the author of many books and articles, including "When Sacred and Secular Mix: Religious Nonprofit Organizations and Public Money" (Rowman and Littlefield, 1996), and "Pursuing Justice in a Sinful World" (Eerdmans, 1984).

Richard J. Mouw Richard Mouw taught in the Calvin College Philosophy Department for seventeen years, and worked with Paul

Henry to organize the first Calvin Conference on Christianity and Politics in the early 1970s. Dr. Mouw is presently president of Fuller Theological Seminary, where Dr. Henry's father was a founding faculty member. He is the author of several articles and books, including "The Smell of Sawdust: What Evangelicals Can Learn From Their Fundamentalist Heritage" (Zondervan, 2000) and "Uncommon Decency: Christian Civility In An Uncivil World" (InterVarsity Press, 1992).

James M. Penning A Professor of Political Science at Calvin College, James Penning was a friend and colleague of Paul Henry. Author of numerous articles in professional journals, Dr. Penning is also co-author of "Christian Political Action" (CSI Publications, 1984) and co-editor of "Sojourners in the Wilderness: The Christian Right in Comparative Perspective" (Rowman and Littlefield, 1997). He is a former Chair of the Calvin College Political Science Department and has served as Acting Director of the Paul B. Henry Institute for the Study of Christianity and Politics.

David E. Price U.S. Representative David Price, a lifelong educator, represents the Triangle region of North Carolina. First elected in 1986, Mr. Price serves on the House Appropriations and Budget Committees.

Mr. Price studied at Mars Hill College and was a Morehead Scholar at the University of North Carolina at Chapel Hill, from which he earned his B.A. in 1961. He continued his education at Yale University, where he received a Bachelor of Divinity degree (1964) and a Ph.D. in Political Science (1969). Mr. Price taught political science and public policy at Duke University, and is the author of four books on Congress and the American political system. Mr. Price is also a founding member of the Democratic Leadership Council, an organization of moderate Democrats, and served as Executive Director of the North Carolina Democratic Party from 1979 to 1980 and as Chairman from 1983 to 1984. In 1990, Mr. Price was awarded the American Political Science Association's Hubert H. Humphrey Public Service Award.

Fred S. Upton Mr. Upton represents the southwestern corner of Michigan in the U.S. House of Representatives. He was first elected to the House in 1986, and serves as a senior member of the House Commerce Committee.

Mr. Upton grew up in St. Joseph, Michigan, and still makes his home there. As both a community leader in that area and as a representative in Congress, Mr. Upton has focused on local economic development and racial reconciliation. He is a graduate of the University of Michigan.

Gary L. Visscher Gary Visscher graduated from Calvin College with a B.A. in Political Science in 1976. He served as Legislative Assistant to Paul Henry in the Michigan State Senate and in the U.S. Congress and as Professional Staff and Labor Policy Counsel for the Committee on Education and the Workforce. He currently is Vice President, Employee Relations, for the American Iron and Steel Institute in Washington, D.C.

Introduction

For my thoughts are not your thoughts, neither are your ways my ways.
Isaiah 55:8

Only the good die young. Billy Joel

These were two of the lines that played and replayed in my mind on August 3, 1993 as I flew to Grand Rapids, Michigan, with dozens of other congressional staff members and over one hundred members of Congress. We were flying to Michigan to pay our last respects to Representative Paul B. Henry who had died four days earlier, after losing a nine-month battle with brain cancer. Congressional delegations to the funerals of members of Congress are typical, but this one was unusual in two respects. First, the sheer number of politicians of both parties flying to Grand Rapids that day was notable and surprising given the acrimonious congressional atmosphere at the time and Paul's minority party status. Second, this group's affection and respect for Paul, already profound, deepened after participating in a funeral service characterized by obvious and widespread public admiration for Paul. We found ourselves in the midst of a community that not only voted for, but obviously deeply loved, respected, and admired its representative in Congress. What was his special gift, the source of this remarkable display of affection?

This book approaches these questions, but does not attempt to definitively answer them. Rather, it presents evidence about Paul Henry's personal character and political views that provide some insight into the man and some guidelines for future scholars and practitioners interested in politics, especially its moral and religious dimensions. Presented here are three types of documents: a selection of Paul's writings and speeches about Christianity and politics, some of his work on policy questions, and reflective essays by a few of his friends and colleagues in academia and politics.

The broad sketch of Paul Henry's life suggests great promise only partly fulfilled. Paul was born in 1942 to noted theologian Carl F. H. Henry and his wife Ruth. He attended evangelical Wheaton College, spent two years in the Peace Corps, and then completed a doctorate in political science at Duke University. After an eight-year professorial career at Calvin College from 1970 to 1978, Paul Henry served six years in the Michigan legislature and nearly nine years in the U.S. House of Representatives until his untimely death.

Paul Henry began his political career shortly after graduating in 1963 from Wheaton and serving the next two years in the Peace Corps in Liberia and Ethiopia. During graduate school in political science at Duke University from 1965 until 1970, Paul spent two periods of time as a congressional staff person working for Republican representative John Anderson of Illinois. Paul's first congressional job was an entry-level position tasked with the most rudimentary jobs in a congressional office, like answering the telephone and running an oily mimeograph machine to put out weekly newsletters.

But his second stint with Anderson was more challenging. By 1968 Anderson had become chair of the House Republican Conference, the party's third-ranking leadership position. Paul served as acting staff director for the Conference in 1968 and 1969. In this position, Paul oversaw all the details necessary to promote a united, collegial, and well-informed Republican congressional caucus.

In 1970, just after earning his Ph.D., Paul and his family moved to Grand Rapids, Michigan to teach at Calvin. His introduction to Calvin, and its introduction to him, is chronicled in the essays by Richard Mouw and Steve Monsma. Paul soon became involved in practical politics, particularly the Kent County Republican Party and the campaigns of various individuals for office. In 1974, local Republicans were shocked when, in the midst of Watergate, a Democrat was elected to the local congressional seat long held by Gerald Ford, who had resigned to become Richard Nixon's Vice President. In the aftermath of that shock local party leaders recognized the need to project an image of the party as more youthful, energetic, inclusive, and intellectually respectable. Paul was asked, and agreed, to become chair of the Kent County Republican Party.

By then Paul's political skills and ambitions were widely known. In

1975, Michigan's Republican governor, William Milliken, appointed Paul to a seat on the Michigan State Board of Education. In 1978, Paul entered politics full time when he ran for and won an open seat in the Michigan State House of Representatives. In 1982, Paul successfully sought to move up to a seat in the Michigan State Senate.

In the spring of 1984, the incumbent Republican congressman from the Grand Rapids area announced he would not seek reelection. Paul entered and won the race to replace him, obtaining a majority in a multi-candidate Republican primary and receiving sixty-two percent of the vote in the fall general election. He won reelection in 1986, 1988, and 1990, each time receiving more than seventy percent of the vote, usually a higher percentage than any other area candidate did. He was also easily reelected in 1992, two weeks after he was diagnosed with a brain tumor. It was hoped that the surgery that took place only days before the election would lead to recovery. Indeed, for a while Paul did regain his strength, enough so that he was able to attend his swearing-in at the beginning of the 103rd Congress in January, 1993. Gradually, however, he became weaker and died while still holding office on July 31, 1993.

One wonders what political heights Paul Henry might have reached. In Michigan the door was wide open for Paul to attempt a U.S. Senate run in 1994, which would prove to be a banner year for Republicans. And exposure on the national political stage of the mid- and late- 1990s could only have made more attractive Paul Henry's unique integration of character and intelligence.

But such what-ifs are misleading. Despite its early end, Paul's life had a profound effect on many people – students, academic colleagues, fellow public officials, his constituents, and others – through his writing, speaking, and actions in public life. I am one of those persons. I remember the first and last times I talked with Paul Henry. The first was as a young congressional staff member looking for work in early 1984; my boss at that time had announced he was retiring at the end of the year and I needed a new one. I wrote Paul in early May, offering to help in his first campaign for Congress, pointing out my western Michigan roots and Washington, D.C. experience. To my surprise Paul called me back a few days later and hired me to work in that campaign and, later, on his first congressional staff. The last time I talked to Paul was late September of 1992, when I was in the position to hire staff for another new member of Congress. Paul called, promoting one of his own staff as an ideal person around whom to build that new staff. Both these times, and doubtlessly many times between and before, Paul was as intent on helping others as he was in advancing his own goals. Some of the essays included here, especially that by Steve Monsma, Paul's colleague at Calvin in the 1970s and fellow office-holder in the state legislature, note that same characteristic in Paul, unusual in the political arena.

The primary materials in the book are selected articles Paul wrote and speeches he gave that discuss the interplay between Christianity and politics. These twelve items, arranged in three sections, cover a variety of themes. In section one are Paul's earliest writings on Christianity and politics. It contains two items dated before his arrival at Calvin College in 1970, but mostly consists of materials from his Calvin years. A common theme in this section is criticism of evangelicals for a deadened social conscience. Sometimes gently, sometimes pointedly, Paul calls evangelicals to expand their concern beyond individual salvation to wider social problems, particularly racial injustice and poverty.

Section two is knit together by a more practical thread. Most, but not all, of these items were written during Paul's time in public service, first in the state legislature and then in Congress, and focus on practical politics. In some, Paul chides politically conservative Christians about their style of activism, their view on the legitimacy of politics, and the issues on which they focus. Other articles strongly defend America's governmental and political party systems and individuals' involvement in them. Finally, the section includes a wide variety of documents that reveal how Paul thought about and acted on the issues he faced in elected office. These items detail how Paul applied his understanding to daily controversies. There are constituent letters, House floor speeches, short articles or speeches intended for secular audiences, and other texts that show how Paul thought through policy questions. The issues run from the obscure, such as detailed requirements for federal arts funding, to the momentous, such as starting a war in the Persian Gulf. They also run from the intriguing, such as military aid to the Nicaraguan contras to the embarrassing, such as Paul's entanglement in the House bank scandal of the early 1990s.

Four articles present broader and more positive contributions to the integration of Christian faith and politics. "Love, Power and Justice" and "Christian Perspectives on Power Politics," in the first section of the book, were written in the late 1970s when Paul was changing careers from academician to politician. The other two, "Reflections on Evangelical Christianity and Political Action," and "Morality vs. Moralism," were talks given in 1989. These two articles compose section three and represent Paul's most developed thinking on morality and Christian action in politics.

At the end of each of the three major sections are personal essays by Paul's academic and political colleagues. The essays round out and fill in the picture of the remarkable person and engaging personality that was Paul Henry. Academic colleagues such as Richard Mouw and Jim Penning contribute memories from Paul's days at Calvin. Political contemporaries such as Mark Hatfield, Paul Hillegonds, Dennis Hastert, Fred Upton, and David Price relate their impressions of Paul during his time in public service.

Published by the Paul B. Henry Institute for the Study of Christianity and Politics at Calvin College, this book is intended to be both a commemoration and a challenge. It honors a dear friend to many, an unforgettable man who, as a Christian, was a gifted political scientist and politician, successful at both endeavors. As such, it is intended to faithfully illustrate to others how Paul Henry integrated his own vibrant Christian faith with high level public service.

The book is also intended to challenge Christians who are political scholars and practitioners. Paul's views about how faith and public life should interact are certainly within the broad Reformed Christian tradition, but they differ in important ways from other prominent voices in that tradition and, of course, from other Christian views. This book does not intend to settle these disputes, but, following the example Paul gave in his academic and political lives, bring them into the open and address them with thoughtfulness and civility.

Section I: The Challenge of Ambiguity

Section I
The Challenge of Ambiguity

Section one presents some of Paul's thoughts on Christianity and politics during the academic portion of his career. The section starts with two items, "Christians Must Face the Social Crisis Today" and excerpts from *Three Young Laymen: A Symposium*, which date from his time as a doctoral student and instructor at Duke University. The former is a brief article for *Christian Life* magazine. Emphasizing that sin is both individual and institutional, he argues that Christians must seek to redeem both, and calls for an evangelical social and political agenda that focuses on combating racism, poverty, and war. The excerpts from the latter article are Paul's thoughts expressed at an American Baptist Convention symposium on May 13, 1970 in Cincinnati, Ohio. Expanding the themes in the *Christian Life* piece, Paul decries the close tie between conservative theology and conservative social and political views, arguing that the excessive individualism of its theology encourages a simplistic approach to social problems. He urges evangelicals to develop institutional responses to social problems to complement and complete the primary emphasis on individual sin and responsibility.

The third selection, "Evangelical Christianity and the Radical Left," dates from Paul's second year at Calvin. In this chapter of an edited volume Paul evaluates liberal political movements, both the "old left" dominated by democratic socialists and a "new left" influenced by more revolutionary thinkers such as Marx. While the analysis is interesting on its own merits, Paul's major concern is to spur evangelicals to devise a better analysis of and treatment for social problems than that offered by either branch of the left.

These first three articles lay the groundwork for the next four selections, a quartet that presents Paul's most developed thoughts on Christianity and politics before his full-time entry into public service. "Evangelical Social Ethics: A Study in Moral Paralysis" and "Coming out of the Wilderness" are the two meatiest chapters from Paul's 1974 book, *Politics for Evangelicals*.

In "Evangelical Social Ethics" Paul elaborates on the themes of his earliest work. For several reasons, he writes, contemporary evangelicalism has a limited and immature social ethic. First, it has relied too much on Lockean individualism for understanding the nature of humanity and the purpose of political life. Individualism has misdiagnosed sin as merely an individual matter and thus truncated the purpose of politics to merely advance individual goals. A Christian who defines politics so narrowly would likely regard it as sinful. Second, evangelicalism has uncritically accepted Augustine's too-negative view of the state, denying its positive possibilities to promote justice. Third, American evangelicalism has been too pietistic, by which Paul means too emotional and personal. This has led evangelicals to downplay the importance of social problems and evangelicalism's responsibility to address them. Fourth, evangelicalism has promoted its own version of gnosticism in that it has denigrated reason, natural theology and natural revelation, the physical world, and cultural engagement.

In "Coming out of the Wilderness" Paul presents a far more positive alternative view of politics that encourages evangelical engagement. He starts with declaring that fallen humanity and its structures still embody real, if tarnished, images of God. Second, he points out the practical necessity of politics and its potentially good, if currently ambiguous, nature. Politics, in Paul's definition, is an ongoing process of conflict between differing concepts of the good. Politics by nature involves conflict and temporary compromise.

If not entirely good, politics is certainly not completely evil. Christians are obligated, Paul argues, to participate in politics to promote their version or versions of the good. It would be morally wrong to withdraw from politics and leave the definition of the good to non-Christians. Christians should seek political justice that, although difficult to define precisely, is characterized by order, freedom, equality, and participation. Anticipating the charge that Christians should not engage in the moral ambiguity of politics, Paul responds that all of life has a moral ambiguity; it is simply more obvious in political action.

The last two selections, "Love, Power and Justice" and "Christian Perspectives on Power Politics," were written in the late 1970s, near the end of Paul's tenure at Calvin. By this time politically conservative evangelicals had entered electoral and partisan politics encouraged by, and then disenchanted with, Jimmy Carter. The first article worries about the rejection of politics by politically liberal or progressive evangelicals; the second article squares off against the religious right.

In "Love, Power and Justice" Paul criticizes the political thinking of Anabaptists such as Jim Wallis and John Howard Yoder who reject politics because it is not characterized by Christian love. Identifying the limits of politics and defending Christian political engagement, Paul focuses on the terms love and justice and the politically relevant distinctions between them. While love should animate all Christian action, including political action, one cannot expect non-Christians to practice love, nor a largely secular society such as the United States to institute or follow a "politics of love." To do so denies the realities of a pluralistic society.

On the other hand, justice is possible. Paul defines justice as a universal good and an appropriate Christian political objective. Because justice is universal, non-Christians can also seek it, or be convinced to seek it, providing a common goal for politics. But because justice can only be known in concrete reality, a simple claim to justice does no good unless it can be tied to specific conditions in a particular social setting. Different persons have different views about the specific content of justice, so the best one can hope for are procedures and practices that resolve peacefully the conflicting claims of justice. A realistic, but noble, Christian goal for politics is to find just means for resolving the continually conflicting claims of justice.

"Christian Perspectives on Power Politics" comes back to these same themes but targets politically conservative evangelicals. Paul finds that these Christians are seeking to use political power to reward particular behaviors they would define as "righteous" and punish a list of behaviors they would define as "unrighteous." Specifically mentioning race, welfare, and crime, Paul argues that conservative evangelicals are seeking to impose a set of values that derives from a particular social, economic, and cultural position and not from any religious or biblical foundation. White middle class values can explain the conservative evangelical position on crime, for example, far better than biblical quotations. And even if the foundation of their views were biblical, Paul argues that universal claims of justice, not Bible-based beliefs about righteousness, are the appropriate grounds for political action.

Section one concludes with reflections by three people who knew

Paul best during his years at Calvin. First, Steve Monsma reflects upon how he "discovered" Paul, encouraged him to come to Calvin, and built a lifelong friendship. Richard Mouw, now president of Fuller Theological Seminary but then a colleague at Calvin College, describes the circumstances of Paul's arrival at Calvin in the context of the college's changing mission. Jim Penning, first a student and then a colleague of Paul's in Calvin College's political science department, presents vivid snapshots of Paul's engaging personal character.

Christians Must Face the Social Crisis Today

Contemporary America is in the midst of social revolution. Established patterns of relationships between the races, the social classes, individuals, voluntary associations, and the institutions of government are in question and brought into conflict.

It is imperative that Christians consider their responses to the forces of change sweeping our country. They have an obligation to see that the change which does occur is change for the good. And Christians also have a vested interest in their own self-preservation as a viable subculture within American pluralism – a possibility only as we are relevant to the social system as a whole.

If we are to meaningfully address men and women of space age America, we must first establish basic principles from which to operate.

(1) Christianity transcends political ideology. Let us begin by frankly admitting that as a community we are essentially conservative and hesitant to respond to social pressures and social changes. I am not asking that we berate ourselves for this, but simply that we admit it. For while there may be a great deal of blind allegiance within the Christian community to conservative political, economic and social causes in our nation, nonetheless we are an essentially white, Anglicized, middle-class people who would be expected to have a natural disposition toward conservatism.

I would not suggest that the corrective for this would be an equally binding commitment to a form of doctrinaire political or economic liberalism. Rather, the message of the Gospel transcends all political persuasions and ideologies. Our first obligation is simply to begin to think critically about the great social issues of the day and to relate

---

"Christians Must Face the Social Crisis Today," *Christian Life*, January 1970, 16-17. Obtained from the Paul B. Henry Collection in the Heritage Hall Archives of the Hekman Library at Calvin College.

them to the message of the Gospel. Only then can we begin to consider our response to these issues as Christians.

(2) Christian political action must achieve a balance between *individual* and *institutional* response to social questions. The *means* by which Christians can best achieve commonly agreed upon *ends* within the social sector continue within the church. Few Christians are in favor of the perpetuation of poverty, the waging of war, or the reversion to racism. Yet they have difficulty coming to agreement on how to deal with these evils.

Some argue that the structures of society can be changed only as individuals composing the society are changed. They believe we must minister to individuals responsible for the perpetuation of these evils. Others argue that man is a social being, and that the institutions of government were established by God to be instruments of justice in the social order. Therefore, they assert that the instruments of the state ought to be mobilized against social injustice.

Could it not be that *both* positions contain truth? The Christian who stresses only the individual means to meeting social problems forsakes his opportunity to be a minister of the Gospel within the institutional framework of human society. Another Christian who stresses only the institutional methods neglects the fact that the social order is a macrocosm of the individuals of which it is composed. Each of these Christians is failing to recognize the *total* mission of the Church to minister to the totality of human life.

In light of these guidelines, let us examine several of the problems facing our nation today.

Racism – Granted that we are only beginning to become fully conscious of the role of racism in the context of our own past and present history, what ought Christians to do today in facing this problem? Let us begin by confessing our own guilt and sin in having both consciously and unconsciously participated in this evil. And let us acknowledge that we are dealing not only with a *legal* issue brought to the fore by Supreme Court decisions and legislative actions, but with a *moral* issue stemming from the fact that all men are essentially equal in terms of their integral humanity before the Creator God.

An evolutionist might be able to justify racism by appealing to the principle of "survival of the fittest." A Marxist might be able to justify racism by juxtaposing racial groups against the economic development of their societies. But for the Christian there is only the model of the

Christ who died for all men. There can be no East or West, no black or white.

Government as a divine instrument of justice has an obligation to prohibit outward discrimination because of race. The Church must reconcile the races by presenting the good news that Christ died for all men, and that before God all men are equal.

The Church could begin by healing racial divisions within its own body. White and black congregations should begin to schedule times of worship together. And Christian families of differing color ought to fellowship together in their homes. Together, they will be able to discuss and devise means by which Christian individuals and the institutional Church can address themselves to the issue of race in contemporary America.

Poverty – This issue goes beyond the rhetoric of the Great Society and the organizational abilities of the government's Office of Economic Opportunity. Christians know that poverty is a spiritual as well as a material phenomenon. A man can be rich in material possessions, and still suffer poverty of the spirit. Likewise, a man can be poor in material wealth, but still have a life of richness.

Just as we have an obligation to see that all men are presented with the good news of Christ which makes a spiritually rich life possible, so we have an obligation to see that all men have the opportunity to provide for themselves a life suitable to the fact of their humanity. Our obligations derive from the fact that we are Christians and that we are human. Christ himself linked those two roles when He reminded us that the mere giving of a cup of water to a thirsty man could be seen as a good work done to the glory of God.

Again, both the government and the Church have obligations in this area. For too long, however, the Church has berated government action in this field while doing too little on its own. It has been estimated that if every church were to "adopt" four families on government poverty rolls in this country, those rolls could be completely eliminated.

War – The plaque the astronauts placed on the moon – "We Came in Peace for All Mankind" – is a reminder that peace has been the irresistible dream of mankind throughout history. Indeed, some 2,000 years ago Christ himself was hailed as the Prince of Peace by the angels who sang in chorus: "Peace on earth, good will toward men."

Christ called the peacemakers blessed. We must relate the Christian message to peace in a world whose history is mapped by conflict and war. We must learn to join in the prayer of St. Francis of Assisi, "Lord, make me an instrument of thy peace." Peace is something more than the mere absence of war. It is a quality bestowed as a gift from God. Nonetheless, that does not excuse the fact that we often allow our criticisms of the weaknesses of international peace-keeping mechanisms to degenerate into sheer cynicism. Nor does it excuse our moral callousness to a situation such as that in Biafra today, or our measuring of "progress" in the Vietnam war by "kill-ratios" of human death and destruction.

While we can make no claims as to our abilities to usher in an era of peace and understanding, we are called to be agents of peace. We are just beginning to realize that ours is a violent nation. We can begin to address this problem by facing it first in our own homes. By learning to forgive and live at peace with those closest to us, we can go beyond to forgive and live with people of our community, our nation, and our world.

There are no easy answers as to how Christians can face social issues in today's world. Nonetheless, we must get Christian perspectives from which to view these problems. Let us pray that God will give us the wisdom to go beyond talking about the problems and actually get to the place of doing something.

Three Young Laymen: A Symposium

I have been asked to share with you some of my thoughts as a young, theologically conservative layman, regarding the problem of relating Christian commitment to contemporary social and political concerns. I want to begin by stressing the fact of my own commitment to theological conservatism and the evangelical perspective – the so-called fundamentals of orthodox Christianity – for the simple reason that some of what I have to say may sound somewhat unusual considering the theological perspective by which it is informed. And while some of my remarks will be critical, I am hoping that they will be received in the same spirit of concern with which they are offered.

As a young evangelical I am repeatedly distraught by the *de facto* alliance of conservative Protestantism with conservative social and political interests. Surely, the conservative's emphasis upon man as a fallen creature raises questions as to what he can look for in man's social relations. Surely, the conservative's belief that the eschaton will be ushered in only at the command of God raises questions as to what man himself can do to reform the fundamental structures of society. And surely, the conservative's belief that the primary concern of the Gospel is a spiritual one raises questions as to the priorities the Church should assign to social and political concerns.

However, at the same time, the conservative's concern with preserving the importance it assigns to the distinctive revelation given to us in Jesus Christ has often been at the expense of neglecting the general revelation given to all men by God by virtue of their humanity. In the conservative's obsession with defending the supernatural and revelatory basis of the

---

Remarks delivered on May 13, 1970, in Cincinnati, Ohio, as part of a three-person panel presentation and printed in *Three Young Laymen: A Symposium*. Reprinted by permission from The Ministers and Missionaries Benefit Board of the American Baptist Convention.

Christian faith – an obsession, I might add, which I believe partially justified considering the circumstances in which orthodox Christianity has found itself in the modern era – it has neglected many of the indicators God has given to man through nature and reason, particularly as they apply to the sphere of man's social and political relations. And just as surely as the revelatory basis of our faith informs us of the limitations of man's existence, so the rational basis of our being informs us of certain potentialities of man's existence. Conservatism must learn to find a middle road between the boundaries of potentiality and limitation, and it must learn to speak positively as well as negatively regarding the aspirations of men toward social justice.

While conservative theology has spent its efforts in defending the historic creeds and the uniqueness of the Christian revelation, it has at the same time been unfaithful to those creeds and that revelation. For while we conservatives are particularly adept and vocal in our exegesis of John 3:16, we are equally inept and silent in our refusal to take seriously the teachings of the Prophets Isaiah, Hosea, Amos, and Micah, or the New Testament teachings in the books of James and 1st John. While we have taken seriously the Biblical imperatives pertaining to man's relationship to God, we have neglected the Biblical imperatives pertaining to man's relationship to his fellow man. The Biblical message taken in its entirety refuses to separate these concerns, and insofar as we insist on doing so, we are no less heretical than others who upset this balance in other directions. While we have sought to protect our doctrinal orthodoxy, we have at the same time lost any claim to ethical orthodoxy.

As a young evangelical, I object to the simplistic solutions offered for our social and political problems by conservatives who glibly state that these problems would be solved if men would just turn their lives to Christ. It is an error, I suggest, to argue that justification before God produces a sort of instant sanctification between men in their social relations. This leads to an ideological utopianism just as illusory as those stemming from the denial of man's nature as sinner.

The sad fact is that commitment to Christ has not solved the racial problem in the "Bible belt." Commitment to Christ did not stop the Christians in Indonesia from massacring the Moslems and Communists in their own country after the overthrow of Sukarno. And commitment to Christ gives us no easy solutions to the problems of pollution, inflation, depression, or full employment.

There is a need for serious thinking on these complicated issues which is informed by Christian perspectives. Evangelicals have failed in this regard and rationalized their failures by asserting that they have been so busy defending the integrity of the supernaturalist and revelatory criteria of the Christian faith that they have not had time for such mundane considerations. A generation ago we admitted this fact when one conservative scholar wrote of *The Uneasy Conscience of Modern Fundamentalism.*[1] The relative lack of action by conservative Protestantism in the thirty years since that book appeared has done little, it seems to me, to set that conscience aright.

As a young evangelical, I object to the ethical schizophrenia which insists on bifurcating personal ethics from social ethics. This schizophrenia proceeds on the assumption that the social order can be changed only insofar as the men composing it are themselves changed. Taken to its logical conclusion, this leads to a sort of religious anarchism which questions whether the state can do *anything* in the quest for the political good. And this, in turn, questions the Biblical concept of the state having been ordained by God as an instrument for the procurement of justice in the relations between men.

This ethical schizophrenia in conservative theology limits its ability to deal critically with problems stemming from man's collective and associative relations. Granted that legislation cannot change the motivational basis of human behavior, nonetheless it can in part change the outward forms of human behavior. No law can make a white man love a black man; but law can at least require that a white man treat the black man according to a minimal and relative criterion of justice. No law can give man the fundamental dignity which is potentially his as a son of God; but law can at least lift him above the animal existence of poverty or the stultifying ignorance of illiteracy.

These three factors – the uncritical alliance of conservative Protestantism with conservative social and political interests, the simplistic and/or non-existent attention given social and political problems, and the emphasis given to solely personal as opposed to social problems – have been bothersome to me individually, and to many of my younger colleagues in conservative circles. For it adds to the difficulty of maintaining a conservative theological apologetic which is, due to historical circumstance, already defensive in its orientation. What then can be done to rectify this situation?

The *de facto* alliance between evangelicalism and political and social conservatism will not be improved by an equally uncritical *de facto* alliance with political and social liberalism. The Gospel stands in judgment on all of man's activities and aspirations, and its demands always transcend the political and social propositions which man as sinner and self-interested participant offers as solutions to his political and social problems. The early Jewish Christians at Jerusalem undoubtedly had different opinions concerning the virtues of the Roman Empire than did the early Gentile Christians at Rome. It is not as important for us to reach a new basis of consensus as to how the Gospel relates to the social and political order as it is to recognize that the Gospel stands in judgment on any and all of man's attempts to come to definite solutions to this problem.

Evangelicals must guard against their own particular brand of utopianism which offers Christ as an easy answer to social and political problems. We are guilty of having accused many of our more liberal Christian colleagues of utopianism as they have sought ethical applications of Christianity within the social order while we ourselves have failed to recognize that we, too, have been utopian in suggesting that a type of Gnostic withdrawal from the world provided an answer to the problems stemming from social and political relations.

Evangelicals must learn to function at the institutional and collective level of social existence as well as at the individual and personal level of social existence. That is not to say that we can completely institutionalize our response to the social needs of men; but it does say that we cannot get about our business in this area of Christian responsibility without formal organization and cooperation any less than we can do so in our responsibilities pertaining to evangelism and foreign missions. As more and more of our lives become collectivized and interdependent, and as we as individuals are caught in the institutional and collective expression of man's sinful nature, so our responses to that situation demand institutional and collectivized efforts as we as individuals seek to redress the wrongs and injustices of our society.

Finally, let me state that my criticisms and suggestions have been directed primarily at the conservative theological community because that is the community with which I identify and whose peculiarities I know most closely. I recognize, of course, that one of the reasons for our positions on these matters has been in response to what we consider to be the errors of theological liberalism. But I think we should have the humility to admit that many of the errors of theological liberalism in these areas have stemmed from what they have considered to be the errors of our position. Neither group, liberal or conservative, can justify itself before God on the basis of arguing that it was provoked by the other.

We are called to be God's disciples in the world, and neither ethical orthodoxy nor dogmatic orthodoxy can stand alone as a basis from which this discipleship can proceed. The task of reconciliation and discipleship must begin with the Church, however, before the Church presumptively marches into the world. And with this in mind, it would be appropriate to remember the words of James when he wrote: "Therefore confess your sins to one another, and pray for one another, that you may be healed. The prayer of a righteous man has great power in its effects."

NOTE

1. The author of this book was Paul's father Carl F. H. Henry. *The Uneasy Conscience of Modern Fundamentalism* was published in 1947 by Wm. B. Eerdmans of Grand Rapids, Michigan.

Evangelical Christianity and the Radical Left

The Shift to the Left

From the perspective of the 1970s, it is almost impossible to remember that America entered the decade of the 1960s with such hope and confidence in the innate strength of its society and governmental institutions that the Eisenhower Administration took the unprecedented step of establishing a commission for the purpose of defining future goals for the nation – as if all the present needs and aspirations of the American people had been met![1] In 1962 the noted political scientist Clinton Rossiter confidently predicted a shift to the right in American politics. In his volume entitled *Conservatism in America* he stated:

> It scarcely seems the part of bravery to foresee no sudden check or reversal in the glacial shift of the American intellect toward the Center and beyond toward the Right. Trustworthy observers have pointed to several developments that are making it easier for ordinary men to live as conservatives and thus for extraordinary men to think as conservatives.[2]

Only two years later, Senator Barry Goldwater – whose best-selling volume, *The Conscience of a Conservative*, helped make him a national political figure – won the 1964 Republican nomination for President of the United States.[3]

Yet, while the establishment was confident that American society was entering a period of quiet building and mending, there were already signs that the country in fact was approaching a time for scatter-

First published in *The Cross and the Flag*, eds. Robert Clouse, Robert Linder, Richard Pierard (Carol Stream, Illinois: Creation House), 1972. Obtained from the Paul B. Henry Collection in the Heritage Hall Archives of the Hekman Library at Calvin College.

ing stones and tearing down. In 1962 Michael Harrington's book *The Other America* brought to the nation's attention that significant numbers of Americans lived in poverty, passed by and unnoticed by the silent majority of the technocratic society.[4] In 1963 Martin Luther King began the much-publicized protest demonstrations in Birmingham, Alabama, against discrimination, and the march on Washington in quest of a new civil rights law. In the fall of 1964 the "Free Speech Movement" broke out on the Berkeley campus of the University of California – and millions of American TV viewers were stunned to hear student leaders shouting four-letter obscenities at their professors and administrators. In 1965 the Johnson Administration escalated American military involvement in the Vietnam War on the pretext that United States naval vessels had been attacked without provocation on the high seas by North Vietnamese troops. And by 1966 such groups as the Students for a Democratic Society (SDS) and the Student Nonviolent Coordinating Committee (SNCC) – originally gradualist and democratic in their approach to social and political problems – were advocating violence as the only means of redirecting and reordering the priorities of American society.

Thus a decade which began in quietness and self-confidence ended in violence and despair. Black uprisings occurred in the nation's largest cities. Students closed down some of the most prestigious educational institutions. Political leaders fell to the assassin's bullet. The national political conventions were forced to meet behind barbed wire fences, protected by thousands of National Guard troops. Thousands of young and old joined together to march on the Pentagon to protest the Vietnam War. Coalitions of students, blacks, and the poor attempted to move the American political system radically to the left, using violence when they thought it necessary to their cause. Within the decade, political life had become so radically polarized that it was commonplace to hear political analysts speak of the crisis of confidence in American society and government.

As the radicals on the left mounted their attacks on the American system, political observers disagreed as to both its meaning and its importance. Was the radical left being blown out of all proportion by the news media? Was it calling America back to its stated ideals of liberty and equality for all, or was it nothing more than the impassioned and undisciplined outbursts of Bohemian students, socialist intellectuals, and militant blacks? Some were convinced that the radical left was secretly being financed and organized by Communist groups. Others maintained that the movement represented a dramatic reawakening of the national conscience to the issues of war, race, and poverty. To some, the radical left represented the rejection of traditional Western standards of civility – it was associated with the rising drug culture, a communal life-style, and acid rock. Yet others saw in the far left a rising idealism which in its refusal to compromise with the materialism, militarism, and racism of American culture was nothing less than the beginning of a new historical consciousness which would eventually bring about "the greening of America."

But for all of the talk and concern over the radical left in the 1960s, it seems to have dissipated just as quickly and mysteriously as it appeared. By 1972 the radical left had become passé in most academic and political circles. Civic discussion groups and polite cocktail party conversation substituted *Jesus Christ Superstar* for Abbie Hoffman, the wage-price freeze for the Vietnam War. On the campuses, black arm bands were replaced by little yellow buttons with smiling faces serving to remind everyone that "happy days are here again."

While there has been an apparent return to normalcy in American politics, the suspicion still lurks that it is much too early to become sanguine about the future of American politics – the sounds of silence may indeed be ominous. Nonetheless, the present calm in American politics affords an opportunity to confront several lingering questions regarding the meaning and importance of the radical left. What were its origins? What were its goals? How can Christians minister to the needs of the people associated with this movement? And perhaps most important of all, what can Christians learn from the radical left?

The Radical Left: New or Old?

Two of the questions most often asked about the rise of the radical left are (1) what are its origins? and (2) in what ways is it distinguishable from the "old left?" Most scholars agree that both the intellectual and institutional roots of the new left can be traced rather directly to mainline liberalism, that is, the old left. And most also believe that distinct differences have arisen between the two. Thus, to answer these questions it is necessary first of all to deal briefly with the characteristic features of mainline political liberalism.

THE OLD LEFT

Political liberalism had its origins in the seventeenth and eighteenth centuries. In some respects, it can be regarded as a political counterpart to the Reformation. Just as the Protestant Reformers opposed the institutional authority of the Roman Catholic Church and asserted the priesthood of the individual believer, so the political liberals argued against the arbitrary powers of the state, contending that it should have no governing powers other than those specifically contracted to it by individuals. Political liberalism was concerned with the problem of maximizing the freedom of all individuals who, the liberals asserted, had inalienable rights to life, liberty, and the enjoyment of their personal property. The American Revolution in 1776 was justified on the basis of these very concepts.

Most of the political liberals believed that man's nature was basically rational and good. If the arbitrary use of state power could be eliminated, individuals would use their freedom to live rationally and virtuously. For this reason, they generally argued that the government which governs best is that which governs at least – for such a government would allow individuals to maximize their individual freedoms, and hence to maximize their capacity for a rational and virtuous life.

In the nineteenth and twentieth centuries, however, the thinking of political liberals changed concerning the proper role of government and the problem of maximizing human freedom. The growth of huge urban centers and a highly industrialized economy created a society in which individuals became increasingly interdependent. And while a person might enjoy a great deal of political freedom, it was apparent that technology was rapidly diminishing the number of individuals who could ever attain economic and social self-sufficiency in such a society. The industrial revolution had transformed a society of independent and self-sufficient artisans, farmers, and laborers into one of increasingly interdependent and intertwined businesses and corporations. If the economic and social freedoms of individuals were to be protected, argued the new political liberals, the conduct of these large corporate enterprises must to some degree be limited and directed by the state. Thus, the later liberalism took a much more positive attitude toward the role of the state than did the liberalism of the seventeenth and eighteenth centuries.[5]

The modern liberals often disagreed as to what extent state intervention was necessary to protect the social and economic welfare of individuals. Some maintained that a minimal amount of regulation of large corporate organizations was adequate. Others argued along more socialistic lines, believing the state should seek outright ownership and management of major corporate entities or should assume the obligation of guaranteeing national standards of economic and social well-being for its people – in other words, a welfare state.

Although modem liberals believed in an expanded role for the state, they did not reject concepts of limited government or individual human rights. To the contrary, they argued that by expanding the role of the government into social and economic spheres, limited government and human rights were strengthened against the threats of radical revolutionaries who questioned the ability of democratic institutions to respond to the rising political, economic, and social aspirations of the working classes. This is illustrated dramatically by Franklin Roosevelt's famous "Four Freedoms" speech which linked such social and economic freedoms as freedom from fear and hunger with the more traditional political ones of religion and expression.

It is important that the modern liberals and democratic socialists described above be distinguished from the revolutionary socialists such as Karl Marx. The revolutionary socialists – which are generally designated as Communists today – contend that violent overthrow of established authority is the only means of achieving desired social, economic, and political reforms. Thus, the distinction between the democratic left and the nondemocratic left is a crucial one.

Although early and later liberalism disagreed regarding the proper extent of state intervention in the social order, they continued to agree on several fundamental points. First, they both believed in maximizing human freedom. The emphasis in all liberal political movements has been on freedom as opposed to order, liberty as opposed to authority. Second, both early and later liberalism tended to believe that the nature of man was basically good. When men did bad things, it was because they had been affected negatively by a bad environment. To make men good, all that was necessary was to remove the inequities and artificial restraints which interfered with man's natural tendency to goodness.

These basic tenets of liberalism are important to remember at this point for two reasons. First, as will be demonstrated shortly, the new left movement of the 1960s had its roots in this intellectual tradition. While the new left often seemed utopian and anarchical to outside observers, it was in fact based solidly on the presuppositions of the old left. Second, it is important to stress that political liberalism as an ideology has several, serious shortcomings from the perspective of the Christian faith.

First, Christians must reject the liberal concept of freedom as nothing more than the absence of restraint. Freedom, for the Christian, involves the spiritual dimension of man's being as well as his relationship to the state and society. Thus, it involves the acceptance of legitimate authority as well as the rejection of illegitimate claims to authority. The Christian insists that freedom is not just an abstract possession, but rather, it must have some purpose. He asks not only if a man is free, but for what he wishes to use his freedom.

Second, the Christian rejects the liberal concept that the human condition is fundamentally a product of the environment. Liberals have tended to believe that improvement in the political community in which men live will result in the substantial modification of the conduct of individuals within that community. While not rejecting the obvious truth that human behavior is in part conditioned by the environment, Christians recognize that the root cause of evil in society rests with man's rejection of God. Therefore, the primary social problem for the Christian is not how social institutions can be modified to change human behavior, but rather how individuals themselves can be changed by God, and how changed individuals can effect change in the larger social order.

These two basic weaknesses in the liberal ideology help in understanding not only the origins of the new left, but its increasing radicalization as well. The new left began by asking why the old left had failed. The answer – at least initially – was that the principles of the old left had not been applied with enough vigor and consistency. But as the institutions of political liberalism proved increasingly unable to solve the problems which the new left sought to attack, it began to turn away from the old left ideology and to create a counterculture with a new set of values all its own.

The New Left

The goal of the old left was the gradualist reform of the social, economic, and governmental institutions of society through democratic means aimed at insuring that all Americans would share justly in the wealth of a highly industrialized society. It sought further to manage the economy to protect individuals from the vagaries of economic depression. And it was concerned — although to a much lesser extent — with securing full human rights for minority groups within society.

The new left, however, was upset with the complacency of what it contended had become "establishment liberalism." This was particularly true of college and university students across the country who had become involved in the civil rights struggle. Student political activism, which has played such a key role in the new left, is nothing new in American history.[6] In 1823, for example, half of the Harvard senior class was expelled for becoming involved in disruptive activity. Between 1886 and 1930 the Student Christian Volunteer Movement was an active force on scores of American campuses — generating interest in causes as diverse as foreign missions, educational reform, and women's liberation. It was in the 1930s, however, that the first signs of organized *radical* student political activity began to appear on American campuses. Groups such as the Student League for Industrial Democracy and the Intercollegiate Disarmament Council supported socialist causes on many campuses.

However, the student activism of the new left was qualitatively different from previous experiences. First, by the 1960s the numbers of college and university students in the United States had grown phenomenally. Students outnumbered farmers, for example, and recognized that if they organized as a visible political pressure group they could as students directly affect American politics in much the same way as farmers influence politics through the American Farm Bureau Federation or the National Farmers Union.

Second, as the absolute size of the student population grew, it increasingly took on its own identity as an independent force in American politics and dissociated itself from the sponsoring organizations in the adult community. For example, until 1966 the Students for a Democratic Society was tied to the League for Industrial Democracy and received substantial financial support not only from the league but from national labor unions such as the United Auto Workers. But as the collegiate groups declared independence from their adult sponsors, they were freed of many of the restraints which had applied to earlier attempts at youthful political activism.

Third, student political involvement prior to the 1960s had generally been educationally oriented. Traditionally, such groups concerned themselves with sponsoring campus forums and lectures. In the new decade, however, they turned to direct political action. It is as a part of the history of student attempts at political activism – and the continuing failures which the young encountered – that the growth of the new left can best be described.

In 1954 the Supreme Court rendered its decision declaring segregation in public education to be in violation of the law of the land. In the next few years students organized to protest noncompliance with the Supreme Court decision in the Southern states. At this point the students were rather obviously operating within the system to make it work – not against the system in an effort to destroy it. The Student Nonviolent Coordinating Committee (SNCC) was established to help fund and coordinate student activism in the civil rights struggle, and among other things SNCC sought to have the Justice Department provide protection for students who were involved in civil rights activities in the South. However, the federal government refused to provide protection for the young people, despite the fact that in many cases they were victims of mistreatment by local law enforcement officials in the South. Hence, a crisis of confidence developed between the students actively involved in the civil rights struggle and the government which refused to use its powers to insure enforcement of the law.

In the summer of 1964 several hundred college and university students participated in a SNCC-sponsored voter-registration drive in the Mississippi Delta, a region where blacks substantially outnumber whites. When they returned to their campuses in the fall, they told of being beaten by local whites and of having seen abysmally shocking poverty. They elicited sympathy among fellow students and tried to raise money to continue the project on a permanent basis. Several campuses sought to restrict these fundraising activities by the students. Attempts at such restriction often resulted in open confrontation between students and campus administrators, and the students insisted that their rights to free speech and political association were being violated. The most dramatic instance of this emergence of the Free Speech Movement (FSM) occurred at Berkeley. The result was that the students, who were already beginning to doubt the integrity of the government's commitment to the civil rights struggle, now began to question the educational establishment as well. Mario Savio at Berkeley led the FSM students into dramatic confrontations with campus authorities which received extensive television coverage. The most significant action was a campus sit-in which resulted in the arrest of over eight hundred students.

As this was occurring, American military involvement in Vietnam was escalating. In the summer of 1964 President Lyndon B. Johnson secured the passage of the "Gulf of Tonkin Resolution," and by the end of the year there were over 23,000 American military personnel assigned to the Vietnam War. The students were the first to see the futility and morally questionable character of the conflict in Indochina; and as the number of troops in Vietnam climbed to over half a million, the students helped to spark a national debate on American policies there. In 1965 the first "March on Washington" in connection with the war drew 20,000 demonstrators, most of whom were students. In 1967 the "March on the Pentagon" attracted at least 55,000 persons, and brief clashes between police and demonstrators took place.

As students became increasingly disillusioned with the political system and with their academic communities, the New Left began to develop into a counterculture, as exemplified by the "hippie" and "yippie" movements. The use of drugs, the growth of long hair, and the development of the underground press became the characteristics of the youth revolt. Before long, the student movement divided between more moderate students (who could best be described as old left liberals) and those who began to develop a new rationale for political action. The assassinations of Martin Luther King, Jr., and Robert Kennedy in 1968 – both heroes of the young – together with the brutalities of the Chicago police at the 1968 Democratic National Convention caused increasing strain within the student movement. It then began to fragment over the issues. This splintering of the new left soon led to its dissipation, and since 1969 there has been a steady decrease in the visibility and vocalness of the radical movement.

In discussing the new left, it is extremely difficult to delineate its "characteristic features." The new left is more of a movement than an ideology. It was more a reaction to a series of historical events experienced by the student community in the 1960s than the product of any fixed ideology. Initially, the momentum of the new left was inspired by the ideological rhetoric of the old left; but as the students involved in the new left became disillusioned with establishment liberalism in the government and the academic community, they began to react strongly to crises as they encountered them. The popular press has tended to label the new left with terms such as *revolutionary, romantic, idealistic, utopian, and anarchic,* but these generalizations fail to withstand the scrutiny of empirical study.[7]

One of the most important documents to emerge from the literature of the new left which delineates an ideology for the movement is "The Port Huron Statement" issued by the SDS in 1962.[8] This document summarizes the objectives of the new left activists and the goals to which they are committed. Attacking the persistence of racism within the country and the military arms race between nations, the document indicts the educational establishment for its institutional complicity in perpetuating these problems:

> Making values explicit – an initial task in establishing alternatives – is an activity that has been devalued and corrupted.... Our professors and administrators sacrifice controversy to public relations; their curriculums change more slowly than the living events of the world; their skills and silence are purchased by investors in the arms race; passion is called unscholastic.[9]

The Port Huron Statement decries not only the institutional failures of American society, but points to the need for a renewed sense of community in a highly technocratic and bureaucratized world. It expresses the longing for a society in which people will participate more directly in making decisions affecting their lives ("participatory democracy") and one in which personal values will regain their rightful place against the culture of technology.

Ironically, as the new left became increasingly radical, it became less political, for students gradually began to lose faith in the political process itself. Charles Reich's best-selling book *The Greening of America* captures the spirit of the new left in the late 1960s when he writes:

> There is a revolution coming. It will not be like revolutions of the past. It will originate with the individual and with culture, and it will change the political structure only as its final act. It will not require violence to succeed, and it cannot be successfully resisted by violence. It is now spreading with amazing rapidity, and already our laws, institutions, and social structure are changing in consequence. It promises a higher reason, a more human community, and a new and liberated individual. Its ultimate creation will be a new and enduring wholeness and beauty – a renewed relationship of man to himself, to other men, to society, to nature, and to the land.[10]

Thus, while the new left began in the liberal tradition of seeking to change men by changing their institutions, it moved during its brief lifetime to a position which in some ways is like a basically Christian approach to social problems; that is, one first concentrates on transforming individuals, and then institutions will change as a consequence. However, Reich's statement omits a crucial factor – man's need to renew his relationship with God as the means by which all other relationships can be transformed. Instead of turning to God, the new left turned to drugs and mystery religions. When these failed, many of the disillusioned new left radicals sought refuge in the Jesus movement![11]

Positive Contribution of the New Left

Because the new left has been associated so closely with the drug counterculture, and its leaders have at times advocated revolutionary tactics, most Americans were more concerned with how the new left could best be controlled and dissipated rather than with its message to society. Now that the threat of the new left has subsided, it is possible to make a more objective evaluation of the movement.

First, the new left has quickened the conscience of America in regard to social injustices such as poverty, racism, and militarism. The left's expression of moral outrage about these issues can be compared to the prophetic utterances of Amos and Hosea who condemned the calloused conscience of ancient Israel in the face of problems not unlike our own. Most Americans had grown accustomed to military spending levels which absorbed roughly half of the budget expenditures of the national government. Most people were oblivious to the pervasiveness of poverty within the richest nation in the history of mankind. They had learned to live with the evil of racism, believing that property rights should be held higher than human rights, and that relations between the races could not be improved by legislative fiat.

All too often, Americans rationalized the injustices in their own society by making comparisons with other countries where such problems were even more glaring, as if that were enough to excuse the perpetuation of injustice in their own land. The new left unconsciously reminded American Christians of the biblical concept that to whom much is given, much will be required.

Second, as the new left encountered opposition to its indictments of American society, it pointed out that the evils of society were much more deeply rooted than many citizens had believed. After all, it was not the revolutionaries of the left who assassinated social reformers such as Robert Kennedy or Martin Luther King. These violent actions served to highlight the depths of the antagonisms which were eating at the soul of the American republic. The new left taught that although social reform was sorely needed to attack the institutional injustices, an even more important goal was the transformation of individual beliefs and behavior which passively accepted the existence of social evil.

Third, the new left brought to light the fact that the growth of technology in the modern world tends to mitigate sensitivities to human values. Students who saw themselves as nothing more than IBM numbers on a computer print-out sheet could sympathize with the plight of blacks and poor people who had also been reduced to statistical tables. They objected to cataloging the suffering caused by the war in Indochina in the simple form of kill ratios and body counts, and attacked the monotony of work in a technological society where human values were sacrificed to a higher GNP. The new left recognized that the dignity of men as individuals created in the image of God was being buried under layers of bureaucratic structures by government, industry, and the "great" universities. Realizing that these trends could become just as totalitarian in their impact on people as the older totalitarianisms of fascism and communism, it called for a reordering of priorities in which technology would serve the human spirit and not the other way around.

Fourth, and perhaps most important, the new left helped to reawaken the social conscience of institutional Christianity in America. For too long the church had remained silent in the face of social injustice, and through its silence it had forfeited the right to speak to the present situation. This was, unfortunately, particularly true of the evangelical and conservative churches which viewed their mission solely in terms of preserving the dogmatic orthodoxy of the Christian faith and thus remained oblivious to their obligation to attack social injustice in the name of the just God. The new left quickly recognized the irrelevance of faith without works, and because of the failure of the churches the movement approached social problems in a secular manner. A Roman Catholic theologian notes with regret that

> the quest for human values in our society… has been radically secularized. It has moved outside the churches. If one wishes to be radically religious in our society — that is to

> say, radically committed to a vision of human brotherhood, personal integrity, openness to the future, justice, and peace – one will not, commonly, seek an ecclesiastical outlet for one's energies. One will, instead, find community under secular auspices, create one's own symbols for community and integrity, and work through secular agencies for social and political reforms.[12]

In view of this situation, leaders of evangelical Protestantism have begun challenging the church to face up to its responsibilities in the social arena. Sherwood Wirt, editor of *Decision* magazine, and Carl F. H. Henry, former editor of *Christianity Today,* have both recently published books urging the evangelical community to recognize the need for and the validity of witness in the social sector.[13] At the 1969 United States Congress on Evangelism, evangelist Leighton Ford called for Evangelicals to repent of their sins of social insensitivity and lack of concern with the great social questions of the day, while Senator Mark Hatfield of Oregon in a 1970 commencement address at Fuller Theological Seminary delivered a ringing call for social concern and activism on the part of evangelical Christians.[14] Both leaders were warmly received by their audiences. In His providential ordering of history, it appears that God is using the past failures of the Christian community to create the opportunity for repentance and renewal.

WEAKNESSES OF THE NEW LEFT

Having pointed out the validity and importance of the new left's critique of contemporary American society – and what should be learned from it – it is equally important to touch on some of the weaknesses of the new left. First, the pride and self-righteousness evident in much of the rhetoric and belief of the new left is open to serious criticism. Having pointed to the failures and institutional hypocrisies of American society, the new left has often been blind to its own moral bankruptcy. While the movement has given many valuable insights into the moral failures of modern technological culture, it lacks any authoritative basis upon which to create a renewed sense of morality or social justice. All too often, the new left merely proposes that individuals be allowed to "do their own thing" when it comes to such personal behavior as the use of drugs or extramarital sexual activities, but not when it involves social concerns such as business or government. The new left divides personal and corporate morality artificially, but oddly enough it reverses the direction in which this bifurcation generally takes place in American culture.

Second, the new left has done a better job of criticizing American society than it has in proposing viable alternatives. While its indictments of the status quo may indeed be accurate, these are not very useful unless they are coupled with specific and concrete policies which can transform these criticisms from mere abstractions into realistic opportunities for change. The new left has a great deal of vision, but not much of a program for implementing it. The Port Huron Statement of the SDS virtually confesses this when it states in closing: "If we appear to seek the unattainable, as it has been said, then let it be known that we do so to avoid the unimaginable."[15]

Third, the new left suffers from the basic weaknesses of the old left discussed earlier in this essay. It basically accepts the liberal belief in the innate goodness of man. If only the social environment can be changed, argues the liberal, the basic human problems can be solved. This is clearly contrary to the Christian affirmation that man is a fallen being and that God alone can transform men and resuit them to the purposes for which they were created. In fact, much of the frustration and radicalization experienced by the new left results from its belief that men are basically good and rational. For if such is the case, how could the new left explain the inability of modern man to solve his great social problems other than to accuse the system itself as being the great corrupter?

Daniel P. Moynihan, addressing the 1969 graduating class at Notre Dame University, summarized the key weakness of the new left when he declared:

> The principal issues of the moment are not political. They are seen as such: that is the essential clue to their nature. But the crisis of the time is not political, it is in essence religious. It is a religious crisis of large numbers of intensely moral, even Godly, people who no longer hope for God. Hence, the quest for divinity assumes a secular form, but with an intensity of conviction that is genuinely new to our politics.[16]

The new left has come and now is on the way out. Hopefully, however, it will leave its mark not only on the political institutions of

American society, but on the churches as well. For only the gospel of Jesus Christ can fill the spiritual void that the secular saints of the new left uncovered in American society. When the Master returns, may He find evangelical Christians working as faithful stewards to carry out the divine mission to call people to repentance and to seek justice for all men.

NOTES

1. President's Commission on National Goals, *Goals for Americans* (New York: Prentice-Hall, 1960).

2. Clinton Rossiter, *Conservatism in America,* rev. ed., (New York: Vintage Books, 1962), p. 237.

3. Barry Goldwater, *The Conscience of a Conservative* (Shepherdsville, Ky.: Victor, 1960).

4. Michael Harrington, *The Other America* (New York: Macmillan, 1962).

5. To many Americans, the term "political conservatism" refers to that seventeenth- and eighteenth-century liberalism which believed the role of the state should be restricted as much as possible insofar as is compatible with the necessity for society to establish order. The term "political liberalism" has come to refer to that nineteenth- and twentieth-century liberalism which seeks a more active role for the state in managing the overall affairs of society.

6. On this see Philip G. Altbach and Patti Peterson, "Before Berkeley: Historical Perspectives on American Student Activism," *Annals of the American Academy of Political and Social Science* 395 (May 1971), pp. 1-14.

7. See Philip M. Burgess and C. Richard Hostettler, "The 'Student Movement': Ideology and Reality," *Midwest Journal of Political Science* 15 (1971), pp. 661-86.

8. This statement is available in Robert A. Goldwin, ed., *How Democratic Is America?* (Chicago: Rand McNally, 1971), pp. 1-15.

9. Ibid., p. 4.

10. Charles A. Reich, *The Greening of America* (New York: Random House, 1970), p. 4.

11. A fascinating study of how new left activists have been drawn into the Jesus movement is provided by Edward E. Plowman, *The Jesus Movement in America* (New York: Pyramid Books, 1971).

12. Michael Novak, *A Theology for Radical Politics* (New York: Herder & Herder, 1969), pp. 17-18.

13. See Sherwood E. Wirt, *The Social Conscience of the Evangelical* (New York: Harper & Row, 1968) and Carl F. H. Henry, *A Plea for Evangelical Demonstration* (Grand Rapids: Baker, 1971).

14. Leighton Ford, "Evangelism in a Day of Revolution," *Christianity Today* 14 (Oct. 24, 1969), pp. 6-12; Mark O. Hatfield, "American Democracy and American Evangelicalism – New Perspectives," *Theology, News and Notes* 14 (Nov. 1970), pp. 8-11.

15. Goldwin, p. 15.

16. Daniel P. Moynihan, commencement address at Notre Dame University, quoted in the *Wall Street Journal,* June 20,1969, p.6.

Evangelical Social Ethics: A Study in Moral Paralysis

Knowledgeable observers – even those committed to an evangelical theology – generally concede that twentieth-century evangelicalism has failed to develop a mature social ethic or political strategy. Indeed, the basic apologetic tenor of the evangelical movement is still focused essentially on relating Christian faith to the natural sciences, despite the fact that increasing numbers of individuals find greater apologetic difficulty in relating Christian faith to the concerns of the social sciences. On a day-to-day basis, the Christian must relate his faith more frequently and more thoughtfully to the theories of social revolution than those of natural evolution. When is the last time somebody told you he turned against the church because he was unable to reconcile the Genesis creation accounts with the demands of modem science? On the other hand, have you not encountered individuals who left the church because they saw the church as an impediment to achieving social justice?

Indeed, many historians of science argue that Christian concepts of nature actually provided the intellectual foundations for the development of modern science. On the other hand, there is no shortage of social historians today who would share the dictum of Karl Marx that religious faith is an opiate which diffuses the struggle for social justice by transferring attention from man's present physical plight to his future spiritual bliss.

One would be hard put to provoke an argument in an evangelical church today as to whether or not Christian faith could be made compatible to the demands of modern science. But the relation between Christian faith and the social order is so potentially explosive that our

---

First published as chapter two of *Politics for Evangelicals* (Valley Forge, Pennsylvania: Judson Press), 1974, and reprinted by permission of Judson Press.

pulpits abstain from giving us instruction where it is most needed. The concept of separation of church and state means, for much of the evangelical community, a separation of religion and politics.

What accounts for the silence of the evangelical community, in the social arena? Why the lack of serious attention to social problems by the established leadership of evangelicalism? The silence of the evangelical church today stands against its own tradition of social pronouncement and social activism Evangelicals have wandered far away from the likes of the pulpiteer Jonathan Boucher (1738-1804), who preached with two loaded pistols on the pulpit to defend himself against his angered congregation! In the mid-nineteenth century, the famous evangelical pulpit of Park Street Church was one of the few in the Boston area made available to the crusading abolitionist William Lloyd Garrison. Jonathan Blanchard, the first president of Wheaton College (Illinois), was not only an active abolitionist, but he also protested against commercial activities on the Lord's Day by leading sit-down demonstrations on the railroad tracks running through the community. What has caused the evangelical community of twentieth-century America to abandon its social activism and its commitment toward creating a just and righteous society? To answer this question, we must first look at some of the factors which have informed, shaped, and limited the development of a mature social ethic in contemporary evangelicalism.

INDIVIDUALISM

American political culture is based upon a highly individualistic concept of man and society. Evangelicals have generally tended to be part of that individualistic culture rather than to stand against it – even though in some respects it violates biblical concepts pertaining to the social nature of man and the corporate moral responsibilities of societies.

The individualism in American political life has its origins in several sources. But without doubt the most important of these is that general body of liberal political theory influenced by John Locke (1632-1704). Locke's political writings were offered as a defense of the English Revolution of 1688, and the American colonists were quick to give Locke a quick baptism in order to use his arguments on behalf of their own revolution of 1776.

So great has been the impact of Lockean political thought upon American political culture that one scholar remarks that all Americans are born as Lockean liberals.[1] The principles of Locke are part of the

American birthright, and to repudiate them is, in part, to repudiate America itself.

Locke argued that all mankind is born into a state of nature which operates under laws which can be made self-evident to the inquiring mind. These laws, both physical and moral, establish a natural harmony in the universe and provide a framework of moral responsibility to which all men are obligated.

However, it was very obvious to Locke in the seventeenth century – a period of great political unrest in his own country – that the supposed euphony of society had degenerated into cacophony. This occurred, argued Locke, because society had reached a level of complexity in which the laws pertaining to it had become equally complex. Hence, there was a need for specialists to find, interpret, and enforce the laws of nature and to pass human laws of convenience which would direct the society into its natural state of harmony. Therefore, individuals create government on the basis of a social contract to handle this difficult task. Since government is created to enunciate, refine, and enforce these natural laws, it has authority only insofar as its actions are in keeping with the natural law. When government violates the natural law, it violates the contract by which it is established and revolution against it is justified.

There are several important implications of Locke's theory which, when pointed out, can be recognized as very much a part of the American political consciousness. *First* is the concept that society and government are created by the individuals of whom they are composed. Government and society exist to serve the individual, not vice versa. *Second*, the function of government is really quite limited – to clarify, enunciate, and enforce the laws of nature. Once this is accomplished, there is a sort of natural harmony which will govern relations between men. Government does not exist to meddle with the laws of nature or to interfere with the natural balance within nature. *Third*, since government is created by the people for this specific task, should it ever violate or exceed the task assigned to it, the people have the right to abolish it. The overall task of government is to maximize individual freedoms by perfecting the laws upon which individual freedom rests. In this sense, government may be said to provide for the general welfare of all.

As the scientific revolution – and the social and technological revolutions spurred by it – began to affect society, the goal of a society in which the benefit of all was achieved by maximizing individual freedom in the Lockean sense became increasingly illusory. Technology began to place disproportionate power in the hands of its masters at the expense of the masses. Further, no individual could ever achieve autonomous freedom in a technological society which bred increasing degrees of specialization and interdependence.

Hence, in the twentieth century, many individuals challenged the "classical liberalism" of Locke with a "modern liberalism" which suggested that government must assume a more active role in regulating the lives of individuals. The cause of maximizing personal freedoms for all people could be better achieved if, in some instances, we placed limited restraints on the freedoms of others. Hence, the distinction between classical liberalism and modern liberalism has been at the heart of the distinction between "conservatism" and "liberalism" in the lexicon of contemporary American politics.

But for all their apparent differences, even modern liberals share the fundamental assumptions of Locke that (1) government is a product of the collective consent of individuals, (2) the purpose of government is to maximize the total amount of individual freedom, and (3) a government which violates its trust is properly the object of revolution. The real differences between conservatives and liberals in the American tradition are those of means, not of ends or of fundamental suppositions about the origins, purposes, and authority of government.

If we look at the Lockean credo from a biblical perspective, however, we find several points of conflict. The *first* regards the nature of man. Locke sees man as essentially autonomous. The purpose of government is, therefore, to perfect and protect his autonomy. The Bible, on the other hand, portrays a picture of man as a social being. God created man and woman so that neither would be alone. (See Genesis 2:18-25.) The nature of the church is pictured as one of extreme interdependence between the parts, each of which has a gift which contributes to the others. (See I Corinthians 12.) We are pictured in the Bible as being responsible not only for our own well-being, but also for the well-being of our brother.

What Locke has done is to elevate the concept of man's *selfishness* as a principle for social organization. Society exists only for the collective wills of the selves of which it is composed. The Lockean model of the autonomous man differs quite drastically from the Christian model of the "man for others."

Second, Locke's concept of the origin of government must also be called into question. Romans 13 rather clearly teaches that government is more than a human convenience. It is divinely ordained and serves divine purposes as well as being humanly instituted and serving human purposes. It is questionable as to whether Locke's argument regarding the "social contract" origin of government was meant to be taken as anything more than an allegorical analogy. Nonetheless, it contrasts sharply with the biblical model of government as an instrument established in the will of God – that rulers on earth are in the last analysis but vice-regents of God's own ordering of the universe.

Third, one must question the purpose of government as it has been defined by the Lockean tradition. For Locke, government exists to prescribe and enforce the natural law for the sake of maximizing individual freedom. Insofar as Locke saw individual freedom as operating under the restraints of "natural law," it may be said that Locke recognized that freedom cannot be separated from moral responsibility and self-restraint. However, the tradition descending from Locke has tended to emphasize individual freedom as opposed to defining the natural law (moral responsibility and restraints) under which freedom is said to operate. The logical outcome of Lockean liberalism in this sense leads to anarchy, of which Marxism is but a variant. (Marx simply wished to get back to the pure state of nature in which the state would no longer be necessary to maintain order.)

Christ, too, was concerned with human freedom. But rather than viewing freedom descriptively as the simple absence of restraint, as the Lockean tradition tends to do, he defined freedom substantively as a life lived in accordance with the will of God. "... You shall know the truth, and the truth will set you free.... Everyone who commits sin is a slave.... If then the Son sets you free, you will indeed be free" (John 8:32-36).

Fourth, one must question the almost simplistic notion of revolution handed down to us from the Lockean tradition. Most middle Americans are now so comfortable with the status quo that the thought of there being any inherent right of revolution for those who don't share as generously in the goods of society is most disquieting. They would like to forget that Thomas Jefferson postulated that in a true republic a revolution would occur roughly every twenty-five years, and that even good old Abe Lincoln insisted that Americans had the "revolutionary right to dismember or overthrow" their government when they "grow weary of the existing government."

Such a teaching not only violates the tradition of the greater part of classical and medieval political theory, but also flies in the face of the apparent biblical injunctions and the traditional teachings of the church in support of obedience to political authority.

These remarks are not to be taken as a flat-out repudiation of the liberal tradition's high regard for consensual politics or individual rights and human freedom. For the individualist bent of American politics has made tremendous contributions toward a truly humane social order. The point is that one must not yield to the tradition uncritically.

For there have also been great costs associated with these gains. We have in many respects been blinded to the social dimensions of human existence. And while the Lockean tradition has heightened our sensitivity and capacity to appreciate the *personal* dimension of human responsibility and fulfillment, it has lowered our sensitivity and capacity to appreciate the *social* dimension of human responsibility and fulfillment.

We fail to see that society is more than a collection of individual wills contracting together at a point in time. Societies are also the products of the past and have obligations toward the future. And they carry moral responsibility for not only the present, but for the past and the future as well.

We fail to see that God judges not only individuals and individual actions, but also societies and social actions. And although our lives have become increasingly interdependent and intertwined with the lives of others, we continue to be guided by an ethic which is unable to address itself to the corporate dimensions of sin, righteousness, and human responsibility.

We conveniently forget that the Old Testament prophets called down God's judgment upon entire nations for their rebellion against God's ordinances – obviously, holding the entire societies collectively responsible before God. For example, God's punishment of Sodom and Gomorrah was placed upon the entire communities – not just the unrighteous individuals within them. God held the "righteous" individuals in those societies responsible for the iniquity which abounded in their communities. And we fail to recognize that the New Testament paradigm for God's people is the new "city" of God established amidst cities of men. Hence, we address the deity as "*Our* Father which art in heaven. . . . " And John's Revelation judges the seven churches of Asia as collective entities, not simply in terms of the individuals of which they are composed.

We must come to see that nations – just as individuals – may be said to have a spiritual life that leads either to felicity or damnation. The status of a nation's spiritual health projects a moral climate which fundamentally affects the public policies a nation pursues. In other words, nations may be said, in an allegorical sense, to possess a soul. And just as the outward life of an individual reflects the spiritual resources and commitments of his soul, so, too, the outward life of a state reflects the spiritual resources and commitments of its soul.

The individualist biases of American political culture encourage us to see the state and society as nothing more than the sum product of their components, as opposed to recognizing that in some important respects state and society have a life and impact of their own which in turn affect the character of the component parts. There is a two-way, reciprocal relationship between the group and the individual.

Nonetheless, evangelical ethics by and large continue to see social betterment as a simple, almost automatic, by-product of personal evangelism; and it sees in personal evangelism the only genuine route to social reform. Thus, Billy Graham captures the spirit of the evangelical approach to social problems by insisting that really there are no social problems – only composites of individual problems. Just as John Locke might say that there really is no such thing as a society or a state – just composites of individuals choosing to call themselves that – so Billy Graham can write:

> The international problems are only reflections of individual problems. Sin is sin, be it personal or social, and the word "repent" is inseparably bound up with "evangelism." Social sins, after all, are merely a large-scale projection of individual sins and need to be repented of by the offending segment of society.[2]

NEGATIVE VIEW OF THE STATE

Evangelicals have rather uncritically accepted yet another characteristic of American political culture. Rather than viewing government positively as a gift from God (as we are enjoined to do in Romans 13), evangelicals have generally viewed government indifferently, as a necessary evil. They have tended to subscribe to a negative view of the state which is fearful of any and all government power. Rather than seeing in government one of the great achievements of mankind which distinguishes human society from brute animal existence, evangelicals have seen government itself as a leviathan seeking to devour our freedoms. Rather than regarding government as providing opportunities for Christian leadership in society, evangelicals share in the popular disdain of politicians and officeholders as a breed of megalomaniacs.

What accounts for such suspicion and distrust of government? Why do we so simplistically accept such statements as "That government which governs best, governs least?" For surely the logical extension of this would be a commitment to anarchy. If the government which governs least is best, then the best government would be that which governs not at all!

There are two basic sources of this negative assessment of state power within the American evangelical community. The first is rooted in the American historical experience. The second is rooted in a rather uncritical acceptance of St. Augustine's teachings regarding the state.

The American historical experience fostered a negative view of the state insofar as self-conscious Americanism has its origins to a large extent in the struggle for independence *against* another government. The independence struggle saw the dangers inherent in government power which was distant from the people. Further, since the struggle for independence was personified into a struggle against the British monarchy, the Americans came to distrust executive power in particular. Thus, the first attempt at American union under the Articles of Confederation established a central government with no executive head, and with powers so limited as to make the government of the confederation inoperative. When, under the Constitution, the American government was reconstituted to give the central government more power, the Congress was still maintained as the "first branch" of government. The role of Congress was viewed, among other things, as that of checking the power of the executive. The prevailing American view was – and in some respects still is – that freedom is won against the excesses of government. The more one succeeds in limiting government, the more one succeeds in protecting his freedom.

Obviously there is some merit to this position – but only within certain limits. A strong case may be made that governments have historically interfered with what we presently regard as the private rights of individuals. In this sense, we can view many of the present social and political liberties of our society as having been the product of a strongly *limited* government.

But one must caution against the danger of absolutizing freedom at the expense of order. And one must also guard against insisting that any extension of government activity is *ipso facto* harmful to the cause of freedom. A government which posts speed limits for automotive traffic is limiting our freedom to travel at any speed whenever we desire – but the net impact is to provide a context of order in which the right to travel and other related rights are all made more secure. A government which regulates the sale of stocks and bonds may be placing limits on the freedom of the entrepreneur pushing various securities – but it makes more secure the property of the potential investor. What is important in assessing governmental action from a libertarian point of view is not simply the extension of government intrusion into our lives, but the net impact of government policies on our freedoms. From this point of view, one can see that freedoms are won not only *against* government, but also *through* government.

This is, of course, a very sensitive issue in the current world struggle between those countries committed to open societies sustained by limited governments and those countries committed to closed societies sustained by totalitarian governments. We have grown accustomed to referring to the latter as police states because the governments of these societies seek to police every aspect of human behavior. However, we should be reminded that limited governments often behave like police states, although in a different sense. It was a revolutionary Marxist, Ferdinand Lassalle, who first coined the term "police state" when he condemned the weaknesses of a strictly limited government as follows:

> This is a policeman's idea, gentlemen, a policeman's idea for this reason, because it represents to itself the State from a point of view of a policeman, whose whole function consists in preventing robbery and burglary.[3]

Too often, evangelicals have blindly accepted arguments for limiting government action to combat social evil in the mistaken belief that expanded governmental intervention is necessarily a greater evil than that to which it is directed. And through this, the well-intentioned convictions of evangelicals have been exploited by those who benefit from the government's inability to attack social evil and injustice. Thus, the *New York Times* has asserted that the famed evangelist Billy Sunday was subsidized by the business community "as a police measure – as a means of keeping the lower classes quiet."[4]

Evangelicals have been so overly concerned about the positive uses of government power that they have simplistically equated social welfare measures with outright socialism, and socialism with outright communism. Richard Pierard summarizes this attitude as follows:

> Schemes such as urban renewal, public housing, Medicare, and Social Security are part of a gigantic conspiracy to undermine the free institutions of the United States.... Christians should resist all "socialist tendencies." This viewpoint has been expressed with varying degrees of intensity by evangelical leaders.... Harold John Ockenga was quoted in the N.A.E. organ as saying that socialist schemes "soften society for Marxism," while Albert J. Lindsey told an N.A.E. convention in Chicago that socialism is "nothing more than a prep school for communism."[5]

But as we have already indicated, the evangelical's negative view of the state is rooted not only in the American experience, but also in the impact of Augustinian thought upon Christian social ethics. Indeed, the impact of St. Augustine's thought has been so pervasive that one observer has commented: "Especially in the area of social philosophy Augustine's influence is determinative for the West."[6]

What was Augustine's teaching about the state? And why has it played such an important role in the subsequent social teachings of the church? In order to answer these questions, we must first of all briefly deal with the dilemma of the early Christian community in developing an appropriate attitude toward the state. The term "dilemma" is appropriate – for we find that the early church had little by way of systematic thought on the nature of politics and political society, and it was to this void that St. Augustine sought to address himself.

We must remember that despite the political and social implications of Christ's messiahship, he nonetheless avoided any direct endorsement or entanglement with the political factions of his time. Although God in Christ was made flesh and the kingdom of God was proclaimed to be at hand, the mission of Christ and the nature of his kingdom transcended the limitations of the politics of his time.

During his ministry, Christ passed prophetic judgment on each of the major political groupings of his day. Although his triumphal entry into Jerusalem for the Passover festival seemingly complimented the ambitions of the Zealots, who sought a revolutionary overthrow of the

Roman occupation, his repudiation of Peter's use of the sword against a Roman soldier clearly dissociated him from zealotry. Although his retreat into the wilderness and his baptism by John the Baptist suggest ties to the Essenes (a group practicing ascetic withdrawal from society), his feasting with publicans and sinners and supplying wine for wedding celebrations indicate that his was not a life of ascetic spiritual withdrawal from society. While he chased the money changers out of the temple courtyards, suggesting an affinity with the Pharisees, who wished to protect the integrity of temple rites, his repeated chastisements of the pharisaical hypocrisy clearly antagonized that community. And when he advocated accommodation to the Romans ("Pay Caesar what is due to Caesar"), he seemed sympathetic to the compromises established between Rome and the Sadducees, only later to repudiate them for their lack of religious orthodoxy.

Christ belonged to no political party. In that sense, his kingdom clearly was not of this world. Yet at the same time, that kingdom was proclaimed to be present among his followers. The question was, therefore, how the kingdom of God related to the kingdoms of men which were still everywhere to be found.

Thus, the early church had little direction in terms of what path it should take in reconciling the demands of God's kingdom with the kingdoms of men. But even more important for later generations of Christians to realize is that not only did the early church have few guidelines within which to develop a social and political ethic, but also that the early church itself did little in the way of trying to develop a systematic social or political philosophy.

The reasons for this neglect were several. *First,* it must be remembered that the early Christian community was viewed by the Gentile world as a sect of a strange Near Eastern religion. As such, Christians were a minority of a minority – hardly in a position to pontificate on the social and political policies of the Roman Empire! The early church was so insignificant, politically speaking, that to engage in social or political action would have been an exercise in futility. There was, therefore, no practical need for the church to develop a social and political theory.

Second, the early Christians were primarily from the lower end of the socioeconomic spectrum. Hence, they were removed even one step further from the possibility of achieving significant political influence, above and beyond the problems associated with their minority status in the context of the Roman Empire.

Third, the early church's conviction that the return of Christ was at hand created pressures within the Christian community to concentrate almost exclusively on the direct evangelization of the world – sometimes to the extent of being imprudent in terms of providing for the exigencies of daily life. Thus in Second Thessalonians, Paul warns against those Christians who have apparently ceased to work in the expectation that the Lord's return would occur shortly. In the context of such expectations, we can understand why the early Christian community could find little need to develop a longitudinal philosophy of history together with its social and political implications.

Fourth, one must not forget that the relationship between the citizen and the state in the Roman Empire was essentially passive. There was no mass democracy with competing political parties in the sense which we now know it. And as opportunity for direct citizen involvement in the affairs of the empire was quite limited, so, too, was the need to develop a theory which might guide Christians participating in such endeavors.

Thus, all these factors combined give us a New Testament which generally speaks only incidentally and obliquely to questions of the state. There are a few exceptions, such as Romans 13, which speak of government as having been ordained of God and thereby rightfully receiving obedience. But this teaching is offset by Revelation 13, which speaks of government as having become corrupted into the power of Antichrist! So long as the church was not in a position to affect affairs of state in the first place, and so long as its interpretation of Christ's imminent return was such that historical consciousness could not emerge, the development of a practical political ethic was unnecessary. But as the church grew from a scattered minority to the officially sanctioned and sustained religion of the Roman Empire in a period of four hundred years, and as it acknowledged that Christ's return might be yet many years into the future, the need for a political ethic to serve as a guide for Christians now bearing responsibility in the empire was enormous. It was to this situation that St. Augustine so brilliantly addressed himself.

In his *City of God* (412-426), St. Augustine divided all mankind into two groups. The one was "the city of man," which was the association of all individuals for whom self-love was the motivating principle of life. The other was "the city of God," which was the association of all individuals for whom the love of God was the motivating principle of life. The two cities, argued Augustine, were in perpetual conflict insofar as their basic motivations were antithetical.

Both cities physically occupy the same earthly territory, and thus those who are of the city of God may still be said to be in the city of man. And while the city of man is alien to the city of God, it nonetheless fulfills a very important purpose in God's providential care over the world. For due to man's rebellion against God and the substitution of love of self for the love of God, the state provides an ordering mechanism to prevent selfish men from destroying one another. In this context of order, the city of God is allowed to grow and prosper.

In some respects, Augustine's social theory is similar to that of Thomas Hobbes. Hobbes argued that man is by nature nasty, brutish, and antisocial. Only through the creation of a state can the war of all against all be halted. The fundamental difference between Hobbes and Augustine is that while Hobbes sees this condition as natural to man, Augustine sees this conflict as the result of the "fallenness" of man.

While this is a significant point of difference, the practical applications of both theories are strikingly similar. Man is not a social creature – but antisocial. The state is not natural to man – but it is necessary to protect him from self-destruction. The chief purpose of the state is not to pursue justice – but to create some semblance of order.

What is important to note at this point is that Augustine could have pursued quite a different argument. He might have suggested that the state is the outgrowth of the social instinct implanted in the nature of man at creation. He might have emphasized the words of the apostle Paul in Romans 13 suggesting that the state is an instrumentality for goodness and justice. Instead of emphasizing the points of tension between the city of man and the city of God, he might have emphasized the shared natural revelation between them in which both share some common areas of moral responsibility. (See, for example, Paul's argument in Romans 1 and 2.)

But the net impact of Augustinian political ethics nonetheless remains. It suggests that the most we can hope for in the state is order. It suggests that the state is fundamentally alien to human nature – and, of course, unnecessary to those who are truly members of the city of God. Augustinianism creates an aura of moral pessimism in which it is difficult to create visions of a better society or inspire men to work toward justice.

Evangelicals have been slow to free themselves from the limitations imposed by the Augustinian social theory. Undoubtedly, a reason for this has been that most of the modern critics of Augustine have attacked not only his social philosophy, but also his concepts of sin, human depravity, and divine grace. But one need not deny the universality of sin, the depravity of man, or their impact on interpersonal relations to take a more moderate position on the nature of the state, the sociability of human nature, or abiding universal norms of justice than does Augustine. But what happens altogether too often is that evangelicals baptize the American experience, which is so conducive to a negative view of the state, with theological justifications drawn from their Augustinian heritage. And once that happens, one is judged to be heretical if he deviates from the party line.

Pietism

A third factor which has strongly influenced evangelical social ethics is its pietist heritage. Pietism per se was a movement reacting against a purely confessional test for religious orthodoxy. Beginning in the late seventeenth century and of major importance in the eighteenth century, the pietist movement emphasized the importance of religious feeling and experience as opposed to the practices of the state churches, which seemingly insisted only on an intellectual assent to confessions of faith. Pietism is in some respects anti-institutional, stressing the spirit of the relationship between believers and their Lord as opposed to the form it takes. Thus, spontaneous prayers replace written prayers. Gospel songs and choruses replace traditional hymnody and liturgy. And testimonials replace creedal confessions.

The pietist influence received impetus in the United States through massive immigration of "Free church" dissenters, and it was reinforced by frontier evangelism, where Christians moved west ahead of the institutionalized churches of confessional Protestantism. In the twentieth century, evangelicals within the main-line confessional denominations were literally driven into the pietist Free churches because, strangely enough, there was greater faithfulness to confessional orthodoxy in the pietist movement than in the main-line confessional churches themselves.

The pietist influence has made some vital contributions to the health of American evangelicalism. Its tendency to disdain established rite and ritual has given evangelicals greater flexibility in testing new modes of mission and worship than has been true in the confessional churches.

And the pietist insistence that we believe in God with our hearts as well as our heads encourages evangelicals to develop a Christian experience which involves more than simply the verbal confession of an historical creed.

But there have been drawbacks to the pietist influence in evangelicalism as well. Religious feeling, for example, is often used as the supreme test of religious commitment. Hence, the need to create a vigorous intellectual apologetic for the Christian faith is downgraded. In the area of social and political ethics, the importance of systematic inquiry into the causes and solutions of social and political problems is brushed away.

The net impact of this situation is that evangelical Christianity often takes on an anti-intellectual cast. Its social and political ethic, rather than being clearly thought out and systematically stated, is a collection of moralisms which tends to romanticize concrete social and political problems as if they were nothing more than vaguely "spiritual" in character.

Thus, Billy Graham addresses the problem of race relations and integration, and states: "Though the race question has important social implications, it is fundamentally a moral and spiritual issue. Only moral and spiritual approaches can provide a solution."[7] And Leighton Ford suggests: "Our greatest need is for an inner revolution that can transform men's hearts.... Moral aspirins and political pills cannot solve our problem. What we need is radical surgery for cancer of the soul."[8] In reference to the problem of the national energy crisis, Ford suggests that what is of greater importance is the crisis in moral power: "Today we are suffering from a widespread moral power failure, and a great portion of man's life is crippled because of a breakdown in our spiritual transformers!"[9] Speaking on the balance of payments problem, Ford suggests that "Moral deflation is a far greater problem for the free world today than monetary inflation. The moral drain is more critical than the gold drain."[10]

There is a degree of truth in each of these statements. But the point remains that simply converting men to Christianity does *not* solve the social and political problems of institutionalized racism, the energy crisis, or the balance of payments! Perhaps what is most needed in the evangelical community is a little more moral humility and a little less spiritual pride. One does not have to be a social historian to recognize that the Christian faith has not provided simple formulas for achieving the most efficient development of natural resources or balancing conflicting economic interests between "free traders" and "protectionists." Indeed, the very fact that evangelical ministers are usually forbidden by their congregations to deal with social and political matters from the viewpoint of Christian convictions (other than in moralistic terms) gives testimony to this fact. So long as evangelicals engage, then, in prescribing only moral clichés to difficult social and political problems, they are in fact avoiding any direct interrelating of their faith with the sociopolitical world around them. We forget that the early church experienced tremendous tension between Jewish and Gentile believers over the issue of fellowship between Christians of different ethnic groups. (See Acts 11 and 15.) The apostles themselves were so divided over who should succeed Judas to their brotherhood that they finally resolved the issue by casting lots! Accepting God's grace in Christ does not provide us with an easy set of answers to social, economic, or political questions. God's grace justifies us before the creator God – but it doesn't provide instant sanctification in dealings with our fellowman.

GNOSTICISM

There is a bit of irony in suggesting that the evangelical community, which takes such great pride in its attempted defense of orthodoxy, is itself guilty of heresy. Gnosticism was the first major heretical threat to the orthodoxy of the Christian confession; and, as we shall see, it is still with us.

There were numerous Gnostic sects in the first three centuries of the church's history. Many of these revolved around the teachings of prophetic figures who claimed affinity with the Christian community. Generally, the Gnostics held to a dualistic view of the universe in which the struggle between the forces of good and evil was a struggle between spirit and matter. The implications of this dualism were, of course, devastating to anybody who took the claims of the incarnation seriously. The Gnostics maintained that Christ was not made of flesh, but was a spirit who "appeared" to be flesh. A Christian view of the world which suggested that God had created the world and found it "good" was obviously alien to Gnostic logic, and to suggest that one could serve God by making his body a temple of the Lord was nothing short of preposterous. To the Gnostic, anything of the world was either illusory or evil. The trick was to escape the world of flesh and to free one's "spirit" for communion with God. (The term "gnostic" refers to the "gnosis" or "knowledge" passed on within the sect which teaches how this escape is accomplished.)

The Apostles' Creed, among others, was written largely in response to the threat that Gnostic teachings posed for Christian orthodoxy. The affirmations that God created the world, that Christ was born of a virgin, that his body was raised from the dead, and that there will be a future bodily resurrection of the dead for all believers – all of these were upholding the physical reality of the incarnation.

The early Gnostics did not deny the world of the spirit; they denied the world of the flesh. They did not deny the possibility of uniquely inspired sacred writings; to the contrary, they added to the canon writings of their own which they held to be of sacred value. And the Gnostics did not deny the supernatural or the miraculous; to the contrary, they claimed hosts of miraculous proofs for the truth of their beliefs.

Contemporary attacks on orthodoxy have been inspired by an almost complete opposite of Gnosticism. Since the seventeenth century, attacks on Christian orthodoxy have been based not on a denial of the physical, but on a denial of the spiritual; not on the basis of additional sacred writings, but on the repudiation of any uniquely inspired written source of revelation; not on the basis of miraculous proofs, but on the repudiation of any concept of the supernatural or miraculous whatever.

In responding to these attacks by the modern world, evangelical apologetics have tended to "spiritualize" or "gnosticize" Christian teachings. In an effort to defend the supernatural, they have tended to downgrade the natural. In an effort to defend revelation, they have tended to downgrade reason or natural theology. In an attempt to defend the uniqueness of sacred writ, they have tended to divorce it from the social and historical heritage from which it emerged. The net effect of this defense is to preach salvation in Christ as spiritual redemption, neglecting the physical aspects of that redemption as it plays itself out in the social and political world. Evangelicals have preached "justification" before God without having defined what "justice" is in the first place.

Thus, even the "neo-evangelicals," who lament the tendency of conservatives to divorce the gospel from real life, are prone to suggest that at least the evangelical community has not abandoned the "heart of the gospel message." Or they suggest that while Christianity does indeed relate to the whole of life and that the church has a mission to address the gospel to all dimensions of human existence, the "primary task" of the church is still to preach the gospel. Nowhere is there the recognition that the very gospel, as perceived in the evangelical community, is itself but half the gospel. In reacting to the immanental theologies of the modern world, the evangelical community has responded with a mystical gnosticism of its own, having abandoned any attempts at reaching toward a genuinely transcendental theology which both reconciles and overcomes the polarizing tendencies of each of the other alternatives.

Thus, evangelicals suggest that one can have a "saving knowledge of Christ" if he accepts spiritual salvation and redemption apart from whether or not he properly understands the earthly and fleshly consequences of that faith. But at the same time, the evangelical is unwilling to suggest that a theological liberal who understands the immanental consequences of Christian faith in the flesh can find salvation apart from reconciling his spirit to the creator God through Jesus Christ the mediator. Let's call a spade a spade. Half the gospel is half the gospel. Neither half alone is truly a saving gospel, at least not in the way that God intended.

It must be granted that much of the reason for this tendency in the evangelical community has been the attempt on its part to combat the heresy of the liberal theologians. But one does not combat heresy with heresy, just as one does not right a lie with another lie.

But I suspect that there has been another reason for the tendency to gnosticize the gospel on the part of the evangelical community. Whereas in the effort to combat heresy at least the motivations of the evangelicals were pure, in this case the motivations themselves are suspect. Evangelicals are, by and large, very comfortable in terms of their socioeconomic position. And any gospel which takes seriously either the Old Testament or the New Testament injunctions to care for the poor and to free oneself of materialist concerns is a hard pill to swallow. How desperately we need to hear the words of James: "Next a word to you who have great possessions. Weep and wail over the miserable fate descending on you" (James 5:1). The suburban captivity of the church has fostered the political captivity of the Christians.

Each of these factors – individualism, negativism toward the state, pietism, and Gnosticism – serve to mutually support one another. If one assumes that social problems are really only compounded individual problems, then it is only logical to hold to a negative view of the state. After all, the state can't really do anything that people can't do for themselves. Or if one begins with a negative view of the state, he will obviously be inclined to seek individualist rather than statist solutions to social problems. Individualism and the negative view of the state are then further reinforced by a pietist view of life which refuses to face the intellectual shortcomings of this position. It turns to the heart and romantic notions of community in Christ as a community in which all disagreements have ceased. (One need look only at the New Testament and church history to gather quite a different picture!) Pietism fails to see that justification in Christ does not bring about some sort of instant sanctification in the relations between men. And it fails to answer the problem of how Christians are to balance their demands with those of non-Christians in the world community. Finally, succumbing to a Gnostic concept of salvation and moral obligation, the evangelical community has tended to dismiss its critics as having misunderstood the essentially "spiritual" character of the Christian gospel.

The ethical consequences of this situation are well known. Evangelicals have concerned themselves with individual sin, individual repentance, and individual renewal. They have addressed themselves forcefully to the problems of drugs, alcohol, lust, and personal example in interpersonal relations. But evangelicals have failed to deal with corporate sin, corporate repentance, and corporate renewal. This is obvious to the outside observer. But the evangelical finds it difficult to see the truth or gravity of the charge made against him. For if all problems are viewed as essentially individual problems, then addressing oneself to individual morality has *ipso facto* solved the problem of social morality.

Obviously there is some merit in the evangelical's argument that as individuals are changed, the world is changed. The question is, however, *how* does one change individuals? Is it a matter of individuals changing themselves (with God's help)? What if some individuals resist change? Is moral improvement thereby out of the question? Can a majority in society set standards for the entire society? If we cannot legislate genuine morality, can we not at least legislate external behavior between individuals in society? It is at this point that the evangelical's answer to social and political problems has been haphazard and inconsistent. We are told that one can't legislate against racism. But at the same time we are encouraged to support laws against drugs, alcohol, and sexual promiscuity. We are told that new gun-control laws won't get at the heart of crime. But at the same time we are told that capital punishment and mandatory incarceration for certain crimes rest on biblical principle.

Because evangelical ethics are rooted more in the political heritage of seventeenth- and eighteenth-century America than in a truly biblical understanding of the nature of man in society, their practical effect has been to marshal support for conservative political interests. The practical effect of this has been two-fold. First, it has bastardized Christianity into a civic religion of the political right. Second, it has elevated conservative causes into sacred principles.

The answer to this problem is not an equally insidious and simplistic bastardizing of Christianity into a civic religion of the left. Rather, what is needed is a serious reexamination of the biblical concepts of man and society as they pertain to the political dimensions of human existence.

NOTES

1. See Louis Hartz, *The Liberal Tradition in America* (New York: Harcourt Brace Jovanovich, Inc., 1955).

2. Billy Graham as quoted in David Lockard, *The Unheard Billy Graham* (Waco, Texas: Word, Inc., 1971), p. 97.

3. Ferdinand Lassalle, *The Working Class Program* (1862), in Albert Fried and Ronald Sanders, eds., *Socialist Thought* (Chicago: Aldine-Atherton, Inc., 1964), p. 386.

4. *New York Times,* May 20, 1916, p. 10.

5. Richard B. Pierard, *The Unequal Yoke* (Philadelphia: J. B. Lippincott Company, 1970), p. 88.

6. George W. Forell, *Christian Social Teachings* (Garden City, N.Y.: Doubleday & Company, Inc., 1966), p. 68.

7. Billy Graham as quoted in Lockard, *op. cit.*, p. 124.

8. Leighton Ford, *One Way to Change the World* (New York: Harper & Row Publishers, 1970), pp. 34-35.

9. Ibid., pp. 51-52.

10. Ibid., p. 49.

Coming Out of the Wilderness

Reciting long litanies of evangelicalism's failure to speak forthrightly to pressing social issues is nothing new. It has been going on for at least twenty-five years. During the past quarter-century, there have been several evangelical spokesmen who have not only bemoaned this fact, but also have tried to show that it is contrary to the spirit and traditions of the eighteenth- and nineteenth-century evangelicals.[1] Figures, such as Wilberforce and Lord Shaftesbury, and movements, such as the Clapharn Society or American abolitionism, can be cited in the effort to demonstrate that evangelicalism is not inherently opposed to vigorous social action and political engagement. But none of these spokesmen provide the foundation for a renewed evangelical thrust in the social sector. They have looked backward – confessing sins of omission. But they have not looked forward – telling us how to pursue acts of righteousness. Failing to escape their individualistic biases, their negative view of the state, their romantic pietism, and their spiritualized concepts of salvation, they are unable to speak to the need for *political* solutions for *social* problems in *historical* existence. We need more than penance for sins of the past. What is needed is a fundamental – even elemental – discussion of the nature of man, society, and politics from an evangelical perspective. Once this basic groundwork is laid, steps can be taken toward developing strategies for social and political engagement.

The Nature of Man and Society

What is the nature and destiny of man? Only as we give answer to this can we answer the question, "What is the nature and function of politics?" For politics, in the last analysis, must be seen as a part of man's

First published as chapter three of *Politics for Evangelicals* (Valley Forge, Pennsylvania: Judson Press), 1974, and reprinted by permission of Judson Press.

attempt to find meaning and purpose within his historical existence. Thus, at the very beginning we see that politics receives its definition and function from our view of man. Here the great biblical teachings of the evangelical tradition may be seen to touch at the heart of everything we shall say subsequently about the political world.

The evangelical confesses that man is a being qualitatively different from any other of God's creation. According to the Genesis creation account, man is the capstone of God's creation, and he shares in the very image of God. Sharing in God's image, he is therefore capable of having fellowship and communion with God. Further, he may be said to share to some extent in the very attributes of God – self-transcendence, freedom, and creative power. God charged man with establishing dominion over the earth, and thus in some ways man mirrors God's sovereignty over the universe through his own assigned sovereignty over the earth. Finally, man was created to live not only with God, but also with his fellowman. God did not create man to be alone, but to be in the company of other persons, all sharing equally in their fundamental distinction from any other product of God's creation: the image of God implanted in man.

But man attempted to assert his God-given likeness beyond the limits set by the Creator. Created in God's image to live in creative freedom, man used his powers to challenge the freedom and sovereignty of God himself. Thus man was cursed by God for having marred the image of God itself. The harmony of parts creating an ordered relationship between man, his fellowman, and God the Creator was destroyed.

Man may thus be said to live a schizophrenic existence. His existential selfhood (what he has become) is perpetually at conflict with his created essence (what he was created to be). His consciousness of the ordered relationships which ought to exist between himself, God, and his fellowman constantly hurls itself against the fact that he has been sent away from the Garden in which God first placed him.

But the image of God in man remains, and God does not forsake man. Man may continually abuse that image and continually set himself against the Creator, but God constantly calls man back to his intended purpose and created nature through acts of goodness and mercy, chastisement and judgment. Through these acts and the testimonies of divine creation, all men still experience the sacredness of their nature and the capacity for communion with God and their fellowman.

Thus, man the sinner does not suddenly become an asocial animal capable of no moral good. Were that the case, man would no longer be morally responsible to either God or his fellowman. Rather, God sustains man. He places limits on the powers of evil. Man remains a being bearing the image of God. He still hears the voice of God when God approaches him. He retains some capacity to fulfill freely the purposes for which he was created in God's image. Because all men share in this capacity, there remains a point of contact and commonness which allows the essentially social nature of man to find expression.

To say that the image of God remains in man is not to say that the image has not been marked and marred by sin. But if the image of God were obliterated, that being which we call man would no longer truly be man. To say that man can still hear the voice of God is not to say that man will listen to the voice of God. But if man could no longer hear the voice of God, he would no longer be man. To say that man is capable of doing moral good is not to say that man is capable of earning merit justifying himself before God. But if man is incapable of any moral good, he cannot be held morally responsible.

These are fine distinctions which are often overlooked by evangelicals in their zeal to combat the exaltation of man by modem liberal humanism. The liberals have often tended to deny that man is a fallen creature. Evangelicals have tended to counter that man is nothing more than a fallen creature. Both miss the critical balance of recognizing that while man is a fallen creature, he nonetheless continues to bear the image of God. The liberals have exalted man's capacity for good to the point that they suggest man can earn salvation. The evangelicals have emphasized man's capacity for evil to the point that man is no longer seen as capable of any good. Both miss the critical balance of recognizing that man still has moral responsibility and capacity to choose for either good or evil. In choosing evil he simply compounds the terrors of a disordered life, and in choosing good he acts to bring life back into harmony with the Word – the very Word which tells him that there is no remission for sin aside from God's sacrifice of himself. The liberals have tended to exalt the social nature of man into a panacea for overcoming all selfishness. The evangelicals have tended to view the selfishness of man as an obstacle to achieving any genuine society. Both miss the critical balance of recognizing that man is a social creature by creation and God's sustaining grace despite the fact that he chooses to exalt self above both God and his fellowman.

The liberal, while recognizing that man is fallen, still sees him capable of achieving his own redemption. Christ is but a prototype of the potential for goodness in all men. If this view is extended to its logical conclusion, then, all men, in fact, can become very God of very God. The consequences of this approach for social theory are obvious. Man's inability to reenter the garden of peace is self-inflicted. But by using his creative powers and turning freely to do the good, man can establish a perfect society which has overcome all evil. Liberals differ radically, of course, on the means of pursuit, their identification of the sources of good and evil, and the immediacy by which they think their goals can be met. But since all men share in the commonness of God-likeness, all men are equal in the resources essential to the reestablishment of social harmony and a just society. Society and the state are therefore rooted in a natural ethic known to all men.

The evangelical has reacted strongly against the almost flippant attitude that the liberal manifests in regard to the problem of man's fall into sin. The danger has been in overreacting to the point that man's "total depravity" is construed to mean that man is capable of no good whatever. Rather than viewing man as bearing the likeness of God, the evangelical reminds himself that as man was created from dust, so shall he return to dust again. In reaction to the liberal's humanistic understanding of Christ and his deification of man, the evangelical has so emphasized the deity of Christ that he seems blind to the humanness of Christ, and he has so undervalued the potential of man that he seems blind to the *imago dei* rooted in man. The consequences of this confusion for social theory are likewise obvious.

According to this evangelical view, man can do nothing to reenter the garden of peace. He deludes himself when thinking that he acts creatively or freely – he is really captive to the powers of evil. Strategies of social reform and renewal are secondary to and dependent upon the more basic question of how man can escape the pervasiveness of sin. Only in finding individual salvation can one find the path to social salvation. But since all men are alienated from God and each other through sin, there can be no really cooperative endeavor toward reestablishing social harmony and justice apart from the redemptive action of God in Christ Jesus. The state and society are thus, in this evangelical view, rooted in a uniquely revealed ethic resting on the redemptive power of God known only to those to whom God has chosen to show himself.

For the liberal, politics is based on a natural ethic rooted in man's divinity as a created being. For the evangelical, politics is based on a revealed ethic rooted in Christ's redemptive power. The liberal therefore sees the possibility of an inclusive political base joining together both the believer and the nonbeliever, united by their common humanity. Such an approach can be rationally perceived, and man has within himself the ability to construct healthy political societies based on this ethic. The evangelical, on the other hand, sees mankind hopelessly divided into factions – the most fundamental being that between the redeemed and the unredeemed. These two cannot really work together because their ethics are based on fundamentally different conceptions of the nature of man and the foundations for society.

What is desperately needed is a via media between these two extremes. What is needed is an ethic which recognizes that all men still bear the image of God and thereby possess the capacity for an inclusive society based on natural ethics and at the same time recognizes that man's fall into sin places fundamental limitations on the success of such an endeavor. What is needed is an ethic which recognizes that God's redemptive power in Christ holds the key to the ultimate success of social and political reconciliation, but at the same time recognizes that God still sustains the prerequisites necessary for an at least rudimentary success at the social and political level. The liberal fails to see that a purely humanist politics is forever doomed because man is a sinner. The evangelical fails to see that a purely redemptionist politics is a contradiction in terms. For redemption, when viewed as a totally accomplished fact, obliviates the need for politics. But to understand this, we must now change our focus to the nature of politics itself.

The Nature of Politics

Because all men have tasted sin, all men share in the consequences of sin. All men consequently elevate the love of self above their love of God or fellowman. That perfect society balancing the love of self, love of one's brother, and love of God which the Creator had intended has been upset. Discord has usurped the harmonious relations between the parts. Self-interest asserts itself over the interests of God and our fellowman.

Politics is simply the means men use to ameliorate the conflicts stemming from this situation. Man finds himself trapped in moral anarchy. But because he is a social being by creation, this anarchy is intolerable to him. He seeks accords with his fellowman which are in keeping with his self-interest. Failing that, he resorts to force and violence to assert his self-interest over the interests of others.

Conflict stemming from self-interest must therefore be seen to lie at the heart of politics. Were there no conflict, there would be no need for politics. Political society, as opposed to what we might call "natural" society, is itself a consequence of sin. Were there no sin, there would be no selfishness. Were there no selfishness, there would be no conflict. And were there no conflict, there would be no need for politics.

In order to pursue their self-interests, individuals associate with others who share the same interests. Thus, interest groups and political parties are established to promote and pursue certain interests. But even within these associations, conflicts of interest emerge between the members as to tactics to be employed and the ranking of priorities.

It is of utmost importance to recognize that conflict is integral to politics. Both liberals and evangelicals have generally tended to try to escape this fact. Liberals try to romanticize conflict away by euphemistically insisting that since men are essentially brothers, they share essentially the same interests. Hence, the purpose of politics is to strip away the veneer of apparent conflict and create a peaceful society based on shared, common interest. This fails to recognize the utter pervasiveness of sin which extends to the very root of the human heart and all human relationships.

The evangelicals, on the other hand, have also tried to escape the fact that conflict is integral to politics. They tend to see conflict as in itself evil, rather than seeing it as a by-product of evil. Therefore, conflict is to be avoided – and if not avoided, at least denied. The evangelical all too often longs for a politics devoid of conflict – a contradiction in terms. Evangelicals generally argue that political conflict would be resolved if all parties to the conflict were reconciled to God. But they fail to recognize that we live in a world where all individuals are not likely to seek such reconciliation. And they fail to recognize that conflicts continue even among the members of God's household. For regeneration in Christ does not completely sanctify relations between men. Conflicts continue to exist – for man continues to sin.

Conflict is integral to politics. So is consensus. Conflict is a consequence of the ego centeredness of man resulting from the Fall. Conflict makes politics necessary. Consensus is the product of man's ability to reach beyond pure self-interest. Consensus makes politics possible. Conflict without consensus would result in pure egoism – social anarchy. Consensus without conflict would cease to be politics – it would be a natural harmony, a return to the garden of peace.

Once again, both liberals and evangelicals have rather simplistic notions as to how consensus can be achieved. To the liberal, consensus can be found rather easily by making moral appeals to man's capacity for idealism and self-transcendence. To the evangelical, consensus is viewed as an automatic by-product of man's reunion with God. The liberal fails to understand that man's selfishness is never totally separate from his idealism. The evangelical fails to understand that his reconciliation with God not only establishes new social division within the human community (redeemed v. unredeemed), but that it can also create a righteous zeal detrimental to the practice of politics. For "true believers" of any stripe are always tempted to become hard-core ideologues seeking to impose their truths on society at large. The more firmly they hold on to their truths, the less willing they often are to compromise them in the political arena.

Political consensus is really a polite term for political compromise. All politics involves compromising the conflicts of interest within a society. Political institutions and traditions are nothing more than the channels through which the conflicts are routed and the rules by which the conflicts are fought. No political consensus – the reaching of an accord between opposing political conflicts – is equally advantageous to all the players. There are always those who are relatively the winners and relatively the losers. Political compromise never puts an end to political conflict. It simply changes the terms and the relative advantages and disadvantages the players have in the pursuit of their interests.

Because politics is a never-ending cycle of conflict seeking consensus, moralists of all stripes become quickly frustrated. They seek absolute answers of eternal significance as opposed to the calculated compromises of politics. They tend to do one of two things. Either they become political extremists seeking to impose their self-assured truths on society in the effort to establish the grand and final solution to social conflict, or they withdraw from political life because they refuse to taint themselves with compromise. But the ability to accept compromise is the mark of political maturity. It is the very stuff out of which politics is made. Purist ideological crusades and ascetic withdrawal must both be seen as the acts of sophomoric arrogance, which they are.

To elevate compromise as a principle of politics is not to insist that all political values or all political interests are equally meritorious. Nor is it to suggest that all truth is relative and that all political solutions are therefore relative. But no one man or party – or even a majority of an entire national population – ever has a pure, unadulterated grasp of truth. While truth is not relative, man's grasp of it is. Compromise in politics is necessary because man's political ambitions never totally transcend his selfishness. Indeed, we have more to fear from the ideological purist who dresses his demands in robes of white than the practical realist who openly confesses the personal interests attached to his political demands. To insist that one has the perfect solution to a political problem is to commit a sin of immense personal pride as well as to reveal a parochialism of understanding.

Withdrawal from politics is as morally reprehensible as is an attack on all politics from the standpoint of ideological purity. When men compete for political goals, implicit in their actions are ethical assumptions pertaining to the good. One person works to achieve change because he believes change will be for the better. Or another opposes change because he believes change will be for the worse. All politics demands ethical commitment. In the last analysis, all politics is then a struggle between competing conceptions of the good – or, if you will, between good and evil.

One cannot, therefore, withdraw from this struggle without affecting a net change in the balance of power between competing political interests. To withdraw is in essence to capitulate, if not to evil, at least to what one perceives to be a lesser vision of the good. Such withdrawal is an abdication of moral responsibility. How ironic, then, that those who do withdraw from politics often rationalize their actions by insisting that politics is a dirty business and they want to keep their hands clean!

But is politics a dirty business? Certainly the withdrawal of those sharing Christian standards from meaningful participation in political life does little to help the situation. But despite the fact that this often happens, one cannot say that politics in and of itself is either good or evil. Political decisions reflect the nature of the inputs or demands which are brought to bear on the political decision-making process. Politics is but a tool which can have consequences for good or evil. But the cause of the good is not helped when political demands sensitive to God's Word are no longer heard. For then half a loaf becomes none. And the entire political system suffers to an even greater extent from spiritual starvation.

THE MORAL AMBIGUITY OF POLITICS

We have suggested above that all political activity is involved in the struggle between good and evil. But at the same time, in the world of politics, it is always extremely difficult to say with certainty what is good and what is bad. Politics is surrounded by problems of moral ambiguity.

We have for example, argued that politics is always an exercise in self-interest. No political endeavor completely transcends the egoism of its supporters. Hence, all politics are partially rooted in selfishness. How, then, does a Christian reconcile political activity with his calling to live a life in conformity to Jesus Christ? We have also argued that all political decisions involve compromises in the search for a politically workable consensus. Politics seeks to find common ground amidst diverse demands, none of which is perfectly pure or righteous to begin with. Politics, then, always demands compromise with evil. The question is not whether or not evil will be mixed with the good, but rather whether and to what degree we will be conscious of the evil involved in our actions. How, then, can the Christian actively pursue compromise in the political world without compromising his own faithfulness to demands God makes on him to live a life of righteousness?

By way of general introduction to this problem, let us remember that politics is not the only aspect of life in which moral ambiguity is present. What distinguishes politics is the *extent* of moral ambiguity, not the simple fact of its presence. The businessman faces morally ambiguous decisions when he negotiates between the demands of labor for higher wages and benefits and the demands of stockholders for larger dividends and capital investment. Both parties often have right on their side. Yet neither side is free of selfish interest. The church faces morally ambiguous decisions in deciding how to budget its resources amidst legitimate demands for staff salaries, building funds, evangelism, and charity. The parents of school children face morally ambiguous decisions between quality education for their own children or, perhaps, an education of lesser quality for their own children, but an education of better quality for the population at large through forced racial integration.

The problem of moral ambiguity is often easier for the liberal to handle than for the conservative, evangelical Christian. The liberal is often willing to accept the concept of contextual morality. He often denies the existence of absolute, objective moral norms. If right and wrong are themselves relative, there is no difficulty in accepting a contextual morality which adjusts itself to the exigencies of the moment. (The irony in all this for the liberal is that he so often engages in moral crusades. How can he justify his sense of moral indignation and outrage over matters which are only relatively just or unjust?)

But the problem of moral ambiguity poses a much greater dilemma to the evangelical who subscribes to an infallible and eternal Word which establishes absolute standards for human behavior. Since right and wrong are absolute, how can one accept compromise or change one's standards to meet the needs of the moment? (Of course, there is irony here as well, for the evangelical, who is so often cocksure of the existence of absolute moral standards, is generally unwilling to engage in prophetic judgment upon society because he sees these standards as being so difficult to relate to specific issues that he is left speechless. Of what use are the standards?)

There are at least three dimensions to the problem of moral ambiguity in politics which must be recognized. The *first* dimension pertains to the problem of establishing absolute ethical foundations for political action. What is desperately needed is the moral humility to accept the fact that while God's standards are absolute and unchanging, we as individuals are never able to know or apply them with perfection. For all our talk to the contrary, we in the evangelical community have taken the concept of sin too lightly! While God has shown us what he wants, our obedience is always affected by what we are willing to see and do in response to his revelation. And even what we do — we might add — is by the grace of God, lest we should boast of our moral superiority!

Further, we pointed out in the previous chapter that the New Testament, in particular, generally speaks only obliquely about the problems of politics. For since political activity was not an option for the early Christian community, there was little need to discuss it. Hence, our guides to political action are based to a great degree on church tradition and our cultural history, not on direct biblical guidelines. If orthodox Christians practicing charity toward one another cannot come to agreement on matters where there appears to be direct biblical teaching (such as the administration of the sacraments or eschatology), it can hardly be expected that they will come to agreement on those matters where biblical teachings are arrived at only indirectly and inductively.

It is important, however, to keep the distinction in mind between the relativist who insists that truth is simply relative, and the moral absolutist who questions not the existence of moral absolutes but rather the limitations of man's ability to grasp moral truth in its entirety.

The *second* dimension of moral ambiguity in politics pertains to the very complicated problems with which politics must deal. Not only do we have an incomplete understanding of the ethical foundations of political action, but also we have an incomplete understanding of the facts upon which ethical decisions must be based. In addition, the facts themselves are always subject to change since social conditions are never static but always in a state of flux and change. Hence, individuals who share similar moral perspectives on issues will often advocate differing policies because they disagree on the facts pertaining to a political question.

Such instances can be illustrated easily. Senator Barry Goldwater voted against the 1964 Civil Rights Act not because he disagreed with the intent of the legislation, but because he believed it to be unconstitutional. Many conservative Christians supported legislation requiring health warnings on cigarette packages and restricting television advertising of cigarettes. Others equally concerned about the ill effect of cigarette smoking opposed this legislation as a dangerous precedent of government regulation of trade and commerce. Many religious leaders oppose the establishment of state-run lotteries because they are against gambling on principle and the social hardships it often creates for those in the lower classes who are prone to gamble heavily. Other religious leaders, however, equally opposed to the evils of gambling, support state-run lotteries as a means of undercutting the financial bonanza that illegal gambling provides for organized crime. Some religious leaders oppose liberalized abortion laws. Others, equally opposed to abortion, support liberalized abortion laws because they don't believe one ought to "legislate morality" or that one can moralize about the rights of the unborn until one shows equal compassion and concern about the rights of those already born. Many political leaders are concerned about the concentration of political power in the national government. Others are just as equally concerned, but see no alternative to the problem unless state and local governments prove themselves able to exercise their powers wisely. Thus, moral agreement – as rare as it may be in politics – does not guarantee political harmony.

The *third* dimension of moral ambiguity in political decision making pertains to the unintended consequences of political actions. Two parties may share the same moral concerns and outlook. They may also be agreed in their assessments of a factual situation. They may even agree that a particular problem will be solved by a particular program of government action. But they may disagree vigorously over the unintended consequences of government action.

Both liberals and conservatives in Congress may support the concept of an all-volunteer army. They may both believe that military conscription is inconsistent with the concept of a free society. They may both believe that the concept of a volunteer army might be a sort of democratic check on the war-making powers of Congress and the president since the strength of the armed forces and the military capacity of the nation would in the future rest increasingly on the popular support of national military policy. Yet, one may still disagree with the proposal for an all-volunteer army since it might encourage a professional military elite to emerge, separated and insulated from mainline democratic values in the society. Another might disagree with the proposal on the basis that the military – now short of much needed manpower – will have to turn to a military strategy based increasingly on massive nuclear confrontation in place of the military strategy of conventional warfare which calls for large armies. In other words, one may very much favor a particular policy – but reject it nonetheless due to the possibility of unintended consequences.

This same principle also works in reverse. Individuals who do not share similar moral or factual assessments of a political situation may nonetheless support similar policy goals. A black person may not have opposed the war in Southeast Asia on moral grounds, but simply on the basis that it diverted national resources away from much needed domestic spending. A parent may not have opposed the war in Southeast Asia on principle, and may be equally opposed to increased spending for human resources on the domestic front, but still have wished the war's end for the simple reason that he didn't wish to see his son inducted into the armed forces. A businessman might have cared less about the war, or poverty, or the parent's child sent to Vietnam or Cambodia, but have opposed the war nonetheless because he was worried about inflation. Thus, for different reasons they supported the same policy. As the saying goes, "Politics makes strange bedfellows."

If Christians are to rise above political naïveté, they must begin by recognizing that political problems are immensely complex and clouded. And they must recognize that the motives behind political action are generally mixed. Hence, politics is not a simple battle between good and evil, or virtuous men and evil men.

However, we should be warned against the danger of using the moral ambiguity of politics as an excuse for moral agnosticism which refuses to speak to political issues. This is just as dangerous as a simplistic and absolute identification of the moral good with one's own pet political cause. While liberals have often identified God's cause with specific pieces of legislation or particular social movements, evangelicals have at the same time rationalized their own lack of social involvement by insisting that since the Bible doesn't speak *directly* to these issues, they themselves can say *nothing* about them.[2]

Our inability to come to a perfect understanding of God's will on political matters does not serve as an excuse for silence. Rather, it calls for humility and restraint. The Christian affirms that God has spoken and shown himself in Christ Jesus. Thus the Christian comes to the political world with insights and moral commitment which at least to a relative degree are capable of transcending the egoism of politics. While Christians ought not hope for perfect and complete political accord, they can at least seek out broad principles upon which to agree. After all, we do not cease in the effort to enunciate church dogma just because dogmatic statements fall short of perfection. Why, then, should we cease in the effort to enunciate Christian social principles just because they too fall short of perfection? The corrective for simplistic moral absolutizing in politics is not abstention, but recognizing the inherent limitations and moral ambiguity of the political world.

Political Justice

Thus far, our discussion of politics has been essentially descriptive. We have suggested that politics is the ongoing search for social consensus amidst a world of competing personal demands. But politics is something more than simply the struggle for personal advantage. It is the attempt of the entire society to organize and manipulate personal demands in such a way that the consensus which is reached will, insofar as possible, be fair to each member of that society. In other words, politics is intimately involved in man's search for justice.

But what is justice? The classic answer to this question throughout the ages has been: "Justice is rendering to every man his due." But what is every man's due? It may seem ironic that a question as fundamental as this cannot be answered with great precision. justice, to paraphrase H.

Emil Brunner, is like a straight line. We all have a concept of what a straight line ought to be, but nowhere does a perfectly straight line exist in factual reality.[3] As unsatisfactory as this analogy may seem, it is nonetheless essential that politics not lose sight of the concept of justice. For if we deny the existence of an abstract and transcendental notion of the political good, then the processes of politics can be reduced to nothing more than brute force asserting its will over a weaker party.

Virtually every civilization and society throughout history has at least paid lip service to the concept of political justice. By it is meant that notion of right or wrong which is implanted in the human heart pertaining to the legitimate distribution of the resources of the given society. (This notion is what theologians often refer to as God's "general revelation" to all people or what philosophers refer to as the "natural law" ethic.) All societies have the concept of law receiving legitimacy insofar as it is in accord with that sense of moral rightness in the minds of its citizens. Obviously, different societies at different points in time have had drastically differing concepts on the particular contents of this higher, universal moral law. But on the broad principle that moral standards exist and should be pursued, there has been a substantive agreement among all civilizations.[4]

In Romans 1 and 2, Paul refers to this moral law as evidence of the fact that God has not abandoned man to moral anarchy. God has provided, through his sustaining grace and general revelation, at least a minimal moral foundation for society which stands as a guide for all peoples. This understanding is of utmost importance for the Christian concerned with politics because it creates the basis for an ecumenical politics. That is, Christians and non-Christians can work together for the political good because all men – regardless of their relationship to Christ – share a degree of common moral unity.

Because each society faces the task of working out the particular content and application of abstract justice in the context of its own particular environment, it is extremely difficult to delineate the criteria of a just society at all specific points. However, history seems to have indicated the utility of at least four *instrumental* values useful in the search for this definition. By instrumental values, we mean certain goals which ought to underlie all political action in the search for justice.

The first of these instrumental values is that of *order*. When we speak of a just society, we are referring first of all to what we commonly call the "just political order." Because of the conflicts and ambiguities inherent in politics, it is necessary to establish institutions by which political conflicts can be regulated and society itself protected from anarchy. Hence, Romans 13 cites the fact that God himself approves of the institutional ordering of society as an instrument for achieving justice. If society has no institutionalized means for creating political order, then it has no means by which to pursue justice. Note, however, that order is an instrumental value and not an end in itself. Institutionalized political authority exists for the sake of pursuing the good. Should the government – as so often happens – become a terror to the good, it will have perverted itself into a beast. (See Revelation 13.)

The second instrumental value is that of *freedom*. By freedom we mean the right of self-expression and self-determination insofar as it is not incongruent with the legitimate restraints imposed upon individuals for the sake of political order. As such freedom must be distinguished from license, which may be defined as simply the absence of restraint.

Freedom and order must be balanced in any society. Yet they must not be seen as opposites. Rather, they complement each other and neither can properly exist without the other. Freedom without order ceases to be freedom – it degenerates into anarchy and license. Order without freedom ceases to be order – it substitutes authoritarianism for authority. When in proper balance, both freedom and order are maximized.

The third instrumental value is that of *equality*. Political equality means that the political system will not make arbitrary discriminations against particular individuals or groups within a society. Of course, the question of what is "arbitrary" is an extremely difficult one. John Stuart Mill argued that citizens who owned land or had a university education should be allowed to cast two votes in national elections on the basis that landowners had a greater stake in the electoral outcome and educated individuals could make more informed choices. Hence, both should be allowed an extra vote. Is this reasonable or is it arbitrary? In the early years of the United States, only taxpaying landowners could vote since, it was argued, they were the ones which supported the burden of government financially. In recent years, the United States courts have upheld statutes which allow only landowners to vote in tax millage assessments since they alone pay for the tax directly. Are these reasonable or arbitrary restraints?

Further, the question of political equality – that is, the concept of dispassionate justice before the law – cannot be totally separated from the question of social equality or egalitarianism. Insofar as society is more than simply a contract between individuals seeking their own self-interest, the concept of equality must include a concept of equity in terms of the distribution of the resources of a society. But how the particulars of this value are to be delineated is just as ambiguous as trying to say once and for all what the perfect balance between the values of order and freedom ought to be.

The fourth instrumental value is that of *participation*. Participation in government decision making was held in such great value by theorists such as Plato, Aristotle, and Rousseau that they refused to conceive of a just political society other than that of a city-state in which all citizens could participate directly on a face-to-face basis. Concepts of mass participation via indirect representation have replaced the simple democracy of these earlier theorists. But they all agree that government must be accountable to the people, and that accountability is best achieved by allowing broad participation in the selection of leaders and determination of policies.

While the presence of these four instrumental values – order, freedom, equality, and participation – is not an adequate definition of a just society, it is safe to say that they will always be marks of a just society. But as we have seen, even in defining instrumental values, there is a great deal of ambiguity implicit in the search for justice.

Christian Insights on Justice

Some readers will be troubled with the preceding argument. First, one may ask why there was no attempt to define justice *substantively* as opposed to emphasizing only the instrumental values of justice. Second, one may ask why in dealing with the instrumental values of justice we refused to engage in precise descriptions of these instrumental values and emphasized again the ambiguity implicit therein. And third, one may ask whether or not the Christian revelation does not solve the moral ambiguity of justice and enable us to become more explicit and substantive in dealing with this problem. The first two of these questions can be answered rather briefly. The answer to the third question will take up most of this section.

In answer to the first question, the distinction between instrumental justice and substantive justice is ultimately an arbitrary one. To suggest otherwise is to believe that there is no integral relationship between political ends and the means used to pursue them. There is always the danger in politics that individuals can believe so strongly in the rightness of their cause that they will participate in unjust means to pursue what they believe to be a just end. In the process, the end itself becomes corrupted.

This problem, among others, was at the heart of the Watergate crisis. Some of President Nixon's supporters believed so strongly that his continued leadership was a political good that they violated the law (the basic institutional *order*ing of society) to pursue his reelection. In the process, the justice and rightness of his entire reelection and forthcoming administration were cast into doubt. In order to achieve their aims, they infringed on the civil *freedoms* of several noteworthy Americans, and in doing so raised the specter of a society in which freedom could be sacrificed if the end were only great enough. In retrospect, many Americans were left wondering whether the electoral procedures by which Americans *participate* in determining their leaders and national policies were so violated as to cast doubt on the legitimacy of the election itself. The crisis of Watergate was not that of defining substantive justice, but of violations of instrumental justice which called into question the legitimacy of any government policy or leader brought about by such means. Hence, means and ends cannot be separated.

Because the Watergate issue has received such widespread attention and because most thoughtful Americans have given it some serious consideration, the above may seem rather obvious. But if this principle applies in the case of Watergate, it must be seen to apply in other instances as well. It applies in the area of criminal justice where the means used to attack the problem of crime must be consistent with the ends. That is, one must not encourage the use of unlawful procedures in order to defend the law. The principle applies in cases of controlling civil disobedience and civil dissent where one must not violate constitutional rights to protect the Constitution. For once the instrumental values of justice are disregarded, substantive justice is reduced to the arbitrary definition of any party or individual successful in forcing its or his will on the masses by any means it chooses. This principle applies to Christians, as well, who are sometimes tempted to endorse policies because they believe them to be substantively correct while paying little regard to the means which might be used to pursue them. Prayers in public schools may be seen as just and good. (Here, of course, many Christians would disagree.) But one must not exalt those political leaders and educators who openly disregard Supreme Court rulings by encouraging prayers in public schools – for such unlawful disobedience only sets the precedent for others who might wish to pursue other goals outside of the law.

Second, we have refused to engage in precise definitions of the values of which instrumental justice is composed. We have done this because these values are strongly conditioned by the political and social environment of each culture. We have stated that political order is a characteristic of instrumental justice. But order always exists in a tandem relationship with the value of freedom. Different societies and cultures are comfortable with different balances between the two. The point to be remembered is that in no case must either freedom or order be exalted to the exclusion of the other.

Likewise, different cultural traditions vary tremendously in regard to the means and extent of participation in the political process. In Western democratic countries, we associate participation with the right to vote on candidates and policies at regular intervals. In traditional societies, the value of participation is mediated through a very stable culture which places constraints on the powers and policies of leaders even though formal electoral procedures do not exist. Thus, in an African tribe, the tribal chief makes his rulings on the basis of a sort of common law passed down within the tribe over hundreds of years. If he violates this law, he will lose his office. It is difficult for us to understand how such traditional restraints and mediated forms of participation are meaningful and effective. Yet in such cultures they are as meaningful and effective as our Western forms of participation. On the other hand, as the cultures change, it becomes imperative that the mode of participation change as well, just as our own modes of electoral participation have changed drastically from the days of a very restricted electorate to the use of mass politics today.

Finally, the concept of equality is strongly affected by cultural factors. Until only recently, women were not allowed to vote in Switzerland. And yet, few Westerners would thereby conclude that Switzerland was not an open, democratic society. Before the passage of the Twenty-sixth Amendment to the U.S. Constitution in 1971, giving the vote to all citizens of eighteen years of age or older, few felt that there was a fundamental problem in that some states allowed eighteen-year-old voting while others did not.

All of these factors – order, freedom, participation, and equality – must be considered on the basis of differing cultures within different political environments. Just as the Christian church universal differs significantly in its various liturgies, social taboos, etc., as they are defined in differing historical settings, so, too, we must expect the same in the political world.

However, our insistence on emphasizing the instrumental values of a just society – as opposed to dealing explicitly with a substantive definition of justice – together with our insistence on emphasizing the cultural relativity of these instrumental values leads to the third possible objection raised above. Does the Christian faith in the revealed Word of God not fill this void? Or are we left in a political world informed only by moral ambiguity and cultural relativism? In other words, is the Christian's ability to provide substantive and absolute moral values for social justice thoroughly mitigated by the moral ambiguity and cultural relativism through which he operates?

The answer to this question is both yes and no. The Christian is indeed in a unique position to give moral direction to the definition of justice insofar as he asserts that God's Word overcomes the moral ambiguity (or moral lostness of man estranged from God) of life with its revelation of God's standards of righteousness. On the other hand, as we pointed out earlier in this chapter, the pervasiveness of man's rebellion against God is such that in the process of utilizing God's revelation he tends to appropriate it for his own selfish purposes. The net effect, of course, is to relativize and demean God's absolute law.

However, while it is imperative that Christians recognize the dangers of moralizing self-interest under the cloak of God's Word, at the same time they must recognize that there is a fundamental difference between that of a simple moral relativism and that of a moral absolute perceived and acted upon imperfectly by confessing Christians. There are several reasons why this is so.

First, even though Christians can appropriate the absolute demands of God only on a relative basis, they are still at a relative advantage over those who have no knowledge or sensitivity to the revelation of God in his written word and in Christ Jesus. Hence, the Christian always has a moral contribution to make to the political debate over substantive justice, even though the contribution is in and of itself an imperfect appropriation of God's Word.

Second, one of the central themes of the Bible is that God calls his people to serve actively in the cause of building his kingdom of perfect righteousness. Thus, behind the conflicts and compromises of politics, there rests the metapolitics of God who in his providence is moving history toward the vindication of his righteousness. Insofar as Christians are called to be agents of the city of God within the cities of men, there is implicit therein the tacit assumption that God the Spirit can and will guide his servants to accomplish his ends. (Also, God used even his enemies to accomplish his purposes – something Christians all too often forget!)

Thus, the knowledge of our own moral inadequacy can never serve as an excuse for inaction based on moral agnosticism. God has spoken and has told us what he demands! However fragmentary our grasp of his truth, we are still called upon to act accordingly. But in so acting, we must at the same time act humbly with the knowledge that we always stand to be corrected. Hence, it is imperative that Christians respect the instrumental values of justice in the pursuit of substantive justice. For these very values protect us from the danger of moral arrogance seizing unwarranted power.

NOTES

1. The first significant call to renewed social concern on behalf of the evangelical community in the post-war period was Carl F. H. Henry's *The Uneasy Conscience of Modem Fundamentalism* (Grand Rapids, Mich.: Wm. B. Eerdmans Publishing Company, 1947). In the last five years, there has been a virtual renaissance of evangelical writing in this area, although it has lacked in dealing with the problems of how Christian conscience can be put into political action. Two of the more significant are David O. Moberg, *The Great Reversal* (Philadelphia: J. B. Lippincott Company, 1972) and Sherwood Wirt, *The Social Conscience of the Evangelical* (New York: Harper & Row Publishers, 1968).

2. On this, see Richard J. Mouw, "Evangelicals and Political Activism," *The Christian* Century, vol. 89, no. 47 (December 27, 1972), pp. 1316-1319.

3. H. Emil Brunner. *Justice and the Social Order*, trans. Mary Hottinger (New York: Harper & Row Publishers, 1945), p. 23.

4. See Brendan F. Brown, ed., *The Natural Law Reader* (New York: Oceana Publications, Inc., 1960).

Love, Power and Justice

The past five years have seen a resurgent awareness in evangelical Protestantism relative to the Christian community's political responsibility. But despite this awareness of political responsibility, *maturity* and *consistency* are sadly lacking in the pronouncements of evangelicals on this topic. The evangelical community, to paraphrase social critic Michael Novak, seeks to leap from piety to practice with little reflection on guiding principles and practical goals.

There are at least three basic concepts which require clear delineation as to what is meant in the contemporary evangelical dialogue regarding matters political. These three are *power, love* and *justice.*

Politics and Power

The very essence of politics is the use of power – the power to determine who in a given society gets what, how, when and where. We can talk about means and ends for a society without conceding the necessity (or desirability) that the sword of the state be the implementing agent. But we must be clear, then, in acknowledging that such talk is no longer talk about politics.

We can talk about the "Power of God to transform lives," but we are no longer talking about the political power of the state, which by definition refers to instituted social authority which enables the state to force compliance upon its subjects regardless of their volitional relationship to the state's demands. One can talk about "the fallen powers" or Christ's victory in resurrection over the "principalities and powers," but that, in and of itself, is not talk about the politics of the Soviet Union or the United States. One can speak of the "sovereignty of God," but one still has not dealt with the sovereignty of the Cook County Democratic Committee.

That is not to say that such talk is useless or unnecessary. Indeed, beliefs relative to the sovereignty of God, Christ's conquering of the principalities and powers, or the transforming power of God in individual lives have profound implications for the way in which we must think about politics. But spoken of in and of themselves, such concepts do little to illumine the path from piety to practice. Indeed, they often serve to obfuscate that path and to mask immoral practices in moral pieties.

There can be no politics apart from the use of power. And yet, as Paul Tillich notes, it is not uncommon to find Christian essayists who develop concepts of "The Politics of God" or "The Kingdom of God" in such a way that they seek a political order in which "powerless love" overcomes "loveless power." The problem to which Tillich refers is clearly evident in the writings of two contemporary individuals who have had a decided impact on the rising social and political consciousness of the evangelical community – namely, Jim Wallis, editor of *Sojourners*, and John Howard Yoder, whose book *The Politics of Jesus* is probably the most profound restatement of Anabaptist social theory in the past quarter of a century.

Yoder and Wallis juxtapose the power politics of the world (i.e., the "powers" of the world expressed in social, economic and political relationships) with Christian love (i.e., servanthood, the cross, self-denial). In the words of Wallis: "It seems to us impossible to be both what the world's political realities set forth as 'responsible' and to take up the style of the crucified servant which is clearly the manner of the life and death of Jesus Christ as revealed in the New Testament" (*Agenda for Biblical People* [Harper & Row, 1976], pp. 122-123). Yoder calls the church to "a social style characterized by the creation of a new community and the rejection of violence of any kind" – by which he means the economic and political orders held in place by the power of the state. "The cross of Christ is the model of Christian social efficacy, the power of God for those who believe" (*The Politics of Jesus* [Eerdmans, 1972], p. 250).

An Apolitical Strategy

It must be noted that while Wallis and Yoder reject "the way of the world" in their refusal to acknowledge any legitimate use of power, they do not advocate a withdrawal from the world or an abandonment of the church's mission to the world. In this sense, they differ profoundly from the separatist tendencies of the older fundamentalism. Indeed, they maintain that the subordination of the cross becomes a "revolutionary subordination" in the name of the Christ who has conquered the powers in his resurrection. The acceptance of political powerlessness, for Wallis and Yoder, creates the basis for the manifestation of the power of God as transforming agent. And thus the Christian community bears witness to the world, not only standing in judgment upon it but also prophetically pointing to the path of the world's redemption.

But what must be recognized is that such thinking provides *political critique and judgment* while rejecting *political involvement and practice* as a corrective strategy. For all of its political relevance and all of its political language, it is in the end an apolitical strategy rejecting power, and thus rejecting politics as well. Theirs is a strategy which advocates *social* involvement, which would effect consequences. But it rejects political involvement directed toward social consequences.

If the evangelical community is going to develop a political ethic, it must be one in which power is recognized and accepted as a legitimate means to the ends it seeks. To reject power is to reject politics. Such a rejection may not in and of itself be improper – but we should at least be clear as to what it is we are doing. The confusion has been great, however, because the very individuals who have done so much to renew the social conscience of the evangelical community have also been those who have rejected politics as a means of fulfilling social obligation. And while the evangelical conscience may indeed have been reawakened, it remains – at least in terms of understanding the linkages between power and politics – as apolitical today as it was 20 and 30 years ago.

The Characteristics of Love

While insisting that one cannot speak of politics without also speaking of power, we have nonetheless thus far not answered the question as to whether love and power are compatible. For if they are incompatible, and the Christian is indeed called to live a life of servanthood in love toward one's neighbor and God, then those who reject politics in the name of Christ are correct. It is imperative, therefore, that we distinguish the characteristics of love so that we can examine its compatibility with the exercise of political power.

First, we must acknowledge that love is something *voluntarily given.* Love can not be forced against one's will. Acts of the political order, however, invariably contain by definition elements of compulsion and involuntarism. Thus, insofar as the power of the state is associated with involuntarisim and the act of love with voluntarism, we must conclude that the state cannot love any more than love can be forced.

Second, love is somcthing that must be personally *mediated.* Since the voluntary nature of love necessitates the existence of a will by which it can become activated, love is always personal. The state, like any other instituted social order, has an objective existence and achieves its ends indiscriminately. The citizen's relationship to the state is an "I-it" rather than an "I-thou" relationship, and incapable of the personal mediation necessary for love to become activated.

Third, love is always *sacrificial.* That is to say that love is always a voluntary (noncompulsory) act in which one wills to allow something to happen at one's own expense for the well-being of another. Let me give an example. Suppose you are a clerk at a turn-of-the-century "mom and pop" neighborhood grocery store. Suppose a poorly dressed and obviously destitute widow comes into the store to buy a loaf of bread. Fumbling through her purse, she finds the last quarter she possesses with which to purchase the ten-cent loaf of bread. Upon the completion of the purchase, you as the store clerk return 15 cents' change to the widow. There is nothing loving in giving the lady her change. The change is hers just as surely as the loaf of bread is now hers.

Now let us suppose that, moved by the widow's evident poverty, you decide simply to give her the loaf of bread. You have no obligation to do so, you are not forced to do so, but you will to do so. You sacrifice your right to a fair price for the bread to the widow's advantage.

Fourth, since love is freely given, it goes *beyond ordinary moral obligation.* To fulfill moral obligation is to respond to moral necessity, and therefore, it is an act of duty rather than of free moral will. It is important to qualify this statement by noting also that going *beyond* one's moral obligation necessarily involves first *fulfilling* one's moral obligation.

Let us return, for purpose of example, to the store clerk and the widow to illustrate the point. This time, suppose the widow, due to her failing eyesight, mistakenly gives the clerk nine pennies and one dime for the loaf of bread which costs only ten cents. In returning the nine pennies to the widow, the clerk is not demonstrating some form of extraordinary love but simply fulfilling the moral obligation of not taking advantage of the widow's weakness of sight.

In summary, I have suggested that love is voluntary and freely given; that since it involves moral volition, it must be personally mediated; that love is sacrificial, and thus limited to the extent to which an individual is capable of personally absorbing the consequences of its acts; and finally, that love extends beyond duty or moral obligation (implying that it must first fulfill moral obligation or duty).

The Use of Coercion

But politics, on the other hand, involves involuntary servitude. Its very nature assumes the sanctioned use of coercion and force to achieve its ends. It is instituted in formal organization and operates impersonally. (Otherwise we should say that it operates arbitrarily and is discriminatory.) And the leaders of the state obviously engage in actions for which others are called on to sacrifice. (Otherwise there would be no need for force or coercion, and there would no longer be a need for the state's existence.) Most of us would be more than pleased with a political order which at least met the demands of moral obligation. Indeed, we would be tempted to rebel if the state sought to require us to exceed moral obligation. For in so doing, it would act as a totalitarian state which recognizes no limits to the power of the state or to the citizen's obligations toward the state.

To use the power of the state as a means of effecting love among its citizens is therefore not only contradictory, insofar as love cannot be forced or coerced; it also destroys the distinction of "moral obligation" by which the difference between a limited and a totalitarian government is marked.

Given the duality between power and love and the apparent conflict between "loveless power" and "powerless love," how shall we choose? So long as the choice is put in these terms, it would be difficult to do other than to choose to be a political eunuch in order to become a servant in the Kingdom of God. Surely, God calls us to the higher and more noble path of love over power.

But critical questions remain. By what is love to be informed other than by its willed motivations? If love is the sacrificial act of going beyond one's ordinary moral duty, how do we define such moral duty so as to know when it has been surpassed and love has taken its place?

It is the concept of justice which creates other alternatives by which the concepts of "loveless power" and "powerless love" can be reconciled. And it is justice which enables us to be servants of both power and love.

The Claims of Justice

The refusal to recognize the claims of justice as universal and eternal – and thus inviolable even in the context of Christian social ethics – has demanded a high price both in terms of the political relevance of the church and in terms of the church's own theological integrity. The theology of Albrecht Ritschl, for example, suffered from this error. Ritschl was reduced to juxtaposing loveless power and powerless love. In so doing, he created an entire theological system which contrasted the Old Testament "God of power" with the New Testament "God of love." In the process he was forced to abandon the concept of God's judgment and retribution for sinners, was forced to adopt a universalist concept of salvation, and gave to the church a love ethic of which nothing substantive could be said.

At the practical level, the love ethic then becomes irrelevant to the problems of politics because, in the words of Reinhold Niebuhr, "It persists in presenting the law of love as a simple solution for every communal problem" (*Reinhold Niebuhr on Politics*, edited by Harry R. Davis and Robert C. Good [Scribner's, 1960], p. 163). Thus, as we deal with the concept of justice, let us not suppose that it is of lesser relevance or importance for the Christian than the concept of love.

We must begin by acknowledging that the claims of justice are universal, eternal and objective. The claims of justice spring from the personhood of the just God, and they lay claim to all that is contingent upon his creative power.

But given the assertion that justice makes itself manifest in the "creation ordinances" of God, why is it then that humanity has never reached consensus as to the substantive elements and characteristics by which justice can be defined? The most commonly accepted starting point defines justice as the "giving of every person his or her due." But what is due each and every individual, or each and every group of individuals, is a constant point of contention. It is here, then, that we must make some important distinctions in regard to notions that have clouded evangelical attempts to deal with the problem of justice.

While some thinkers have posited *love* and *power* as the only values from which Christian choice must be made in evaluating Christian political responsibility, at the exclusion of the concept of *justice*, others have included justice – but in such an ambiguous and ill-defined manner as to make the term as meaningless and without content as discussions relating to the "love ethic."

The claims of justice, if they are to become operational in a political society, must be defined with some meaningful degree of particularity. "Justice," in the words of Niebuhr, "requires discriminate judgements between conflicting claims" (*Love and Justice*, edited by D. B. Robertson [World, 1967], p. 28). Justice as an abstraction is not enough. We must work out an understanding of justice in particulars, lest we fall into the trap of moralizing about politics while having nothing to offer in terms of a moral critique that speaks to particular situations in time and space.

A classic example of this problem is illustrated in the *Politics* of Aristotle. Aristotle points out that if we define justice as rendering to each man his due, there are nonetheless two logically attractive and yet mutually contradictory principles by which this concept of rendering rights can be interpreted. In the first instance, there are those who argue that since all persons have a fundamental spiritual or moral equality, then that equality ought to extend to all social, economic and political relationships in which they find themselves. In the second instance, there are those who argue that since individuals are unequal in the contributions they make to a society, the inequalities of contribution ought to be recognized in consequent social, economic and political relationships. Both arguments have merit. Indeed, this age-old dilemma is at the heart of much contemporary political debate between democratic socialists and democratic capitalists in modern Western societies.

'REDEMPTION ORDINANCES' IN POLITICAL THEORY

Granting the need for dealing with justice in more than simple abstractions, we face even more clearly the problem that people disagree as to the applications to be drawn from such abstractions (such as that of giving each man his due). Of what good are "creation ordinances" if, through the fall, the human being's perception of what is just, let alone one's moral motivation to act on those perceptions, is thoroughly clouded?

Hence, it is not uncommon in Christian political theory – particularly contemporary Christian political theory – to reject the concept of a universally known justice via creation ordinances and turn, instead, to the notion of "redemption ordinances." Given the fall of humanity, these people argue, there can be no sure knowledge of justice aside from the Scriptures and God's incarnate Word in Jesus Christ. I surely would not wish to argue that the fallen human's knowledge of or capacity for justice was unimpaired by the fall. But I would like to point out several dangers in the thinking of those who reject the concept of justice based on creation ordinances known to all persons, regardless of their religious persuasion or soteriological and revelational systems.

First, to reject creation ordinances out of hand places our reason as creatures bearing the image of God (however fallen) into conflict with revelationally based knowledge. It is an epistemological problem which extends itself, logically, to asserting that in all areas of knowing, reason has nothing to say aside from revelation. In the realm of culture, it suggests that Athens has nothing to say to Jerusalem.

Second, this position has very serious practical consequences for strategies of political involvement. For if only those within the household of faith and conversant with the revelation of God in his redemptive ordinance can speak with authority on matters of justice, then Christians are unable to communicate or work with non-Christians in political endeavor. There can be no "secular" basis for political involvement by the Christian – only a religiously informed and motivated involvement which is sectarian by definition. If we deny natural knowledge of the political good, the only alternative for the Christian is to (a) withdraw from politics because it is worldly or fallen, or (b) establish a "Christian" politics which is sectarian in ambition and motivation.

The disjoining of God's "creation ordinances," and the consequent universal norms of justice attached thereto, from God's "redemption ordinances," which establish a unique rationale for a "Christian" politics, has demonstrated itself in various forms in contemporary Christian thinking. Many evangelicals and fundamentalists have sought uncritically to impose revealed norms of religious righteousness on the secular society with little if any justification insofar as how such policies would affect nonbelievers. Hence, crusades to make America a "Christian nation" are not infrequent, and Christian standards of morality and ethics are uncritically (and usually inconsistently) upheld as normative for the secular state.

Many neo-orthodox thinkers, subsuming "redemption ordinances" to "christological ordinances," have uncritically (and equally inconsistently) sought to apply the "love ethic" of Jesus with little regard for the objectifying norms of justice which must inform the spirit of love. And many Anabaptist and revolutionary thinkers, subsuming "redemption ordinances" to "eschatological ordinances," have uncritically (and equally inconsistently) sought to apply the ethic of the Christ who makes all things new and has conquered the "fallen powers" into an ethic of revolutionary consequences, disregarding the fact that the powers given to Satan have *always* been held in check by the Creator God, and that while the conquering power of God has indeed been visibly and dramatically revealed in the resurrection of our Lord, we are told nonetheless that Satan's powers shall be unleashed in new fury before the final consummation of God's kingdom.

The Character of Justice

Let me, then, suggest the following criteria in establishing the character of justice. *First,* justice must be based on *universal* claims of right. To establish justice on the basis of sectarian authority alone is to do violence to our very confession that *all* persons bear the image of God, and that *all* persons carry a knowledge of the good. And consequently it follows that *all* persons are bound to the demands of justice.

Second, justice must be defined within the context of a given social order, and it must be enumerated in terms of specifics. To base one's plea on "justice" alone is not enough.

Third, given the universality of the norms of justice and the universality of the consciousness of justice, one can derive procedures and practices which, when honored, increase the likelihood of policies and programs which eventuate in justice. Indeed, this is exactly what our concepts of "civil rights" seek to do in our constitutionally based democracies; it is the recognition that the *means* employed must not do violence to the *ends* pursued. (We must point out that nonwesternized societies of a traditionalist character have sought to recognize the same principles of constitutionalism in less articulated ways.)

Fourth, we must recognize that the norms of justice are objective and that they exist independently of human volition. Hence, claims can be made in the name of justice, and claims can be rejected in the name of justice. Whereas love must be volitionally given, justice demands to be recognized independently of human volition.

Fifth, since the "God of love" is also a just God, love and justice cannot stand juxtaposed. Love may go beyond justice – but it can never seek less than justice. Love may inform and inspire reverence for justice — but it can never be an excuse for absolving the claims of justice.

Sixth, since justice is an objective quality establishing rights and obligations, calculations can and must be made by individuals and societies as to how their actions serve the claims of justice. Given the fact that not all persons willingly seek justice, power can be used legitimately if and when it serves the cause of justice. While we have suggested that love *cannot* use power to achieve its ends, justice *must* use power to achieve its ends.

Such distinctions are necessary — not only because to call upon the state to "love" is self-contradictory, insofar as the state's actions are rooted in power and not voluntarism, but because the claims of love are rooted in sectarian acknowledgment as opposed to universal norms of justice. As the church proclaims the gospel, it sensitizes the community at large (as well as the Christian community) to the demands of justice. Hence, while justice remains the servant of love, it is love which serves as the enabler of justice.

Further, to seek to use the state as an instrument of love implies not only a sectarian state but a totalitarian state. For it is the discriminating norms of justice which are used to delineate the questions as to what is mine and what is thine. To deny justice in the name of love is to deny the very civilities which are at the root of constitutional government itself.

By adding the concept of justice to those of love and power, new alternatives for evangelical Protestantism's thinking about politics are created. Politics, rooted in power, nevertheless fulfills a legitimate function when it serves the claims of justice. Love, while rejecting power and going beyond the rights and duties established by justice, establishes a will for justice and a moral motivation which crowns the just act. Love, while personally mediated, complements justice with its objective demands.

Christian Perspectives on Power Politics

There has been a great deal of attention paid to the evangelical community's renewed concern with social issues. Yet, in the midst of the social awakening of American evangelicalism, it is already becoming clear that there is a great deal of inconsistency and incoherence within the evangelical community when it comes to addressing social issues.

No doubt the very diversity of evangelicalism contributes to the kaleidoscopic character of evangelical social ethics. The "confessional" wing of evangelicalism, rooted in classical Calvinism and Lutheranism, approaches questions relative to the relationship of church and society quite differently than does the "free church" wing of evangelicalism. The unique flavor of "American fundamentalist" evangelicalism contrasts sharply with the "mainline" evangelicals to be found in denominations such as the Episcopal Church.

This diversity within evangelical Protestantism is one of its strengths – and at the same time one of its weaknesses. In seeking to establish what evangelicalism stands for theologically, one can refer to evangelicalism as a broad community of Christians concerned with maintaining theological orthodoxy in the larger Christian community. But when it comes to establishing what the relationship between that theological orthodoxy and the social concerns of contemporary civilization may be, the diversity of opinion and response from the evangelical community is so overwhelming and contradictory that it has dissipated its capacity for social influence. When a movement stands for everything, it effectively stands for nothing. Such, I believe, is the present situation of evangelicalism with respect to the great social issues of today.

First published in *Christian Social Ethics*, ed. Perry Cotham (Grand Rapids, Michigan: Baker Book House), 1979, and reprinted by permission of Baker Book House Company.

While this broad generalization is true relative to evangelism and social ethics in general, it is particularly true when dealing with questions of politics. This failure on behalf of the evangelical community is a devastating indictment of its self-professed capacity to restore integrity and vitality to the nation's political system. It is particularly tragic given the fact that our world is one in which seemingly all questions relative to life and death have become politicized. And it calls into question the sincerity of evangelical claims to being a "world and life view" addressing the total human condition. Large segments of evangelicalism have supported the cross-breeding of the cross and the flag, thereby compromising evangelicalism's ability to offer prophetic judgment on acts of state. Other segments of evangelicalism have defined Christian discipleship so radically as to effectively remove Christian presence from affairs of state, and in the name of "radical discipleship" have fostered a new movement of withdrawal from the world in the hope of establishing model Christian communities separated from the ambiguities of moral choice which face those who seek to live within, so they may witness to the secular world.

It is true that evangelical Protestantism's failures to deal adequately with social and political questions have protected it against other failures. The apoliticism of a large segment of evangelicalism has protected it from the errors of Protestant liberalism which too simply equated the kingdom of God with the cause of social democracy. The sectarian and institutional pluralism of evangelicalism has protected it from forming a political party seeking to engineer a "Christian politics." And the individualistic pietism of evangelicalism has protected it from seeking to link the gospel to political particulars without appreciation for the finitude and relativities of political decision-making. But the "virtues" of evangelicalism in this regard are not grounds for pride. It must simply be recognized that our sins and shortcomings have been of a different character than those of liberal Protestantism. Our job is not to determine which is the greatest of sinners, but continued repentance and renewal in the quest for mature Christian discipleship.

Political Ethics Juxtaposed to Social Ethics

Why has evangelicalism failed to deal with *political* questions adequately? One of the chief reasons, I believe, is the failure of the evangelical community to take seriously the unique feature of politics as a phenomenon to be distinguished from other social questions by its peculiar relationship to the possession and use of power. For all of the renewed concern within evangelicalism relative to questions of race, economic justice, world hunger, ecology, sex, violence, war, and other pressing social issues, there is little meaningful discussion of the moral questions facing the use of the state as the instrument by which many of these questions will be settled.

Evangelicals are prone to talk about "changing hearts to change behavior" — but what happens when hearts are not changed? Under what circumstances and conditions ought the state to use its power to seek ends which the community will not voluntarily pursue? And what means are appropriate to the use of the power of the state?

In the nineteenth century, Karl von Clausewitz defined war as "politics by other means." He might just as well have defined politics as "war by other means." For the very essence of politics is the use of power — the power to determine who in a given society gets what, how, when, and where. The political system is nothing less (although hopefully something more) than the institutionalized means a society employs to resolve questions incapable of being resolved voluntarily without the use of the sword. When Jimmy Carter spoke of a government "which is as loving as its people," he should have been reminded that government acts not as an agent of love, but as a final resort to force when love, compassion, and voluntarism have failed.

We have grown accustomed to moralizing about our government to such an extent that we forget that at the bottom line, government holds institutionally legitimatized rights to use the sword to effectively carry out its decisions. Struggles over control of the government and the policies of a government are, therefore, struggles over the right to use the power of the sword.

Such talk sounds distasteful to many Christians. It is for that reason that they seemingly do anything they can to escape facing the *political* significance of social questions. For the significance of politics is the significance of power. Paul Tillich referred to the moralizing so common in the Christian community when he wrote:

> One speaks of "power politics," and one often does so with moral indignation. But this is the consequence of mere confusion. Politics and power politics are one and the same thing. There are no politics without power, neither in a democracy nor in a dictatorship.[1]

If we fail to deal with the issue of power, we fail to distinguish between the state and other social institutions such as the family, the church, and voluntary associations. As Karl Lowenstein states:

> The basic urges that dominate man's life in society and govern the allness of human relations are threefold: love, faith, and power.... Of this triad of societal motivations, power, while operative in all human relations, is of paramount significance for the socio-political realm. Politics is nothing else but the struggle for power.[2]

Or again, in the words of sociologist Robert Strausz-Hupé:

> To explore the nature of politics is to encounter the enigma of power. Power is the staff of orderly government. Without the exercise of power, political order could neither be established nor maintained. Power guards society against anarchy. Yet power spawns tyranny and violence, corrupts the mighty and crushes freedom.[3]

I emphasize the power relationships in politics for the simple reason that evangelicals generally tend to shy away from facing the brutal reality that power is at the essence of the political relationship. When evangelicals speak of restoring broken relationships through renewed God-man and man-man reconciliation, they are speaking of social realities which will affect the context in which politics operates. But they are not dealing with politics. When evangelicals speak of demonstrating love and compassion to the poor, the downtrodden, and the oppressed, they are speaking of changing relationships within our society which will have a profound impact on the quality and character of our social existence. But unless and until they speak explicitly of what role the state should take in reordering and reforming relationships between white and black, rich and poor, or young and old, they are not speaking of politics proper.

Politics As Allocation of Resources

The resources on our planet are limited. The people on our planet hold differing views as to how those resources should be distributed. And not surprisingly, given the fall of man, individuals are prone to support allocation of those resources in such a way that the distribution formula is personally advantageous. Hence, conflict over resources and their distribution is an integral part of human existence.

Because this situation, left alone, is anarchic and inherently unstable, societies generally find it to their advantage to designate an agent to settle disputes concerning the distribution of those resources. This agent, of course, is the state. And the interrelationships and activities surrounding the decision-making authority of the state are what politics is all about. Indeed, the most commonly accepted definition of politics used by political scientists is the following: "*Politics is the authoritative allocation of values and resources for all society.*"[4]

Implied in that definition are several concepts which must be looked at carefully if we are going to discuss meaningful Christian concerns relative to the political order. First, let us note that politics is an "allocative" activity. It is engaged in the process of decision-making which rewards and penalizes members of society through the distribution of a society's fixed resources. There is no such thing as a political decision which affects all members of a society equally. Some decisions will be of benefit to the masses at the expense of the few. Other decisions will be of benefit to the few at the expense of the masses. Still other decisions may well be of benefit to everybody, but they will benefit some people relatively more than others. There is no such thing as a political decision which makes all members of society equally happy – for every political decision reallocates the fixed resources of a society among its members.

Recognition of this fact means that when Christians address political questions, they must be extremely careful to acknowledge that while they may seek to help some through political decision-making, they necessarily implicate themselves in hurting others. It also indicates that all political questions are at least in some way economic questions. Politics necessarily becomes involved in questions of "distributive justice." (This must be noted since several prominent evangelical spokesmen, articulating conservative political philosophy, have suggested that the state should limit its concerns to questions of "retributive justice" – that is, should be solely concerned with protecting order and the execution of freely negotiated contracts. While I would not wish to question the concept of limited government which such a position seeks to protect, I would point out that such a policy does affect distributive justice simply because it seeks to protect the rules which have sustained the present allocation of resources in a society. Hence, it by default assumes that present patterns of distributive justice are consistent with Christian concerns.)

Politics As Allocation of Values

Second, let us note that our definition of politics points out that political decision-making allocates not only resources, but "values." What is meant here is that the distribution of resources reflects value judgments concerning what is or is not a "just" allocative formula within a society. In other words, political decision-making is never "value-free."

A "conservative" who opposes a certain change in government policy operates on the assumption that change would be for the worse. A "liberal" who supports change in government policy operates on the assumption that change would be for the better. Of course, what must be remembered is that the points of view taken by the conservative or the liberal are strongly influenced by the relative effect given policies have on his or her own well-being. In other words, we must recognize that what appears to be good or bad, in terms of political decision-making, is strongly influenced by our own calculations of self-interest.

This is not to say that individuals are incapable of transcending their own self-interest for the well-being of the community at large. Were this the case, politics would be nothing more than a struggle between competing private interests. It would reduce itself to a power struggle in which people sought power and influence simply and solely on the basis of private greed.

Though mankind is prone to maximize his self-interest at the expense of others, he also has the capacity to transcend self-interest for the good of the community. Mankind is driven not only by selfish egoism, but by his inherent nature as a social animal which mitigates and questions his predisposition to seek only personal well-being. Thus, while mankind has a predilection toward favoring his self-interest, he has an abiding capacity for altruistic concern of his neighbor's interest.

Politics thus operates amid the conflicts of self-interest and the conflicts within individuals and groups relative to private interest versus public interest. Thus, politics is always a struggle over moral decision-making which affects the allocation of resources in a society. The distribution of resources reflects moral assumptions inherent in the political choices being made.

Further, these moral choices are made in the context of mankind's acknowledgment that he is a being with moral responsibility. The entire concept of constitutionalism (or limited government) implies acknowledgment that government itself operates under moral constraint.

One of the chief opportunities for Christian witness in the political order is the constant call to recognize the moral implications of political decision-making. Since all political decisions allocating the fixed resources of a society rest upon value judgments of what is "in the best interest of all" or "in the interest of certain groups or individuals" (always at the expense of other interests), the clear articulation of Christian principles affects the context out of which final political decisions are made.

Thus, when the Christian community speaks forcefully about concerns relative to racism, sexism, world hunger, environmental limitations, war, and so forth, it is effecting a political role – insofar as it shapes the civic culture and the public philosophy which informs the moral assumptions of public policy. The Christian community, through its recognition of God's call to justice in society, affects the social context from which political decisions are made.

While this is an extremely important role for the church in any given society, it must be emphasized that it is not a complete political strategy. While the values of a society underlie and influence political choice and decision-making, and while politics is therefore never morally neutral or amoral, this role does not completely fulfill the church's political responsibility.

To simply acknowledge that resource allocation (the final political decision) reflects value allocation (the moral assumptions which underlie and sustain resource allocation) is not enough. For it is those very resource allocations which define in substance the values to which we subscribe. Conscience, in matters of state, necessarily involves very difficult "weighing of moral choices" in which values compete and in which complex choices concerning the prudential application of values must be made. To say that the church must call the state to be conscious of world hunger is not enough. For if we simply insist that America's surplus wheat should be shipped to starving nations (rather than dumped in the ocean as it was in the 1950s to keep domestic prices high and give the farmer an equitable return on his investment), we risk destroying the economies of those nations which are dependent on grain exports for their own economic (and political) stability.

Let me elaborate on this example for purposes of discussion. If the United States would encourage maximum wheat production by raising price-support guarantees for wheat farmers, removing lands presently reserved from production by means of "soil bank" programs, etc., and then ship our "surplus" grains to China, the USSR, and third world countries, we would seriously disrupt the Canadian economy, which relies on its grain exports. The disruption of the Canadian economy would seriously disrupt our export of industrial goods to Canada (our largest trading partner) which in turn could cause severe unemployment in our own country. The loss of government revenues through decreased economic output and increased welfare benefits would create not only serious domestic political unrest, but would threaten the government's ability to "guarantee" price supports for the grain producers. Hence, the moral-sounding appeal to develop a government food policy to feed the world's hungry, if not properly designed in particulars, may have devastating moral effects which outweigh the well-intended policies advocated by those concerned with world hunger.

The situation is more complicated when we recall that during the 1970s, the United States shipped enough food to the famine-struck countries of Ethiopia and Bangladesh to completely absolve the hunger in those countries. But the receiving countries themselves were so corrupt and inept in their distribution of the food that substantial famine relief did not take place. Thus, questions must be raised as to whether we should seek to administer such programs directly (neo-colonialism?), and whether we should continue to "waste" foodstuffs through price supports which encourage "excess" production – using tax resources which could otherwise be applied to other social needs.

The point to be remembered is that every resource allocation must be morally evaluated in relation to other resource allocations. It must further be evaluated in relation to the possible unintended consequences which may result from possible decisions. Abstract calls to "feed the hungry" and the simple sensitization of the populace through raising Christian concern are not enough in themselves to bring about policy decisions which are morally adequate.

Politics As Authoritative Use of Power

Third, our definition of politics states that allocation of values and resources is *authoritative.* One of the unique features of politics is its association with the use of the sword to establish compliance with the allocative decisions being made in the name of the state. The state, therefore, cannot be an instrument of "love." For love must be an act of personal volition, whereas the very nature of things political is that they ultimately rely on the power of the sword to accomplish their ends. It is true that states rely on the consent of the governed (either explicitly, as in contemporary democratic governments, or implicitly, as in traditional autocratic governments) as a source of moral legitimatization which enables the state to act "authoritatively." It is also true that states seek to exploit public opinion and support for their policies in order to legitimatize their actions (either through monopolisitic control of opinion formation, as in modern totalitarian states, or through exploitation of the deference normally shown to political leaders in traditional and democratic societies). But in the final instance, decisions of state are enforced with sanctions which render compliance, therewith as something short of being voluntary. While it is less than voluntary, however, we nonetheless acknowledge that the state is "authoritative" in the sense that it possesses a sense of legitimacy.

Hence, if a coalition of minority groups would engage in guerilla activities which effectively "taxed the rich to aid the poor," we would have to maintain that however noble the cause, the action of such a guerilla band would be illegitimate. We would designate their activities as robbery and stealing. But when the state seeks the same goal through an established system of taxation, it is no longer stealing or robbery, but an act of authority which (however misguided the policy may be in the eyes of some) possesses a particular character of moral legitimacy.

The state's use of force is called forth in just those situations where there is not voluntary compliance with social goals. Hence, when Christian spokesmen suggest that we would not have to pass laws on racism, sexism, or welfare rights, if our nation would but repent, humble itself, and conform to the teachings of Christ, they are absolutely correct. But, they must realize they are speaking of an *alternative* to politics, not merely a Christian political style. The fact of the matter is that peoples are not prone toward complying with the demands of justice, and for that very reason states have always served to seek the demands of justice through the power of the sword. Granted, Christian voluntarism would have a tremendous effect on the social structures of our society and upon the political demands with which government has to deal. And granted, a "Christianizing" of the public philosophy would have a tremendous effect on the value system informing allocative decisions which government must make. But this obviously is not a satisfactory solution to the total political question.

The state establishes and protects economic and social systems which render goods and resources in a society. Hence, Christians must deal critically with the *systemic* character of policies and institutions rooted in the power of the state which reflect moral decision-making. And as modern society becomes increasingly interdependent, the state as "economic manager and coordinator" has become increasingly involved in regulating the nature of those interrelationships. And we, as Christians, are increasingly implicated in the decisions of the state. Every dollar we earn we have earned within a system which is upheld by the power of the state. Every dollar we are taxed is used for different purposes – the building of neutron bombs, subsidies for the trucking industry through interstate highways, subsidies for the mariner unions through cargo-preference legislation, the exportation of tobacco products as "food for peace," or aid to dependent children.

Thus, while we correctly believe that the state is not the soteriological answer to the moral dilemma of man as sinner, we must nonetheless recognize its practical necessity in a fallen world where force is necessary as a means to insure a modicum of justice. We must likewise recognize that the force which states use to insure compliance with their policies is a force which can be used for relative good or relative evil. As we have pointed out above, all decisions of state are value-related. Hence, to abandon concern about affairs of state through simple dismissal with slogans such as "The state can't save us!" is to abandon concern in a significant area of moral decision-making. And to denigrate the state as an instrument of force – "The state's way is evil compared with the love ethic taught by Christ!" – is to denigrate concern for the relative justice which the state seeks to insure through its deployment of power.

Finally, to repudiate involvement in affairs of state in the name of Christian love implicates us in sins of omission for not having done what we might have done to affect public policies for the good. I shall concede that involvement in affairs of state implicates us in sins of commission, and that the policies of state fall short of absolute justice and the demands of Christian love. But to avoid involvement in the struggle for justice under the power of the state is to bear responsibility for the unspoken word, the unfulfilled deed, and the withdrawal from the decision-making process which removes Christian witness from the political struggle. And how can one claim fidelity to the norms of love and righteousness at the top of the moral ladder if he is unwilling to serve also the norm of political justice with all of its relativities at the lower rung of the moral ladder?

The Universal Scope of Politics

Fourth, our definition of politics stresses the fact that political decisions are made for *all of society.* Political decisions are involuntary not only insofar as they are enforced by the sword, but involuntary insofar as their scope includes all people in a society regardless of whether they desire to be so included. All other associations in society are voluntary, and all other associations in society are limited in scope. One joins all other associations through direct or indirect consent. But where the state is concerned, one is bound by fact of birth into the existing political system. All other associations make decisions governing only segments of the society at large, and those decisions are not backed by the power of the sword to force compliance. The state, on the other hand, governs all peoples within a society and enforces its decisions with the sword.

The ecumenical inclusiveness of the state thus requires that the values and norms governing its actions be sufficiently inclusive and latitudinarian. It must not serve the value preferences of one set of particular individuals in a society to the exclusion of others. This principle creates an environment of moral ambiguity and moral inconsistency which is difficult for many evangelical Christians to accept and operate within.

Righteousness and Justice in Political Ethics

The evangelical Christian accepts the lordship of Jesus Christ and the Scriptures which bear witness to him as the standard by which all human endeavor is to be evaluated and judged. It is understandable, therefore, that evangelicals are prone to suggest that their understandings of right should serve as norms of national righteousness in political life. The difficulties of this for politics are manifold, however.

First, it must be remembered that Christians themselves disagree substantially on the meaning and interpretation of Scriptures. The Bible is not self-interpreting. Calvinists and Lutherans disagree over the Scriptural teaching concerning the Lord's Day observances. Evangelical Christians with strong ethnic ties to continental Europe feel quite differently about the appropriateness of alcohol and tobacco in private and public life than do many Christians with Anglo-Saxon evangelical traditions. To put the matter simply: if evangelical Christians have difficulty coming to agreement on substantive theological questions relative to eucharist, the second coming of Jesus Christ, and matters of church governance to which the Bible speaks directly, how can they presume to establish coherent and unitary positions on matters of social and political ethics to which the Bible speaks only indirectly?

Second, it must be remembered that substantial portions of the population adhere to varying Christian, non-Christian, and agnostic religious traditions which must be respected in the political arena. Even if evangelical Protestants could come to common understanding concerning the particulars of public policy based on Christian teaching, they would still have to take into account the necessity of respecting the civil rights of those who disagree with their positions on public policy. While all political decisions reflect moral decision-making and value choices, it is nonetheless true that it is bad public policy to root political decisions strictly and solely on the basis of a particular sectarian goal.

The reasons for this are several. It must be remembered that the means a state employs to secure its ends affect the ends themselves. A nation cannot seek to curtail civil rights as a means of securing civil rights. Thus, means of the state which are always rooted in force and involuntarism cannot be used to secure Christian standards of love in society. A father may beat his child into compliance with parental standards. But such acquiescence of behavior by the child reflects not a relationship of love, respect, and voluntarism but simply a relationship of force. To use the sword of the state to enforce standards to which a broad spectrum of society does not agree undermines the broad consensual foundations of legitimacy upon which the state's authority must rest. And to use the sword of the state in the name of Christian love is contradictory – for the compliance to Christian norms would result not in voluntarily returned love but merely in a passive acceptance of superior physical force.

What, then, is a Christian to do when he has learned all his life that "righteousness exalts a nation, but sin is a reproach to any people?" Is not the use of the sword appropriate in the quest for righteousness for the well-being of a people even if they are not able to recognize that it is for their own good?

Several distinctions must be made here. First, let us remember that the Old Testament prophets were speaking in particular to a covenant people existing as a nation-state – a nation-state uniquely used in the providence of God to usher in his salvation to the world. Thus, the standards of national righteousness established for Israel cannot apply in the same manner to the New Testament era unless one assumes that nation-states today are direct inheritors of the promises made to Israel. While the Christian community and the confessing church may be the "new Israel," the nation-states of the twentieth century are not. (The Constantinian Church and Calvin's Geneva are examples where the attempt to wed the state to the Christian church were made, and attempts at applying explicitly Christian standards of righteousness to national politics were deemed appropriate applications of Old Testament principles to New Testament situations. The results were so disastrous both politically and religiously that few evangelicals would covet an attempted return.)

Thus, we must be willing to admit that there is a gap between what may be a just, as distinct from a righteous, political policy. It may be said that any injustice violates the will of God and hence may be considered unrighteous. It does not hold, however, that any effort to arrive at public righteousness is necessarily just.

Let me give an example. When people are discriminated against because of their race by virtue of social structures and public policy, we may say that such an injustice is unrighteous. However, not all attempts at resolving the problem are necessarily righteous or just. Should, as in the case of South Africa, the Bantu natives gain political power and systematically apply discriminatory policies against their former white oppressors, the outcome of such a practice is simply a return of evil for evil without a substantial movement toward justice in that society. However, should a policy of non-discrimination and equal opportunity genuinely evolve, the outcome is a move toward justice and thus also a step toward righteousness. In this case, justice serves the cause of righteousness.

But to suggest that the cause of righteousness necessarily serves the cause of justice is another matter. God's standards of righteousness exceed justice and demand that justice be crowned by a moral motivation which complements the moral act. But the motivations which inspire mankind to action are beyond the control of the state. The state, through force, can compel the external behavior of individuals to conform to the demands of justice. But the state cannot measure or control the motivations which inform external behavior. Indeed, since the element of force or coercion is always implicit in policies of state, to compel "righteousness" would be to force love.

In other words, while injustice is always unrighteous, justice falls short of righteousness. Further, the use of the state to compel righteousness, as opposed to justice, may in and of itself be unjust. Not only would the state have to exceed the demands of justice and seek to "compel love," but it would have to disregard the limits which govern our concepts of civil liberties and constitutional limitations on the state's proper use of power. An example might be when a state seeks to enforce Sabbath observance through public law for sectarian purposes. God does call us to honor the Sabbath by setting it aside as a day of rest. More particularly, he desires that the day of rest be one in which the saints gather together to worship him and sing songs of praise to him. If the state would seek to enforce church attendance because church attendance is righteous, the state would obviously violate justice in the search of righteousness. If the state would seek to enforce Sunday "blue laws" for the sake of honoring the Sabbath (as opposed to secular criteria which might conclude pragmatically that it is to the well-being of all to have established times of relief from commercial activity), the state would violate the limitations of just government because it would exceed the demands of justice *per se.*

Our considerations thus far have dealt mainly with theoretical considerations and distinctions which must be made if evangelicals are to think clearly about the nature of politics. But in the last analysis, politics is not a theoretical activity so much as it is a practical activity. Politics is not simply the distinguishing of principles, but the application of those principles in particular circumstances. While political scientists may define politics as "the authoritative allocation of values and resources for all society," political practitioners would much prefer the popular definition, "Politics is the art of the possible."

I shall, accordingly, shift my discussion from some of the theoretical questions with which evangelicals must deal in regard to politics to matters of practical concern. These must be considered in relation to the potential for evangelical political influence on society.

The Social Context of Evangelicalism

First, we must remember that evangelical Protestantism represents a very distinct segment of the American polity. It is not representative of the multifaceted and diverse character of American society. Evangelicalism is largely composed of white, Anglo-Saxonized, middle to upper-middle class, suburban Americans. Thus, the issues which possess political saliance for American evangelicalism are not necessarily representative of the broad interests of American society, nor are they necessarily the critical issues facing the country as a whole.

Recalling our earlier discussion of the propensity of groups and individuals to maximize their own self-interest at the expense of the whole, we should remember that evangelical Christians are no exception. Political issues are perceived largely through the context of those socio-economic variables which describe the evangelical community. Hence, it has a tendency toward political and economic conservatism since such positions generally best reflect its own self-interest. Often evangelical moralizing about politics is little more than theological rationalization for positions derived independently of genuine Christian reflection.

Thus, evangelicals moved by the significant ministries of organizations such as World Vision International may be sensitized to the needs of the world's hungry. But they are less often sensitized to the hungry of their own communities. Evangelicals may, however belatedly, have become sensitized to the needs of racial minorities. But when the Department of Health, Education, and Welfare issues guidelines for minority participation in the governance of their own religious and educational enterprises, they react indignantly about excessive government interference, oblivious to the fact that the churches themselves are now the most segregated social institutions in American life. Evangelicals have a tendency toward taking a "hard line" on matters of criminal justice, forgetting that their own community has seldom been at the receiving end of the criminal justice system. Evangelicals can rally around welfare abuse much more readily than can the United States Catholic Conference, for example, because evangelicals are more likely to represent the socially advantaged than is the Catholic community with its large concentration of Latinos and other ethnic groups. Evangelical Christianity should include a substantial portion of America's black community. But the fact of the matter is that sociologically speaking, white evangelicalism has cut itself off from the black evangelical, the rural white fundamentalist, and even the inner-city ministries of the Salvation Army.

Thus, the socio-economic predispositions of evangelicalism have tended to interfere with thoughtful reflection of Christian standards of justice as they apply to the value and resource allocation of the political process. The political behavior of the evangelical Christian can be predicted more precisely through standard sociological analysis of income, education, ethnic identity, and geography than anything relating to the confession of Jesus Christ as Savior and Lord. Evangelical

Christians have an obligation to rethink the political implications of their faith for political responsibility so that it transcends the simple reflection of socio-economic interests. And they must be particularly careful, in the meantime, not to engage in crusades which simply baptize political positions reflecting those interests as somehow possessing particular moral authenticity.

THE STRUCTURAL CONTEXT OF EVANGELICALISM

We must remember that there are some very practical consequences of evangelical Protestantism's very loose organizational structure. While estimates of the number of evangelical Protestants in the United States frequently range up to the forty million figure, there is no umbrella organization or common institutional tie where evangelicalism can unite for the purposes of unitary social and political impact.

First of all, the very Protestant character of evangelicalism tends to stress the priesthood of the believer at the expense of the organized church's authority over the life of the individual believer. Further, it must be remembered that a great number of evangelical churches are governed on the principle of congregationalist polity which diminishes institutional relationships between church bodies. The situation is taken to the absurd, organizationally, by the extremely sectarian nature of much of evangelical Protestantism. Hence, leadership in evangelicalism takes place in terms of identifying with personalities and movements which sweep through it and cut across the multiplicity of organizational structures. The Catholic tradition, on the other hand, places more emphasis on the organizational integrity of the church. The latter is much more effective in terms of potential for political impact – it is clear who speaks for the Catholic church, and there are in existence ready lines of internal communication of the church's posture on social and political issues.

This situation has both its strong points and its weak points. We have alluded to the strength of this loose organizational structure when pointing out that the organizational diversity of evangelicalism protects it against simplistic organizational commitments to secular causes in the name of the kingdom of God. (It must be remembered, however, that there is nonetheless an evangelical subculture which does indeed create predispositions toward informally linking certain public policies with Christian standards of virtue.) The weakness of this arrangement is that it substantially prohibits the leadership of the church from acting prophetically on those social and political issues where the church most severely needs direction.

An example of this weakness can be found in racial patterns in the church. During the 1960s, for example, the Catholic churches of the South were able to play a substantially more active and crucial role in the civil rights movement in states such as Louisiana (where Catholicism is strong) because the hierarchical character of the church's organizational structure protected the leadership of the church from cavalier dismissal or repudiation due to its aggressive posture on civil rights. When contrasted with the congregationalist structure of the Baptist tradition, as illustrated in the well-publicized events leading to the dismissal of the pastor at Plains Baptist Church in Plains, Georgia, the comparison becomes obvious.

It must be further remembered that while there may be some forty million "evangelicals" in the American society, most of that number do not consistently and self-consciously identify with evangelicalism as a religious movement. The leadership of the Southern Baptist Convention, for example, which accounts for the largest segment of evangelical Protestantism (broadly defined) has stated at several times that it does *not* consider itself to be properly so classified. If one talks with leaders of the Southern Presbyterian church, one is surprised to find that they little understand the informal and parachurch organizations by which the communication of evangelical Protestantism's character is transmitted in the North.

Even if we turn to the North, we must remember that the self-professed National Association of Evangelicals which spearheaded the leadership of modern evangelicalism accounts for only roughly 5 percent of the forty million evangelicals. (There are probably more evangelicals in the United Methodist Church alone than in the entire NAE fellowship.) It is also interesting to note that estimates of evangelicalism tend to dismiss the black community's extensive ties to conservative Protestantism. Further, there has been little effort to establish working ties with the Roman Catholic and Orthodox communities even though conservative Protestants probably hold more in common with these groups than with liberal Protestantism.

Evangelicalism, as the term is increasingly being used, is not an organized, self-conscious movement within the church or American society. It is really a very general term designating an eclectic group of Christians from differing Christian traditions who resist the theological humanism which has captured much of establishment Christianity. It has no organizational superstructure. It has no self-conscious posture as a movement. And thus, it can hope to accomplish little by way of direct political action. This, I hasten to add, is not necessarily a bad situation. But it is an important consideration when examining the potential strategies which evangelicalism may adopt relative to social and political issues.

The Cultural Isolation of Evangelicalism

Finally, it must be remembered that the disparate character of evangelicalism is nonetheless marked by a degree of cultural isolation from the major purveyors of influence in our society. There are few journals of evangelical opinion which speak widely enough to attract the following of a broad section of evangelicalism, and those which do tend to be largely concerned with matters internal to evangelicalism itself as opposed to directed witness and challenge to secular culture.

Evangelicalism is poorly positioned for expressing its points of view in the national media. It seldom reaches heights of artistic expression in the cultural life of the nation. This is due not only to the organizational weakness of evangelicalism, but also to a tendency of the community toward otherworldliness. Fundamentalism has been defined by some as "orthodoxy gone militant." The fundamentalist movement, the forerunner of contemporary evangelicalism, was basically reactive in temper. It was reacting against secularism, scientism, humanism, the rejection of theism, and so forth. Accordingly, the psychological environment of contemporary evangelicalism is still tempered by tendencies toward social withdrawal and rejection of the world's concerns.

Sociologists have studied the social involvements of church members and have found, for example, that members of conservative, evangelical churches tend to devote their time and energies disproportionately to their churches as opposed to their communities at large.[5] The church becomes a primary association to the exclusion of other associational activities. Even when evangelical churchmen join secondary associations, they tend to be parachurch groups. Instead of the Kiwanis Club, evangelical leaders are prone to join "Christian Businessmen's Fellowship." While this accounts for many of the strengths in evangelicalism, it also fosters many of its weaknesses. It cuts its influence off from the general social structure outside of the church, and prevents its concerns from being affected by questions the world is asking. As others have stated, "How can evangelicalism say that Christ is the answer when it is deaf to the questions being asked?"

If evangelical Protestantism is serious about social and political witness, it must develop strategies of cultural penetration and social involvement with which it is presently unfamiliar. If I might speculate for a moment, I would suggest that there is tremendous potential for evangelical Christianity to vitally impact our culture if it would be willing to consider linkages with the black religious community and the conservative elements of American Catholicism (both Roman and Orthodox). This addresses itself immediately to problems of race, problems between Anglo-Saxon dominance in our society *vis-á-vis* the ethnic groups in the Catholic churches; it offers the potential for a massive movement of resistance to the secularistic rejection of the Judeo-Christian traditions upon which our social structures and political system have been built. But the organizational fragmentation of evangelical Christianity, its cultural isolation, and its inability to distinguish major issues from parochial concerns have all kept evangelical Christianity at the periphery of our social and political order, despite the numbers of individuals who share the basic tenets of evangelical Christian faith.

I am proud of my evangelical Christian faith. But I am embarrassed by its sectarian temper, its cultural isolation, and its "bourgeois captivity." I believe that God calls us to more noble discipleship. However much I value the diversity of social and institutional structures within evangelicalism, I believe we stand in judgment for allowing these structures to dissipate opportunities for witnessing to our world. Although I recognize that this world is not my home, I believe that God created, sustains, and gave his Son to save this world. Obsession with the world's concerns in the name of Jesus Christ is no sin. And however "bourgeois" I may be as a white, middle-class, midwestern male, I believe the captivity of American evangelicalism to such interests is just as devastating to the integrity of the church as the Babylonian Captivity was to the church of the Middle Ages.

Evangelical Christianity must do some serious thinking about the theoretical problems I have outlined above, of relating the Christian faith to the political order. But it must also put its own house in order. Otherwise the cause of evangelical Christianity, while achieving political effectiveness, may foster a movement which it will live to regret.

NOTES

1. Paul Tillich, *Love, Power and Justice* (New York: Oxford University Press, 1954), p. 8.

2. Karl Lowenstein, *Political Power and the Governmental Process,* (Chicago: University of Chicago Press, 1957), p. 3.

3. Robert Strausz-Hupé, *Power and Community,* (New York: Praeger, 1956), p. 3.

4. This definition, or variants thereof, is derived from David Easton's *The Political System* (New York: Alfred A. Knopf, 1953). Easton was one of the first political scientists to introduce systems theory to the discipline of political science.

5. See, for example, Lowell Streiker and Gerald Strober, *Religion and the New Majority,* (New York: Association Press, 1972).

Tremendously Impressed

Stephen V. Monsma

I still remember clearly the first time I met Paul Henry, even though it was over thirty years ago. As a member of the Calvin College political science faculty I had taken a group of students to the National Association of Evangelicals' annual legislative seminar in Washington, DC. One morning we were scheduled to meet with then Representative John Anderson. As often happens in Washington something had come up at the last minute that prevented Anderson from keeping this engagement, so he sent one of his young staffers, Paul Henry, to fill in for him. I cannot claim that I remember exactly what Paul said to the group of students that morning, but I do remember I was tremendously impressed by what he had to say. I thought, "This would be a great person to get on the Calvin faculty." So afterward I went up to Paul, introduced myself, and asked if he would be potentially interested in joining the Calvin faculty. He replied that he might be, and things developed from that point.

I also remember clearly the last time I saw Paul. It was June of 1992, and I was in Washington for a board meeting of Bread for the World. The board members and other Bread for the World supporters had been deployed one day to do some face-to-face lobbying on hunger issues with members of Congress. I stopped by Paul's office on Capitol Hill to see if by any chance he was in so I could offer an official word of thanks from Bread for the World for his consistent support of many of our issues. It turned out that Paul was in and we chatted in his office for ten minutes or so. At one point the conversation turned to the possibility of his running for the Senate in 1994 – something I knew he was seriously considering. I urged him to do so if things looked favorable and promised a significant financial contribution to his campaign. He, in a very unpolitical reaction, seemed embarrassed at the offer of help and told me it would not be necessary to help in that manner.

During the twenty years that separated those two meetings, I came to know Paul as a faculty colleague, a personal friend, and a fellow holder of public office. As faculty colleagues we served together in the Political Science Department at Calvin College for four and a half years. Paul cared very deeply about students and was a very popular instructor. His office was near mine and I could not help but notice that students were constantly stopping by to see him for help with their work or just to chat. His commitment to students can also be seen in an internship program he started in Washington during Calvin's January interim semester, even though it took a huge amount of time and effort on his part.

What I remember most of all from those years are the walks we would take together around Calvin's campus during the summers when we both would be working on one writing project or another. Our lunch hours would often extend longer than planned as we talked of God, the church, justice, politics, and our own personal political aspirations.

It was during his Calvin years that Paul solidified his thinking concerning the meaning and limits of Christian politics. In 1974 he published his thinking on these issues in his book, *Politics for Evangelicals.* Several sentences from that book summarize as clearly as possible the Christian framework of beliefs that motivated Paul's sense of public service: "The Christian who enters politics must do so with the aim of achieving political justice. He does this by subjecting his own personal ambitions and desires to the scrutiny of God's revelation in the Scriptures. And as God gives the grace to do so, he learns to make the needs of his neighbor his own. In so doing, his search for justice becomes an act of sacrificial love."[1] It was by the grace God gave that in the nineteen years Paul had remaining he indeed learned to make the needs of his neighbor his own. It was in his years as a Christian professor and scholar that Paul learned what it was to pursue politics as a Christian calling.

Paul was always very clear that he did not think Christian politics translated into a narrow set of positions on concrete policy issues. He felt that a Christian in politics ought to be committed to certain basic values, but that there was no one certain set of policy positions into which these values neatly and simply translated. He was very conscious of the limited wisdom and virtue possessed by human beings, and therefore he was deeply fearful of a triumphalistic approach to politics that would brand one's own policy predilections as God's own. Later, while in the U.S. House of Representatives, Paul was hurt when his efforts to find a reasonable, responsible compromise on the question of funding of the National Endowment for the Arts resulted in a Christian group labeling him as one who had sold out.

I also knew Paul as a personal friend. Our children were about the same age and often played together. More than once we as families went camping together. "Dr. Henry" was an important figure – and always one of joy and fun – in the lives of both of our children when they were growing up. I remember when Paul and Karen's daughter, Kara, and our son, Marty, were in nursery school together and Paul and I volunteered to be "mothers for the day." (Back in those days it was assumed that fathers would never play this role.) We played with the kids, helped them get their jackets and boots on and off, helped with the snacks, and Paul showed a set of great slides of kids at play. I am still impressed by the fact that Paul was able to relate equally well with nursery school children, college students, and – later – nationally-known journalists and political figures.

Paul had the unusual gift of being able to combine a love of irony and a great sense of humor with an interest in a wide range of topics of a serious, even profound nature. Often the jokes he would tell would be on himself: Once he went into a long rendition of his adventures in growing some backyard tomatoes that he figured cost five dollars each, given the meager crop and the expenses for the plants, fertilizers, stakes, insect killer, and so forth. Often I did not know when to believe him; there was the time, for example, when he told me he thought it wrong to purchase cigarettes but not to smoke them, so he only smoked when he could bum a cigarette from someone else!

But Paul also thought deeply and seriously about life and especially about the public life of the nation and Christianity's role in it. The son of a famous evangelical Protestant theologian, Carl F. H. Henry, Paul was never simply his father's son. In fact, he maintained a certain distance from the evangelical wing of Protestantism. Some of its foibles were often the subject of his wit and sense of irony. Yet running even deeper was an unwavering faith that was very much in the tradition of evangelical Protestantism. He cared deeply for the broader church of Jesus Christ and his personal faith was central to who he was. The time I saw Paul the most excited and upbeat was in November, 1973, when he returned from Chicago and a meeting of a group of evangelical leaders who had drafted what came to be called the "Chicago Declaration." This was a statement drafted over a weekend by a group that included both older, "establishment" evangelical leaders and young, restless evangelicals, such as Paul. In it these leaders acknowledged the failure of the evangelical church to deal with the social and political ills of the nation. Later Paul wrote of his great satisfaction in "the fact that the major leaders of mainline evangelicalism are conscious of the apostasy in the evangelical community in failing to articulate the social and political claims of the gospel."[2]

I also knew Paul as a fellow public office holder. Paul served on the State Board of Education while I was in the State House of Representatives; our careers in the Michigan state legislature overlapped by four years; and Paul ran successfully for the same seat in the U.S. House of Representatives in 1984 that I had run unsuccessfully for in 1982. The fact that we were in different political parties on occasion complicated our friendship. Once when we were having dinner together with our wives in a restaurant the political reporter for one of the local television stations came in, stared at us in amazement, and exclaimed, "What are the two of you doing together!" After that we would go out of town when we met for dinner. Occasionally, persons from both of our parties who were more die-hard partisans than either of us were would raise some eyebrows at our relationship. Somehow our partisan differences never seemed to matter very much to us.

This was never truer than one day when I was in a tough race for the Michigan state senate. My opponent called a news conference to accuse me of being in league with the pornography industry. Paul — who was a member of the state board of education at the time — reached me before the media did and urged I suggest the media contact him for his reactions. I did so and the result was that the news stories centered on Paul's condemnations of the attack instead of on the allegations. Ever after I felt indebted to Paul for his help at that very difficult time.

In writing these remembrances I am reminded all over again how much all of us have lost and how much I personally still miss Paul. His premature death was a major loss to the Calvin community, the broader Christian community, the people of the Third Congressional District of Michigan, and the nation. In Paul's day and in ours there is much too much politics of the self-interested variety and much too little concern for justice. We have more than enough cheap, self-interested, egotistical politicians with inflated opinions of their own importance. They are still too much with us. Paul was one of those public servants who truly earned the appellation "public servant" by diligently seeking to care for the weak and needy by promoting justice in our land, an effort he himself had called for in his writings.

The saddest part of a public life that is cut short lies in the questions of what would have happened if Paul had lived. Would he have run for and been elected to the U.S. Senate from Michigan in 1994? Would he have today been on George W. Bush's short list of vice-presidential possibilities? Or maybe the media would one day be discussing who was on Paul's short list of vice-presidential possibilities! We will never know the answers to those "what if" questions.

What we do know is that Paul is now out of the "shadowlands" – to use C. S. Lewis's phrase – of flawed human institutions and imperfectly realized hopes and lives in the brilliant sunlight of God's justice and peace that the rest of us cannot imagine. Also, we can know that God's purposes – such as Paul dreamed of and worked for in both academia and the political realm – have not been thwarted by his death but are moving ahead, in God's way and in his due time.

Notes

1. Paul B. Henry, *Politics for Evangelicals* (Valley Forge, Pa.: Judson Press, 1974), 123.

2. Paul B. Henry, "Reflections," in *The Chicago Declaration*, ed. Ron J. Sider (Carol Stream, Ill.: Creation House, 1974), 137.

A Bit of a Gadfly

Richard J. Mouw

The title page of my copy of *Politics for Evangelicals* bears this inscription by the author:

> "To Rich Mouw – A dear friend in Christ and one of God's favorite gadfly theologian-philosophers. Paul Henry."

Paul obviously was not astute at discerning who the Lord's favorites might be, but he was certainly right about his and my friendship. And he got the gadfly part of it right too. In this case, though, it took one to know one. Paul was a bit of a gadfly himself. Literal gadflies are insects that bite horses. When applied to a human being, the label is usually accompanied by a measure of respect, even affection. But the term also clearly suggests that the person is a bit of an irritant.

I had arrived at Calvin College a few years before Paul and had already begun to engage in some irritating behavior. Some of it I hope is long forgotten by the folks who knew me then. (Now that I am an administrator I would not want too many people like the youthful me on our faculty!) But there are some modes of irritating activity that are good for all concerned – as, for example, when the literal gadfly motivates the horse to overcome inertia. I had a part of helping to make some good things of that sort happen during my time on the Calvin faculty. One of those good things was the hiring of Paul Henry.

Paul came to Calvin at a time when there were not too many "outsiders" on our faculty. George Marsden nicely captured the experience of that small subgroup in his oft-quoted manifesto: "I am not one of us!" But each of us had come to Calvin with at least some obvious theological affinities. George had been raised Orthodox Presbyterian. I was bred in a parsonage of the Reformed Church in America – which was not by itself enough for full acceptance at Calvin, but it did help a lot that I had attended a Christian school as a kid. Charlie Miller and

Don Wilson had long found their places in the subculture. Ron Wells made his entry with an unashamed testimony that he had been converted to the cause by reading Kuyper's *Lectures on Calvinism.*

Paul Henry was a special case, however. Jim De Borst was the chairman of the political science department at the time, and one day he stopped me in the hall: "We have a shot at getting Carl Henry's son in our department," he reported, and he asked me for help in making it happen. The help that Jim needed had to move in two directions. Not only did we have to convince Paul Henry that he could flourish at Calvin; we also had to overcome some misgivings in the faculty and administration. From a purely scholarly point of view, of course, Paul certainly looked excellent on paper. He obviously was an outstanding young political scientist, and he was also very interested in interdisciplinary questions. But would he really fit in at Calvin?

Two of his nonacademic credentials posed the biggest roadblocks. The first was that he was Carl Henry's son. Not that the senior Henry was disliked at Calvin. His was a respected name, but nonetheless it was a name associated in the Calvin environs with generic evangelicalism. This was a time when the "third party" mentality was still strong in the Christian Reformed Church. As orthodox Calvinists, the Grand Rapids intellectuals certainly did not identify with mainline Protestantism, but neither did they want simply to be absorbed into the evangelical movement. Carl Henry was the icon of this latter option. The Dutch folks respected him, but he also made them a little nervous. What would be happening to us, then, if suddenly his son were a highly visible member of the Calvin faculty?

The second credential only reinforced the first set of worries. Paul was a Baptist, and he wasn't enthusiastic about joining the Christian Reformed Church, a nonnegotiable requirement at the time. If there was not to be an exception granted for him, he allowed as how he might go along for pragmatic reasons. But under no conditions would he and Karen have their children baptized until they had made their own age-of-accountability decision to follow Christ.

It was clear to all of us – both those of us who wanted to see him appointed and those who were nervous about him – that he would be a gadfly in our midst. While he was committed to authentically Christian political thought and action, he was more inclined to quote Reinhold Niebuhr than Abraham Kuyper. And while many folks at Calvin thought that we were already an important intellectual center, Paul kept talking about what we might become if only we would open up a little. Some of us saw these things as giving us good reasons to take up the pro-Henry cause with enthusiasm. On his first visit to our campus a few of us spent a relaxed evening with him, and it was clear beyond question that he was the kind of colleague we wanted in our midst. The next day Paul made a strong impression on all who interviewed him, including President Spoelhof and Dean VandenBerg. For his part, Paul decided that Calvin was a place where he could flourish. When his family moved to Grand Rapids, La Grave Avenue Christian Reformed Church embraced them as new members, baptistic theology and all. And Paul Henry quickly established himself as a key member of the faculty and an influential person in the West Michigan community.

The appointment of Paul Henry to the faculty can be seen as a symbol of an important transition that was taking place at Calvin College in the 1970s. During that same period quiet discussions were taking place in the admissions department about the need actively to recruit students from beyond the Dutch Reformed community. At that point a vast majority of Calvin's student population came from the Christian high schools associated with the Christian Reformed community. But Calvin was no longer the only school of choice for the denominational constituency: Dordt and Trinity Christian had become four year schools, and there was talk of new undergraduate programs in the Dutch communities in Canada. With the increasing assimilation of the Dutch ethnic community into the larger North American culture, the "secular" schools were no longer as "other" as they had appeared to be in the past. If Calvin was to grow, new constituencies would have to be found. The broader evangelical community was an obvious place to do some recruiting. These explorations were manifestations, I think, of the same underlying "evangelicalizing" currents that brought Paul Henry to the Calvin campus.

Some folks speculated from the outset of Paul's service at Calvin that the school would not contain him for very long. The possibility of a political career was on many minds (including his) early on. He quickly established his credentials as a Republican activist. Even here, though, he was a gadfly. Paul Henry went to the state convention in 1972 as the only delegate committed to Paul McCloskey, whose main campaign theme was his opposition to the Vietnam war.

But Paul also reached out beyond the campus from the platform of a political science professor. He led the way in instituting the Calvin Conference on Christianity and Politics, where dialogue took place between the Dutch Kuyperians and the broader evangelical world, between Catholics and Protestants, and between Reformed and Anabaptists. This annual conference was, as I see things, one of the most important instruments for the opening up of Calvin College to the larger Christian world. There had always been good lecture series on the campus, where distinguished scholars from the larger world would make an appearance. But in the Christianity and Politics conferences, the outsiders came in droves. Calvin came to be seen as one of the places in the religious arena where important intellectual dialogue was taking place.

Occasionally someone will say to me that the decade of the 1970s was the "golden age of Calvin College." I think that is hyperbole, and it is unfair to the present: As I see things, Calvin College has never been stronger than it is right now. But those were indeed wonderful days – certainly the most exciting in my own intellectual life. The Lord allowed some of us to be together for a time and to experience new conversations that, because of their very newness, we will not see the likes of again. And for me, Paul Henry was one of God's special gifts to the campus on which I was privileged to be present for those exciting times.

When I left Grand Rapids for California in 1985 Paul was already in Congress. We stayed in touch for the next half decade mainly by means of the wonderful Christmas letters that Karen wrote – in which she was not afraid to poke some fun at a congressman husband who talked about "little cows" to an audience of farmers, because on his feet he could not remember the word calves!

But Phyllis and I did see Paul again when, while in Washington for the National Prayer Breakfast, we visited a briefing that he gave to some folks visiting from Michigan. He saw us in the crowd and he signaled at the end that we should wait around. After greeting his constituents he hustled the two of us through the tunnel to his office, where we sat and talked about old times at Calvin – and his own old times at Fuller Seminary, where his father had been one of the founding faculty.

In those minutes together we simply picked up where we had left off years before. He mentioned the night we first met, when he had come to Calvin to be interviewed. Together we agreed that those years had been wonderful – that the Lord had been good to us in letting us be at Calvin during those exciting times. As Paul talked about his present activities and his future plans, it was clear that he was still a gadfly. And I have no doubt that now that he occupies an office, access to which comes only by an election far more glorious than any earthly constituency can afford, there is still something of the gadfly in him.

Warmth, Wit and Wisdom

James M. Penning

I first met Paul Henry in 1970 when I was a senior political science major at Calvin College and Paul was a recently hired assistant professor of political science. Because I had completed most of my major course requirements by the time Paul arrived on campus, I never had the opportunity to take a class from him. However, that didn't prevent me from speaking with him on various occasions regarding politics and political science.

Since I was a college senior who was seriously considering pursuing a Ph.D. in political science, and Paul was a freshly minted Ph.D., I naturally sought his advice about graduate school and the dreaded Graduate Record Exam (GRE). Paul advised me to pay particular attention to the specialized test in political science, making every effort to prepare myself in each of the discipline's major subfields. "For example," he said, "be sure to familiarize yourself with notable political thinkers… people like Georges Sorel." I nodded sagely, refusing to admit that I knew more about Al Kaline than about Georges Sorel. In fact, I had never heard of Georges Sorel.

As a student growing up in the 1960s I had developed a healthy skepticism of authority figures, but something in this young professor's demeanor prompted me to head for the library and look up Georges Sorel. What harm could that do? As it turned out, one of the first questions on the GRE exam concerned the political thought of Georges Sorel! Was it blind luck or did Paul Henry have a rare gift of prophesy? I wasn't sure at the time but my respect for him soared nonetheless.

Four years later I returned to Calvin College and joined the political science faculty. Paul was now a colleague rather than a mentor. It was difficult addressing my former professors by their first names rather than their titles, but Paul soon made me feel welcome. In fact, he went out of his way to do so, providing both academic and personal guidance. For example, I soon discovered that it was necessary to have a credit card in order to travel to academic conferences and the like. Unfortunately, as a "new" professor with no credit history, I was turned down when I applied for a VISA card. Paul, always sensitive to gross injustice, decided to remedy the situation by doing what all good politicians do – pulling some strings. He immediately marched me to Union Bank in downtown Grand Rapids where one of his friends was a branch manager. Within ten minutes the bank authorized my card. (Viewing my latest VISA statement, I'm not sure whether or not Paul deserves thanks for this act of generosity!)

At Calvin College my office was adjacent to Paul's and I had the opportunity to speak with him and observe him "in action" on a daily basis. "Action" is the right word, because Paul demonstrated tremendous energy and activity in all areas of his life. In his teaching Paul was always looking for innovative classroom methods. He once, half seriously, considered using the Bible as a required "text" in his Introduction to Politics course. He was devoted to his students and willing to teach courses (e.g., public administration) that were outside his areas of "expertise" if he thought that it would benefit them.

Paul loved the world of ideas, especially when those ideas involved relating faith and politics. As a scholar, Paul is perhaps best known for his book, *Politics for Evangelicals*, a work designed to give guidance to the growing numbers of evangelicals who were "returning from the wilderness" and getting involved in politics. To me, the most salient feature of the book was Paul's warning to avoid simplistic engagement in politics. Politics, he asserted, is "morally ambiguous" and Christians must approach politics with considerable humility. Paul's other scholarly work also reflects this theme; whether writing about the relationship between "love, power, and justice" or about the political thought of Jacques Ellul, Paul refused to accept easy answers to complex problems.

Although Paul excelled as a teacher and scholar, he was at his best in the "real" world of applied politics – particularly Republican Party politics. With his intelligence, hard work, and personality, Paul soon became a leader in Kent County Republican circles and was selected as county GOP Chair. Paul, always skilled in the art of "political networking," purchased a membership in the Press Club, watering hole for many of the local movers and shakers. I can remember accompanying him to the Press Club and seeing such local luminaries as the Grand Rapids mayor and the superintendent of the Grand Rapids Public

Schools engaged, I supposed, in discussions about the good of the community. Paul, it seems, was well known and well liked by everyone, even the few Democrats with the temerity to enter the "Club."

Paul networked not only with local officials but also with national officials. As a former aide to Congressman John Anderson of Illinois, he had made many friends in Washington. Paul was delighted when Anderson decided to launch his, ultimately unsuccessful, presidential bid in 1976 and took special pleasure in inviting me to a "private" lunch at the Kent County Airport when Anderson came to town.

Paul's networking skills, however, had their limits. Although one often hears of politicians and businessmen "doing business" on the golf course, golfing wasn't his forte. One fine spring afternoon Paul, acting on impulse I think, demanded that we go to the local public golf course and play nine holes. Suffice it to say that neither of us proved ready for the PGA tour. In fact, other golfers would have been well advised to wear hard hats that day.

Paul had a particularly good time as a delegate to the 1976 Republican National Convention, the ultimate GOP networking site! He reported, with a twinkle in his eye, that the only way to calm the frenzied delegates was to sing "God Bless America." Ultimately, the Convention selected Grand Rapids' own Gerald Ford as its nominee. Paul was delighted at the choice and extremely disappointed at the election outcome.

I could go on to recount Paul's many accomplishments in the Michigan legislature, the Michigan Board of Education, and Congress, but they have been well documented elsewhere. What is most impressive about his political career is that Paul never avoided hard issues and never flagged in his effort to relate his Christian faith to his public service. Indeed, Paul occasionally acted as a political "maverick," crossing party lines if necessary to pursue his vision of justice.

In retrospect, what I remember best about Paul is that despite his many accomplishments and prominent government positions, he never lost his sense of boyish mischief. I recall how much he enjoyed showing me the "secret" coffee room hidden behind the restrooms. I also remember him laughing as he rode my new racing bicycle down the halls of the College (now Spoelhof) Center building. And I still smile when I recall his assertion that the Central Intelligence Agency had "bugged" our classrooms in order to ensure that no "radical" ideas were being taught.

Although Paul took his faith seriously, he never failed to see the humor in organized religion. He enjoyed telling the story of visiting two different churches on the same Sunday – and hearing the same sermon. And he could provoke laughter with his account of losing a game of SCRABBLE to a Swiss theologian when the theologian challenged his attempted use of the word votum.

In his last week as a Calvin College professor, Paul, clearly headed for bigger things, asked me to have lunch at a local restaurant. We had enjoyed having lunch on a regular basis over the years, but this was to be our last as faculty colleagues. I was saddened at the thought of losing my daily dose of Paul's wit and wisdom but also happy to think of his future political career. With a laugh, Paul promised to keep in touch and to pass on information about the "real world" of politics. He did.

Section II:
The Real Work of Politics

Section II
The Real Work of Politics

This section features some of Paul's thoughts on the more immediate application of Christian faith to politics. Most but not all of these selections date from Paul's time in public service, first in the Michigan legislature and then in the United States House of Representatives. The section begins, however, with extended excerpts from "Strategies for Political Action," the last chapter in *Politics for Evangelicals*, written while Paul was still at Calvin. Paul presents a unique call for the church's engagement in political efforts. While he cautions against official political pronouncements by denominational boards, he urges local congregations to initiate internal dialogue about pressing political issues and to work hard to raise up lay political leadership among their members.

"Christian Political Action: NACPA Reconsidered" also dates from Paul's early days at Calvin. Reacting to a call by a professorial colleague for a separate Christian political party, Paul lays out an extended defense for Christian action in the American constitutional and political party systems.

In "The New Christian Right: A Practicing Politician's Perspective," Paul returns to his criticism of politically conservative Christians. By the time this was written in 1979 a new body of such Christians had made its entrance and was flexing its muscle: the Moral Majority. Starting with a concise historical overview of conservative American Protestant Christianity, Paul restates his longstanding disagreements with the new Christian right, and adds his opinion that the movement has both claimed and received too much credit in the political world for defining the terms of debate.

The remainder of the original material in this section is grouped under seven topics. The first topic illustrates Paul's views about applying Christian principles to a vocation in politics. Many people, from leaders of the evangelical community to young constituents, asked Paul how he viewed the integration of his job and his Christian faith. Selected for inclusion in this area are a 1985 interview with *Christianity Today*, a 1988 interview with Eternity magazine, a brief 1988 article he wrote for the Just/Life political action committee newsletter, and a response to the questions of a young constituent.

The other six topics illustrate Paul's thinking on six specific controversies or policy areas that he encountered in his public career: prison reform, aid to the contras fighting the Sandinista-led Nicaraguan government, the Persian Gulf War, environmental issues, religious and moral issues like abortion and religious freedom, and political parties and partisanship.

While in the Michigan House Paul was appointed to a statewide commission on prison reform, sparking an interest in criminal justice issues that would persist throughout his career. He would later work closely with Charles Colson and his Prison Fellowship and Justice Fellowship ministries. The selection offered here is an essay Paul wrote for the September 15, 1980 issue of the *Banner*, a Christian Reformed Church publication.

Early in his congressional career Paul faced critical decisions on U.S. policy in Central America. The most important debates concentrated on military and humanitarian aid packages to Central America to fight against Communist insurgency. Nicaragua's previous government had been replaced in 1979 by a Marxist-influenced regime, and El Salvador, Honduras, and Guatemala began to experiment with democracy after years of military domination. Nicaragua's governing Sandinistas began to support revolutionaries in these other countries. To counter the perceived threat, President Reagan asked for aid to Nicaraguan contra guerillas, which were harassing and sought to overthrow the Sandinistas. Reagan emphasized military aid, most congressional opponents preferred humanitarian aid, and a few in Congress wanted no aid at all to the contras. Predictably, compromise packages usually emphasized humanitarian aid, with the Reagan Administration seeking other means to send the contras military aid.

Paul supported a nonmilitary aid package in April 1985, raising the ire of many of his constituents who wanted no aid at all. In March 1986, Congress debated a $100 million aid package with both military and humanitarian assistance, and Paul spoke on behalf of the President's proposal. President Reagan eventually succeeded in this request, but it would prove to be his only clear victory on the issue. Paul's stance on contra aid changed over the years. At the beginning, he supported the President's policy while reserving the right to change his position as he further studied this complex issue. Over time Paul became more skeptical of Reagan Administration policy and less inclined to vote for aid requests that seemed only to cause the conflict to continue. Early in 1987 he announced that he would no longer support contra aid unless it was accompanied by a "multinational" and "multilateral" policy that included the United States and several Central American countries. Diplomatic efforts initiated in 1988 by the Reagan Administration eventually ended the fighting and scheduled elections that replaced the communist government of Nicaragua. In the aftermath, Paul received some credit from colleagues in Congress for having helped redirect Administration policy. Numerous selections, including constituent responses, private communications with Secretary of State George Schultz, and a newspaper opinion/editorial illustrate the evolution of Paul's thinking on this issue.

In August 1990 its large neighbor, Iraq, invaded Kuwait. Almost immediately President Bush sent American troops to Saudi Arabia, along that nation's borders with Iraq and Kuwait. The United Nations, in response to the invasion, issued Resolution 678, urging Iraq's permanent and full withdrawal by January 15, 1991. After that deadline, member states were authorized to use "all necessary means" to bring Iraq and its leader Saddam Hussein into compliance. Congress had two issues at hand: whether or not to go to war and whether or not the president has the power to declare war without the authorization of the Congress. Up to the last days before January 15, a majority in Congress appeared to believe that the President had not made a strong enough case for how Hussein threatened U.S. vital interests. However, as the day approached, bipartisan agreement coalesced behind a resolution drafted by Stephen J. Solarz, D-NY and Robert H. Michel, R-IL that called for immediate military action if Iraq did not comply with the United Nations resolution. House Joint Resolution 77 authorized the president to use U.S. military forces to put an end to Iraq's "illegal occupation of, and brutal aggression against, Kuwait." This measure was in competition with a resolution composed by most House Democrats that supported only a continuation of economic sanctions against Iraq. On January 12, the Solarz-Michel resolution passed the House on a 250-183 vote, and the Senate passed the joint resolution the same day. Paul's floor speech during House debate is reprinted here. President Bush signed the resolution on January 14, and on January 15 he signed an executive order authorizing an aerial attack on Iraqi fortifications. On February 24, after five weeks of aerial bombardment, the ground offensive began. Three days later, on February 27, President Bush ended the offensive and pronounced the liberation of Kuwait complete.

Paul had a strong environmental record in the Michigan and U.S. legislatures. While in Congress Paul was most known for promoting a national bottle bill to mandate the recycling of beverage containers, and reprinted here is one of the many articles he wrote in support of the bill. Michigan had passed a similar law for the state, and Paul viewed that law an unmitigated success. U.S. Senator Mark Hatfield of Oregon, who sponsored companion legislation in the Senate, regularly joined Paul in this effort. A brief interview with *Christianity Today* illustrates how Paul connected his faith and political views with the environmental cause.

Paul would inevitably be drawn to political issues directly involving religious or moral questions. In December 1987 Soviet leader Mikhail Gorbachev visited the United States to discuss arms control issues with President Reagan. Paul took the occasion to raise the issue of religious oppression in the Soviet Union. In early 1988, after an adverse Supreme Court ruling, Congress needed to pass legislation to clarify its intent in sex-discrimination laws. In that debate the freedom of religiously controlled institutions became an issue that needed resolution. In 1989 the National Endowment for the Arts came under great scrutiny for its funding of art projects that were found obscene by a vocal portion of Americans. The Congress banned the NEA from funding projects containing "obscenity, homoeroticism and sadomasochism," though there was almost no change in the amount of money given to the NEA to distribute to artists. The ban was lifted in 1990 when Paul devised and successfully passed new requirements for the NEA that stated it must consider "general standards of decency and respect for the diverse beliefs and values of the American public" in making its grants. And in the early 1990s the federal government began to push more vigorously for research involving fetal tissue, a move that disturbed many in the right-to-life community. Paul was strongly pro-life, although he was not an outspoken congressional leader on the issue and ultimately voted to support fetal tissue research in a 1992 House debate on the issue. The heading "Religious and Moral Issues" includes some of Paul's reflections on each of these matters.

Paul Henry was a Republican, willing to defend his party and criticize Democrats when he felt it necessary. But Paul constantly urged Republicans to reach out to groups and movements not traditionally associated with the GOP. Paul was known in Congress and among his constituents for his outstanding personal integrity and forthrightness. So it was that perhaps the most personally tumultuous time of Paul's legislative career came in the House "bank" scandal of 1991-1992. Many members of Congress apparently had taken advantage of loose accounting and management in the House payroll office (which also provided a checking service exclusively for members of Congress) to "float" checks that in any other financial institution would have "bounced." The scandal entangled many members of Congress, including Paul who, according to some readings of fragmentary records, had bounced a handful of checks. With many other members, and with some justification, Paul blamed the Democrats and their long control of the House. This response, whatever its merits, had little resonance with a public always skeptical of politicians and weary from several previous congressional scandals. In any case, Paul was deeply hurt by what he thought was misleading reporting and subsequent public confusion about the "bank" issue. He joined forces with a dominantly, but not exclusively, Republican group of members to push for comprehensive congressional reform of support offices such as the bank, post office, and printing services. Regrettably, because of his illness and death Paul never saw the significant congressional reforms of 1993 and the far more sweeping changes that came after the 1994 election.

This section closes with personal essays that focus on Paul as a political practitioner. Former U.S. Senator Mark Hatfield first became acquainted with Paul in the early 1970s and maintained a close personal and legislative relationship with him throughout the remainder of Paul's life. Paul Hillegonds, former Speaker of the Michigan House, served with Paul Henry in the state legislature and shared his Reformed Christian faith and commitment to personal integrity. Gary Visscher, one of Paul's students at Calvin and later an employee in Lansing and Washington, D.C. also contributes an essay, sharing insights that cut across Paul's academic and political careers.

Strategies for Political Action

[H]ow does one go about applying Christian concerns in the political world?"

Denominational Resolutions

One of the primary means the institutional church utilizes in relating the gospel to political issues today is that of mustering endorsements on behalf of certain policies and causes at church conventions and/or through denominational social-concerns boards. Once again, the liberal churchmen tend to praise such activity as a necessary part of the church's prophetic role in society. The conservative churchmen, on the other hand, tend to decry such efforts as inappropriate for a "spiritual" body. They insist that the church is not a political institution and that it should get on with its task of saving souls. The tensions between the two factions often lead to open confrontation in church councils, and sometimes even to church schism. Thus, in 1973, the Presbyterian Church in the United States (Southern Presbyterians) suffered a denominational split, one of the chief reasons rather clearly having been the social and political stands of the PCUS leaders. Citing the literature of the new "Continuing Church" – the conservative faction breaking from the PCUS – we read: "Today the Assembly [of the PCUS], through its boards, agencies and committees has replaced the Church's mandate to be first-of-all missionary and evangelistic, with a primary emphasis on social, economic and political mission."[1]

... [W]hat is indeed ironic and tragic about such confrontations generated by the resolutions and pronouncements of denominations and church councils is that they are in effect little more than hot air! In

Excerpted from chapter four of *Politics for Evangelicals* (Valley Forge, Pennsylvania: Judson Press, 1974), and reprinted by permission of Judson Press.

terms of having any real effectiveness in the political world, such resolutions and pronouncements amount to little. Yet, in terms of damage done to the institutional church, they can be devastating.

There are at least six arguments which can be made against the practice of denominational and council pronouncements on social and political issues. *First*, the pronouncements themselves are generally not given the thorough and dispassionate consideration which is necessary if they are to make genuine contributions to the political debate of American society. Typically, a denominational social-concerns board writes drafts of resolutions for presentation at the annual church meeting. Too often, not enough is done to guarantee expertise in the initial draft of the resolution. Nor is there always a careful solicitation of viewpoints from different interests which might have light to cast on the pros and cons of the resolution.

Then the denominational social-concerns board reports the draft resolutions to the church convention. The leadership of the convention recognizes that the resolutions will likely cause intense debate, so the debate on the resolutions is usually scheduled for late afternoon on the closing day of the convention so as not to throw the program for other business off schedule. Only the most politicized of the delegates remain to debate the resolutions, and depending on what sort of majority controls the floor, ill-considered amendments and changes to the resolutions can occur with little or no thoughtful preparation. The next day, the press reports that the delegates of such and such a church have concluded that Angela Davis was the victim of political persecution, or that prayers in public schools should be restored. The truth of the matter is that any local county committee of a major political party probably brings as much if not more expertise to such an issue than an entire denominational gathering when it is governed under such sloppy and inadequate procedures.[2]

Second, denominational and council pronouncements often tend to be overly simplistic. One can predict that in the light of Watergate, church councils will condemn political fundraising procedures used in this country and call for government-financed campaign spending. While there is obviously much merit to such a proposal, there are also difficulties and ambiguities. If we disallow private contributions to a political campaign, are we limiting the political freedoms of those who wish to contribute to a political campaign? Is funding to be channeled through the national committees of the major parties, or directly to individual candidates? The answer to this question would have a major impact as to whether or not we would foster party control or independent judgment of public officeholders. When one begins to recognize the complexities of most political issues, one next begins to ask where the church gets its vast moral prerogative to make official pronouncements on such issues.[3]

Third, denominational and council pronouncements are not necessarily representative of their constituency. In other words, in claiming to speak for all Baptists or all Methodists, one is, in fact, telling a lie. Just because conventions of other groups, such as labor unions or the American Medical Association, engage in the practice of making resolutions, it does not give the church license to do the same.

There are several reasons for the fact that "interest group" pronouncements often are contrary to rank-and-file beliefs and attitudes. First, all organizations suffer from what is called by social scientists "the iron law of oligarchy." The larger an organization gets, the more the business of the organization is delegated to administrative heads. Successors to the administrators are generally promoted from within the administrative bureaucracy. Before long, the "leadership" has lost touch with the rank and file. There is little the rank and file can do to recapture leadership inasmuch as the administrative and organizational machinery necessary for an effective challenge to the leadership is generally in the control of the leadership itself. To suggest that large denominational bodies are immune to this tendency is to be naive.

But within the typical Protestant denomination, there is another reason for the break between the rank and file and the leadership of the social-concerns committees. This gap occurs because the conservative "faction" of most denominations regards social and political pronouncements as inappropriate or pointless in the first place; so they do not seek appointment to such boards, leaving them completely in the control of the more socially and politically active liberal "faction." Thus, there is indeed some truth to the charge so often made by conservative churchmen that liberals have "taken over" the policy-pronouncement machinery of their denominations. However, they fail to recognize that this is not so much the result of a plot by the liberals as the result of the abandonment of potential influence by the conservatives.

Fourth, denominational and council pronouncements on social and political issues can be divisive and contrary to the well-being of the church, particularly when they are poorly handled. Thus, their potential for good must also be weighed against their potential for harming the well-being of the church. I have met several ministers who would never think of drinking a cocktail in front of their parishioners on the basis that some might take offense. In deference to their feelings, their behavior on this matter is usually quite discretionary. Yet when it comes to such matters as denominational pronouncements on controversial social issues, they feel little if any hesitancy in speaking out vigorously, insisting that the clergy must provide leadership on such issues for the church. Little regard is left for prudential restraint on behalf of protecting the unity and institutional well-being of the church. In fact, some clergy even view the institutional decline of the church in the wake of vigorous social pronouncements as a sign of health.

Fifth, denominational and council pronouncements on social and political issues are often used as rationalizations and excuses for the failure of the church to involve itself in more significant and meaningful forms of social and political engagement. Church leaders look to past resolutions and statements with pride as if their formal stands on issues provided some sort of moral absolution for more substantive failure in the obligation to minister to social and political needs. Since the churches have been unable to mobilize their constituencies for meaningful social and political involvement at the local and national level, they settle for words instead of deeds. Until denominational and council pronouncements can be brought into some meaningful relationship with the actual conduct of the Christian community, they are actually indictments of the church's own pious hypocrisy — and not the prophetic pronouncements on social injustice that their advocates insist.

Sixth, denominational and council pronouncements on social and political issues are generally ineffective at the political level. Community leaders and political decision-makers are not so naive as to be unaware that such resolutions are usually and generally ill-considered, simplistic, moralistic, and nonrepresentative of the grass-roots sentiment of the communities being represented. Such being the case, one can hardly expect resolutions to receive serious consideration. There are literally scores of denominational and religious lobby groups in the nation's capitol alone.[4] It is not unusual for them to take contrary stands on a number of issues (e.g., abortion, prayer in public schools, amnesty, busing, or Vietnam). A practicing politician looking for moral guidance cannot help but be cynical in such a situation when those claiming to speak with the voice of God are all busy saying different things. It is enough to make the most confirmed monotheist convert to polytheism! (Unless, of course, one defines God's omnipotence as including the ability to hold more than one opinion on the same subject matter at once.)

However, the preceding argument must not be interpreted as a simple indictment of any and all political activity on the part of the institutional church. There will no doubt be many evangelicals and conservatives reading this book who will agree with all of the preceding arguments and wish to let the case rest there. At least three provisos must be added at this point. *First*, it must be remembered that sociologically the institutional church is *ipso facto* a political institution in the sense that what it does has political significance whether it seeks such political influence or not. There can be no such thing as political neutrality in the church – for even when the church remains strictly silent on social issues, its very silence is a factor in the political climate of the nation. The withdrawal of the institutional church from politics has the same effect as the withdrawal of individual Christians from politics – it leaves the political world to institutions and individuals who do not share the moral concerns of Christian commitment. This in itself is a very important factor in the conduct of national politics.

Second, the preceding arguments against church resolutions and pronouncements as a means of social and political engagement must not be interpreted as a pat on the back for those evangelicals and conservatives who insist that the evangelizing mission of the church can be separated from social and political concerns.... Such concerns are integral to the gospel, and if the church is going to proclaim a full gospel, it must not neglect the social and political dimensions contained therein. Further, the very conservative churchmen who decry the social and political pronouncements of the "liberal" churches engage in similar activities of their own – although more subtly and covertly. The blending of right-wing politics with fundamentalist causes is a well-established fact of American church life, and the blending of "moderate" conservative political causes with "moderate" theological conservatism is also a well-established fact of American church life.[5]

Third, despite the procedural weaknesses and political ineffectiveness surrounding most denominational resolutions and pronouncements, there are some cogent arguments which can be made on their behalf. Resolutions and pronouncements can be used in attempts to stir the conscience of the Christian community to show what they *should* be doing as opposed to what they *are* doing. In this sense, they serve a prophetic function within the community. Further, they can serve as protestations of conscience from within the Christian community against the failure of the church to show true discipleship in the social and political spheres.

THE CHURCH CONGREGATION AS A POLITICAL UNIT

The beliefs and behavior of the Christian community must be awakened at the congregational level if we are genuinely going to reform the church. Resolutions and declarations may serve to prick the conscience of the church – but the really important thing is to transform the attitudes and conduct of Christian believers at the grass-roots level. If this is going to be done at all, it will have to be done where the "real majority" of Christians find the source of their spiritual fellowship and guidance – the local congregation.

Yet, we have too often separated our religious confessions and practices from real-life problems. We try, insofar as possible, to protect the church from politicization by refusing to consider serious social and political problems at all. The sociologist Jeffrey K. Hadden shows how this affects the quality of our preaching when he reports:

> While congregations seem to have little influence on a minister's political *beliefs,* the evidence is substantial that they affect his *behavior.* In spite of the fact that a large proportion of ministers feel that they should have the right to speak out on significant political issues, only a very small proportion actually do so. This discrepancy between belief and action apparently results from their desire to avoid head-on conflict with their congregations. It is as if an unwritten rule says that a minister is entitled to believe as he likes on political issues so long as he doesn't try to proselytize his own views.[6]

There are two things which are wrong with this situation. The first is that the congregation seems to have little opportunity to discuss political matters with the minister and thus influence his beliefs. The second is that the minister is not allowed to share his theological guidance in political matters with his congregation. In other words, the church has ceased to be a community in which Christians all serve to build one another up in the faith.

We must learn to face social and political issues directly at the congregational level. While the pulpit must never be allowed to degenerate into simply a political forum, it must nonetheless be supported as a place to speak courageously on social and political issues. While church schools and church discussion groups must never be allowed to degenerate into civic-affairs groups, they must nonetheless be encouraged to deal with difficult questions as to how Christian discipleship relates to the affairs of the community at large.

One may ask, "What difference does it make whether my denomination tells me via a resolution how to vote on an issue or my pastor tells me the same thing via the pulpit? Aren't they equivalent?" The answer is no. The minister speaking from the pulpit is speaking within the context of a community of discourse which allows open and honest dialogue to emerge on the issue under discussion. If he takes simplistic approaches to difficult and complex social problems, there is opportunity for exchange, interaction, and correction. Further, there is less likelihood that the minister will take extreme and simplistic solutions to problems if he is part of a congregation which has already made an honest attempt to develop a degree of political literacy, for his congregation will likely represent a blend of competing viewpoints and interests; and he will recognize that, if he is going to be even minimally effective, he will have to take into consideration the diverse opinions and convictions represented in the congregation.

Again, there will be those who object to this line of reasoning by stating: "If my minister is so restricted by competing viewpoints within the congregation as to be literally forced into Caspar Milquetoast social proclamations, what can be achieved by any discussion of issues?" The answer is really quite simple. *First,* one must recognize the tremendous amount of political illiteracy among the American populace at large. Only 53 percent of the eligible voters in the United States can even name their congressman. Less than 25 percent can tell how he voted on even *one* major piece of legislation in the previous year![7] When it comes to state and local matters, illiteracy runs even higher. Only as the American population becomes politically literate can it begin at all realistically to talk about reordering national priorities, solving the problems of racism, or making government more responsible to the people. Politics tends to become "special interest" politics because only those with special interests tend to be concerned with what the government is doing. Only those with more diffused interests can change this situation. The problem with American government is not that it is unresponsive, but that it has only special interests to which it responds. If the general public could be mobilized to stay attuned to political issues and developments, the policies pursued by the government would change accordingly. Thus, while discussion groups and the goal of raising political literacy do not sound very exciting, they are nonetheless very fundamental and basic ingredients to political reform.

Second, when such discussion takes place within the Christian community, there is the hope that Christian values and commitments will inform the direction and character of the discussion which takes place. While Christians will not always agree on all particulars when it comes to political goals and policies, they will nonetheless bring concerns to the political scene which might otherwise be unrepresented and/or underrepresented in the political process.

Most people simply don't care about politics. One of the reasons for this is that undoubtedly the political system seems to run well enough as it is without their involvement. Hence, a person may be tempted to make a simple trade-off between the time and effort it takes to be informed and involved and what he sees as the relatively modest and marginal gains he may make for himself and the community through his or her involvement. The Christian, however, dares not be so callous in weighing the balance. For if he is indeed called upon to make the concerns of his fellowman his own, he has a moral obligation to become involved in the political scene even if he sees no direct benefit to himself. The community leader and activist who gives of his time and energy sacrificially for the well-being of another is a twentieth-century good Samaritan! Until Christians in their local communities begin to understand and act on this basic notion, they should refrain from grandiose pronouncements on how to make this a better world.

How to Become Politically Active

It is one thing to become politically literate. It is quite another to become politically active. If the Christian community is to be true to the political imperatives of its faith, it must not be simply a hearer of the Word. It must be a doer of the Word as well. The usual failure of the church has been that it has sought political influence without giving opportunity for serious consideration of the facts and principles which underlie meaningful political involvement. The preceding section has emphasized the need for such consideration within the Christian community, particularly as it might take place within the local congregation. However, such efforts must not be a substitute for political action. Indeed, if practical modifications in the political behavior of the Christian community do not result from such efforts, then they are no improvement whatever over the flaunting of denominational and council resolutions.

Social scientists estimate that only about 1 percent of the adult population can be classified as political activists. Thus, in a community of 100,000 people (if we assume only 65 percent of the total population are adults), only about 650 individuals are actively following and participating directly in the political affairs of the community. In a community of one million people, only about 6,500 individuals would be properly classified as political activists.[8] Clearly, one congregation of Christians seriously committed to involving itself in community affairs can have influence beyond all proportion to its numbers!

But what means should Christians use to exercise their potential influence in the community? Christians should be cautioned, first of all, from the idea of entering the political world as a block engaged in some sort of holy crusade to usher in a new era in the political life of a community. We have emphasized repeatedly the proper educative role of the institutional church in focusing the attention of its members upon the social and political problems of the community. But when it comes to actually mobilizing for political action, there is reason to believe that the institutional church should show great restraint in becoming politically involved. The complexity of political questions and the conflict inherent in the political processes are such that while the church must encourage its membership to become knowledgeably involved in the political process, it should remain institutionally separate from particular political causes. This distinction is a fine line, of course. In extraordinary circumstances the rule will have to be violated, such as in the case of resisting political oppression or securing basic human rights. But even in these cases, it is important that the church as an institution associate itself not with specific political programs and parties per se, but with the principles of justice at the more abstract level.

The reasons for this are several. First of all, political problems are generally complex. The church as an institution does not have the resources or expertise, as a rule, to speak authoritatively to such problems. Second, because of the complexity of political problems, there is room for honest disagreement between men of goodwill as to how political problems will best be solved. The church gains nothing by arbitrarily choosing and advocating one solution over another. Its role is to continue to call society to the need for solving the problem, not to provide the solution itself.

These restraints would suggest, therefore, that while the church has an obligation to become involved at the educational and motivational level of politics, it has an equal obligation to separate itself from the implementational level of politics. Here the Christian lay person as a citizen of the world must act. He acts within the context of the shared insights of his fellow believers in the Christian community as stimulated by prophetic social proclamation from the pulpit. And he is upheld by the prayerful support of his congregation. The church, in turn, can measure its own success or failure to the degree that it produces men of Christian conscience who are willing to venture into the political world.

But how, then, can laymen become active in politics? One cannot give simple cut-and-dried answers to this question. The practice of politics is an art – not a science. And political strategies are the product of numerous factors depending on the political culture of each local community, the resources one has to work with, and the nature of the goals one is pursuing....

The Christian community must learn to recognize that civic involvement is in itself a legitimate form of Christian service. To deny this is to suggest a truncated Christianity which arbitrarily separates the sacred from the secular. Such a viewpoint refuses to acknowledge that Christian calling and commitment pertain to all of one's life, not just what goes on inside the church walls. It makes the mistake, further, of placing the institutional interests of the church in competition with the needs of the community. It fails to recognize that the former is served only as it shares in the work of the latter.

The preceding discussion on practical political involvement has been very simple and elemental. But exactly at this point our involvement must begin if we are serious about bringing God's Word to bear on man's social existence. Moralists are all too often desirous of moving mountains without having to lift a finger. With indignation, they point to the decline of public morality and the crisis in American political institutions – but when it comes to doing something about them, they are seldom to be found.

The regeneration of American political institutions and an accompanying renewal of the American spirit will come about only when the

American public begins to care enough to allow its vocalized concerns to transform themselves into political action. Just as faith without works is dead, so, too, moral indignation over evil without an accompanying struggle for the good results in nothing.

Politics is the organized struggle for the ascendancy of one's own self-interest over that of another. Justice, on the other hand, is the giving to every man his proper due. The Christian who enters politics must do so with the aim of achieving political justice. He does this by subjecting his own personal ambitions and desires to the scrutiny of God's revelation in the Scriptures. And as God gives the grace to do so, he learns to make the needs of his neighbor his own. In so doing, his search for justice becomes an act of sacrificial love.

Justice thus becomes the servant of love. Insofar as the Christian community commits itself to sacrificial love, it must also commit itself to the struggle for justice.

> "I hate, I despise your feasts,
> and I take no delight in your solemn assemblies.
> Even though you offer me your burnt offerings
> and cereal offerings,
> I will not accept them,
> and the peace offerings of your fatted beasts
> I will not look upon.
>
> Take away from me the noise of your songs;
> to the melody of your harps I will not listen.
> But let justice roll down like waters,
> and righteousness like an everflowing stream."
>
> Amos 5: 21-24, RSV

"You are the light of the world. A city set on a hill cannot be hid. Nor do men light a lamp and put it under a bushel, but on a stand, and it gives light to all in the house. Let your light so shine before men, that they may see your good works and give glory to your Father who is in heaven."

"Think not that I have come to abolish the law and the prophets; I have come not to abolish them but to fulfill them. For truly, I say to you, till heaven and earth pass away, not an iota, not a dot, will pass from the law until all is accomplished. Whoever then relaxes one of the least of these commandments and teaches men so, shall be called least in the kingdom of heaven; but he who does them and teaches them shall be called great in the kingdom of heaven. For I tell you, unless your righteousness exceeds that of the scribes and Pharisees, you will never enter the kingdom of heaven" (Matthew 5:14-20, RSV).

NOTES

1. Quotations taken from the brochure entitled "Reaffirmations of 1973," published by the organizers of the "Continuing Church" advocates within the PCUS.

2. On this general problem, see Paul Ramsey, *Who Speaks for the Church?* (Nashville: Abingdon Press, 1961).

3. A respected political scientist, Reo Christenson, pleads for moral humility by church leaders in his article "The Church and Public Policy," *Christianity Today*, vol. 17, no. 7 (January 5, 1973), pp. 12-15.

4. On this, see James L. Adams, *The Growing Church Lobby in Washington* (Grand Rapids, Mich.: Wm. B. Eerdmans Publishing Company, 1970).

5. On this, see Jeffrey K. Hadden, *The Gathering Storm in the Churches* (Garden City, N.Y.: Doubleday & Company, Inc., 1969), chapter 3.

6. Hadden, *op. cit.*, pp. 89-90.

7. *Gallup Opinion Index*, report no. 64 (October 1970).

8. Austin Ranney, *The Governing of Men*, Third Edition (New York: Holt, Rinehart and Winston, Inc., 1971), p. 294.

Christian Political Action: NACPA Reconsidered

In the December, 1971, issue of *Dialogue,* Professor Gordon Spykman issued a clarion call for political action on the part of the Christian community. More particularly, he attempted to demonstrate the need for Christian political action which is distinctive of and transcendent from the "tweedledee and tweedledum stances" of existing two-party politics in the United States. He suggested, further, that the newly organized National Association for Christian Political Action (NACPA) was a means by which such action might take place.

While sharing Prof. Spykman's concern regarding the woeful lack of vision, commitment, and participation in relation to the political order on the part of the Christian community, I take vigorous exception to the particular vision, commitment, and means of participation which he outlines for us. This essay seeks to reconsider the problems Prof. Spykman has placed before us, to raise questions pertaining to the solutions he has proffered; and to delineate alternatives by which Christians can become more effectively involved in the American political system.

Spykman's Argument: A Summation

Prof. Spykman raises a number of issues regarding the present ineffectiveness of the Christian community in the political world. He asks the question, "... Who in the American political world is raising a voice in the name of Christian principles?" He suggests that the uncritical alliance of God and country (religious patriotism), on the one hand, and the disjunction of personal and social ethics (religious pietism), on the other hand, have both muted the potential for Chris-

Reprinted from *Dialogue* (May 13, 1972), a Calvin College publication. Obtained from the Paul B. Henry Collection in the Heritage Hall Archives of the Hekman Library at Calvin College.

tian political action. And even when Christians do become active politically, he argues, since half vote Democratic and the other half vote Republican, "The net impact of Christian citizenry [is] nil." Prof. Spykman laments the fact that the two-party system has become sacrosanct in American politics, that "campaigns are reduced to popularity contests," and that office holders "appeal pragmatically to voter interest."

What, then, can Christians do to achieve a more meaningful impact in the political world? Acknowledging that political action involves teamwork, Spykman suggests that the first thing to be done is to organize the Christian community for "communal reflection on our Biblical task." Out of this reflection there will emerge "ways of expressing concretely our civil obedience to Christ in the light of His Word." It should be stressed that Prof. Spykman believes that Christians, studying God's Word, will come to a uniform understanding as to what particular political actions are necessary in given situations: "For, as Christ himself said, 'You are the light of the world' – *light* in the singular, not *lights,* not merely individual candles flickering in the darkness, but the body of Christ acting in concert. . . . "

Once an effective mode of authentically Christian political action is discovered – civil disobedience to protest present government policies in education is suggested as a possibility – the Christian community will seek to break "the tyranny of majority rule."

A Reconsideration

Admittedly, the American political system is presently in a period of crisis. The continual tensions between rich and poor, labor and management, black and white, and young and old testify to the failure of the system in resolving the fundamental conflicts within American society. Above all, the political system has failed to address itself to the underlying spiritual crisis of Western civilization. But to admit this is not to accept either the diagnosis of these problems as offered by Prof. Spykman, nor the remedy he suggests. If anything, Spykman's approach to a "Christian politics" is symptomatic of our present political discontents, and not an answer to them. I should like to touch briefly on what I believe are six basic weaknesses in Prof. Spykman's argument.

(I) *Is the "System" at Fault?* Prof. Spykman's argument implies that the unresolved crises in American politics and the ineffectiveness of Christian witness in the American political system can be traced in part to the existence of two-party politics. This argument, of course, bears striking resemblance to those on the radical left and the reactionary right who argue essentially the same thing. The problem with such argumentation is that changing the formal structure of the political system and the political parties within it in no way changes the nature of the human beings of which the political system is ultimately composed, nor does it alter the underlying social and economic forces within the society which tend to rise to dominance in the political system. When political institutions are rearranged, the selfishness and self-interest which governs most political action in this fallen world simply takes on new forms – it is not eliminated.

For all of its faults, the American two-party system has served us remarkably well in comparison with other Western nations. For all the inequalities in the distribution of wealth in this country, America's poor are nonetheless wealthy in comparison to several European socialist countries. For all the unresolved religious and ethnic conflicts in this country, the two-party system has performed well in comparison to the multi-party systems of Germany and Belgium, or the modified two-party systems of Great Britain and Canada. Two-party systems generally seek to resolve conflicts in society by generating policies which will receive majority support at the polls. Multi-party systems, on the other hand, are potentially divisive for a society insofar as the parties seek to exploit distinctive ideologies which will mobilize the party faithful at the expense of the broader interests of a society. Countries which are geographically compact and less pluralistic than our own can afford to run the risk of multi-party politics. But in a country as large and diverse as the United States, a multi-party political system could prove quite harmful.

While the American political system as it presently exists may not be the best of all possible systems, Prof. Spykman's critiques do nothing to demonstrate that his suggestions for reform would in fact create a better system. Anybody who attacks the "tyranny of majority rule" under a two-party system had better be a little more explicit as to what kind of rule he is going to put in its place.

(II) *The Church-State Issue.* A second problem in Prof. Spykman's argument is that he clouds over the church-state issue. I do not question the fact that God's judgment extends over all human endeavors, including the political. But there are both theological and practical questions which suggest that perhaps we should let God do his own judging and not try to do it for him when it comes to attempting to identify good and evil in the political arena. Both the church and the state are granted authority from God, and it is questionable to suggest that the authority of either ought to seek to extend over that of the other.

Is it prudent for the Christian community to identify itself with particular political issues? By doing so, it tends to absolutize the "rightness" or "wrongness" of political solutions to human problems which in the last analysis are susceptible to only a spiritual solution. As Reinhold Niebuhr has suggested, democratic government is a matter of "seeking proximate solutions to insoluble problems."

This is not to say that the Christian community should not seek to enlighten itself on political questions, or that each member of that community does not have moral obligation to both God and his fellow man to seek social justice. But it must always guard itself from identifying the absolute will of God with the prudential calculations which are implicit in political action. Not to do so would be simply to create a new form of political religion as a substitute for the one we already have in this country.

(III) *Are There Christian "Solutions"?* Prof. Spykman's argument assumes that "communal reflection on our Biblical task in political life" will enable us to come to common agreement as to what that task is. This, of course, is a very questionable assumption. First, it assumes that a Christian community which is unable to achieve theological agreement is somehow going to come to agreement on the political principles it derives from its diverse theological traditions. Second, it would create an awkward position for those Christians who may find themselves in honest disagreement with the "official" position of the Christian community – should one be found.

Prof. Spykman may have anticipated this criticism by suggesting that we begin first within the Reformed community, where at least some basic agreement on doctrinal principles can be found, and then later extend ourselves to the more ambitious task of unifying the political clout of all Christians. (After all, he points out that NACPA already "counts its support among a scattered band of Christians in Iowa, Minnesota, Wisconsin, Illinois, Indiana, Michigan, Pennsylvania, and New Jersey" – sound familiar?) If this is the case, then one might suspect that their "Christian politics" is simply a means of using God's name to mask their own parochial interests, shaped not only by doctrinal but also by social-economic factors, ethnic cohesiveness, and shared history. Further, such a group would only add to the scores of such groups which already exist, ranging from the American Council of Christian Churches on the political right to the National Council of Churches on the political left.

To argue that Christians are capable of reaching a unified mind on particular political issues is to suggest that justification before God also sanctifies relations between men. I believe that a stronger case can be made – both theologically and empirically – that justification produces no guarantee of total, instant sanctification. That is not to say that Christians ought not endeavor to lead sanctified lives by God's grace – but rather to say that no matter what degree of sanctification does take place within the Christian community, it will never reach perfection (*i.e.* transcend all pride, self-interest, and parochialism) until its day of glorification in God's presence.

(IV) *The Single Member District System and Third Party Movements.* As a rule, the United States employs a "single member district system" in electing its public officials. This has profound importance for those who would seek to create effective minor political parties. The 435 members of the United States House of Representatives, for example, are chosen on the basis of 435 separate elections in 435 electoral districts. Each district is therefore won or lost on a "winner take all" basis. If three candidates ran for a Congressional seat and Candidate A receives 40% of the vote, Candidate B receives 35% of the vote, and Candidate C receives 25% of the vote, Candidate A will be the winner even though he received less than an absolute majority of the votes cast. Let us suppose that A was a "liberal" and that B and C were "conservatives". Even though more conservative than liberal votes were cast, the liberal voters won the seat because they did not split their vote between two candidates. Single member districts generally reward those candidates who can put together broadly based coalitions of support. That, among other reasons, is why American politics generally avoids commitment to firmly fixed platforms – specific issue candidates are generally not likely to succeed given the rules by which the system operates.

In considering the possibility of establishing a Christian political party, one must therefore assess the utility of such a movement in light of the realities of a single member district system. A Christian political party would, in effect, encourage Christians to waste their votes on candidates who have little if any chance of electoral success. For all of the talk about creating radical alternatives to the present, a Christian political party in effect encourages withdrawal from the arena in which the real political decisions will be made.

Those who argue for a Christian political party usually point to the existence of such parties in Europe. But it must be recognized that most European countries employ what is referred to as a system of "proportional representation." In this system, all candidates run at large throughout the entire nation under party labels, or in large, multi-member districts. If a party receives ten percent of the vote, it then gets ten percent of the seats in the legislature. If a party receives forty percent of the vote, it gets forty percent of the seats in the legislature. It is also worth noting that in those multi-party political systems of Europe, there is often more than one "Christian" party. The Netherlands, for example, has no less than five "Christian" political parties.

(V) *The Party as a Public Corporation.* Another fundamental difficulty with attempts at establishing a disciplined and ideologically committed party in the United States is the fact that the United States generally regards political parties as *public* corporations. That is, in order to participate in a party's affairs, one need simply declare himself as a Republican, a Democrat, or a "Christian." One need not pay dues, subscribe to the party platform, or even register with a party identification in order to vote in a party primary or seek election under that party's label.

This means that should a Christian political party be formed, and if it should somehow agree on specific principles of Christian political action, and if it should establish viability at the polls, virtually anybody could vote in the primary elections to choose that party's candidates or run under that party's label in a primary or general election. Just as George Wallace declares himself an American Independent one year and a Democrat the next, or just as Republicans will undoubtedly vote in Democratic primaries this year so as to disrupt the Democratic party, so too the "Christian" political party once formed might well find itself the victim of demagogues or organized groups which will seek to use the party for its own purposes.

In the multi-party systems of Europe, on the other hand, parties are regarded more along the lines of a private organization. They are given powers to establish their own rules for membership and participation. But since such mechanisms for preserving the purity of political parties do not exist in American law, it is naive to presume that ideological purity could be maintained.

(VI) *Fear of Compromise.* One of the attractions of third party movements is that they offer individuals the hope that an ideologically based party can help us escape the compromise and logrolling associated with politics as usual. Principle, we are told, will be substituted for pragmatism as the basic rule of the political process. Unfortunately, this is an illusory hope.

All politics involves compromise. *All* political action is caught in the web of interest conflict. To suggest that the political process can transcend the selfish contests of interests in a society is to suggest that it can transcend the dilemma of the pervasiveness of sin itself. What distinguishes different forms of government is not whether or not they are involved in making political compromises, but how and under what conditions those compromises are made.

The difference between multi-party and two-party systems is not that one involves compromise and the other doesn't, but rather the time and manner in which compromise takes place. In two-party systems, pragmatic compromise over ideology takes place *before* the election in the effort to gain majority support at the polls. In multi-party systems, compromise takes place *after* the election in the effort to gain majority support within the legislature and to form a government. In the two-party system, compromise is in the open for all to see before they vote. In a multi-party system, compromise may take place behind closed doors – and the people don't know what the new government will be until a few party leaders reach agreement.

Prof. Spykman and that "scattered band of Christians" who have joined with him in NACPA deserve our support insofar as they remind us that the redemption of the world is, among other things, political. Surely there is a very real need for the Christian community to give more serious attention to this task. But let us not delude ourselves into thinking that dramatic but ineffective confrontation against the political system serves to build the Kingdom of God. Third party movements are all too often nothing more than sophisticated rationalizations for copping out of the drudgery of less dramatic, but more effective, means of political involvement.

The New Christian Right: A Practicing Politician's Perspective

Who speaks for evangelical Protestantism in the contemporary political world? And what is it trying to say? The struggle of contemporary evangelicalism to articulate a responsible, biblically-based political ethic amidst the cacophony of a pluralistic and secular culture continues with mixed results. But in order to understand the true dimensions of this struggle, it is first of all necessary to deal at some length with the historical experience of conservative American Protestant Christianity. The question of the relationship between Athens and Jerusalem has been perennial throughout the history of Christendom – and we shall likely not resolve it at this conference. But in addressing the problem, it is important that it be placed in the context of the American political and historical experience. Thus, I begin my remark with a rather extensive summary and overview of the struggles of twentieth-century American culture as a means of gaining perspective on the present problem.

The misunderstandings between evangelicalism – and its contemporary political involvements – are not simply to be understood by sociological analysis. They are in large part a consequence of the overriding rejection of Christian theism as a world-and-life view by the secular culture, and the difficulty which the evangelical community experiences in trying to respond to a culture which dismisses evangelical convictions as the vestige of a pre-modern, pre-scientific era.

In many respects, the origins of modern science were rooted in the Judeo-Christian perspective on the universe which rejected the pantheism of pagan culture. With its understanding of a created universe, established and governed by an unchanging and transcendent God,

---

Speech given at Huntington College, Huntington, Indiana, on April 17, 1979. Obtained from the Paul B. Henry Collection in the Heritage Hall Archives of the Hekman Library at Calvin College.

the philosophical foundations for the objective study of the physical world governed by "laws of nature and nature's God" were established. But in the eighteenth-century, in particular, science began to evolve into scientism. Whereas science had its origins in the de-mythologizing of the universe made possible by the acknowledgement of a transcendent God, by the twentieth century it had turned against the Creator-God with the insistence that whatever could not be affirmed by means of the "scientific method" *per se* was either non-existent or not worthy of acknowledgement by the "scientific" mind. Scientism asserted that the methods of research known to the natural sciences were essential to all disciplines of human learning, and what could not be derived by those methods was to be regarded merely as "belief" rather than "knowledge."

Thus, by the turn of the century, scientific rationalism attacked the fideistic assumptions of biblically revealed religion. The evangelical retort that science itself rested on its own set of fideistic epistemological assumptions – and, ironically, that true science had its origins in Christian theism – was not deemed to be worthy of honest reply. Scientific evolutionism attacked the biblical concept of *ex nihilo* creation, the evangelical retort that scientific evolutionism was demonstrably failing itself as a theory of origins and likewise possibly deficient as a theory of biological change and adaptation likewise fell on deaf ears. Indeed, while the responsibility for the holocaust of World War II can at least partially be assigned to the social darwinism which is implicitly – if not explicitly – the logical consequence of scientific evolutionism, there was seemingly no turning back the tide of scientific evolutionism which stripped mankind of its divinely endowed nature just as surely as it stripped mankind of its divinely demanded responsibilities. Finally, scientific humanism directly assaulted and overwhelmed the Christian world-view in the psychological and social sciences just as scientific rationalism and scientific evolutionism had done in the natural sciences. According to scientific humanism, God was no longer the creator, but the created being. And man was no longer the created being, but the Creator God. Despite the protestations of evangelical Christianity that the scientific humanists were opening the door of an ethical relativism which undermined even the values to which the humanists themselves ascribed, their dissent was once again dismissed as a vestige of pre-enlightened, anti-intellectualism deemed unworthy of honest reply.

The lines were thus drawn between the "modern" world-view of rationalism, evolutionism, and humanism, on the one hand, and the classical biblical theism of the past. The biblical theists were scorned by the likes of H. L. Menchen as intellectual recidivists harkening back to the Dark Ages of primitive superstition and pre-scientific understanding. The parental metaphysical foundations of the newborn child science were dismissed as having already lived their allotted three score years and ten.

A very important consequence of this revolution in world-views is that with the dismissal of metaphysics, the modern mind lost the ability to think metaphysically. This, in and of itself, is one of the primary problems faced by the evangelical community when it seeks to address the modern world. The very language of the secular world reflects a mindset that is unable to converse about questions it either does not understand or dismisses as irrelevant. Hence, when evangelicals raise questions about the morality of public policies, the secular mindset responds that one should seek to impose morality into the political sphere – despite the fact that *all* political decisions are implicitly moral choices. When evangelicals seek to relate politics to religious values, the secular mindset responds that one shouldn't mix religion and politics – despite the fact that *all* political decisions are implicitly religious questions. As a secular culture, we have lost the ability to talk about questions of transcendent concern.

When Christian theists insist that civil rights and first amendment freedoms have their origin not simply in the political acknowledgement of social pluralism, but *also* in the acknowledgement that all human beings bear the image of God, are the children of God, and thus have God-given inalienable rights – and that a thorough going scientific evolutionism therefore undermines metaphysical foundations of democracy – the secular media which instruct our culture regard such warnings as something to be put into the religious news columns rather than a problem germane to socio-political debate.

When Judeo-Christian theists insist that the procedural norms of democratic government are dependent on a metaphysical world-view which acknowledges that the transcendent value of human life demands the applications of *means* which are appropriate to the *ends*, he is misunderstood by a culture which is unable to understand questions of absolute end and in turn absolutizes the means.

In fairness, however, it must be admitted that the reasons theists have had such difficulty in communicating their concerns in this regard are not the fault of secular culture alone. For the tragic fact is that while theists have most insistently proclaimed the metaphysical foundations of democracy, they have behaviorally all-too-often denied the practical consequences of their metaphysical stance. Hence, while evangelical theists have warned against the social darwinist implications of evolutionism, it has been the "Bible belt" which has most rigidly resisted the application of equal human rights to all individuals regardless of race, religion, or sex. While evangelical theists have warned against the gods of science, they have all-too-often been in the vanguard of those trusting in military technology to protect the nation from catastrophe at the expense of honoring divinely-sanctioned human rights as the ultimate test of a rightly-ordered society.

Thus, we find ourselves in a world where those who fail to understand the metaphysical foundations of democracy nonetheless seemingly honor the behavioral characteristics of democracy; while those who honor the metaphysical foundations of democracy all-too-often seemingly deny the behavioral consequences of their own metaphysical foundations.

The rise of the religious right must be understood not simply in terms of the philosophic revolution in secular culture, but also in terms of the manner in which that revolution affected the ecclesiastical structures of the Christian church as well. It was not long into the twentieth century until American Christianity began to divide itself over the question of how to respond to the new world-view of scientism. On the one hand were the self-described "modernists" which sought to reconcile the philosophic presuppositions of the secular culture to the doctrines of the church. Seeking to wed Christian views to the philosophic framework of scientific secularism, they attempted to develop a theology which was compatible with the modern mindset. In response, the "fundamentalist" movement was born. The fundamentalist believed that there was a quantum gap between the modern world-view and classical Christian orthodoxy in terms of metaphysical foundations, whereas the modernist believed the two could be reconciled.

The modernist, in the quest for reconciliation, repudiated classical Christian metaphysics while at the same time seeking to honor the ethical traditions of the Judeo-Christian heritage. Hence, for the modernist, the biblical accounts of the Virgin Birth of Jesus were reduced to literary hyperbole by which the Gospel writers sought to draw attention to the central character of the Gospel drama. The physical resurrection of Jesus was reduced to a metaphor by which it was illustrated that "you can't keep a good man down." The inspired Scriptures were authoritative and "God-spoken" in the same way in which Bach, Brahms, and Beethoven were "inspired" composers. The return of Jesus and the establishment of His Kingdom were reduced to historical self-fulfillment of good triumphing over evil in the name of modern science and progressive democracy. The theological modernist believed that by accommodating to the philosophical presuppositions of scientism, the Christian ethic could still be preserved.

Given this scenario, the fundamentalist reaction to modernism should come as no surprise. The fundamentalist movement was above all else an attempt to articulate a defense of Christian orthodoxy against *both* the scientific secularism of the day and the modernist theology which was spreading within the ecclesiastical structures of institutionalized protestantism. Hence, while its chief objective was the articulation of the Gospel of classical Christian theism against post-Christian and anti-Christian world-views, it was at the same time fighting an internal battle for the control of institutional ecclesiastical structures as well.

What becomes important at this point, for purposes of our discussion, however, is the perception of fundamentalism by those outside its movement rather than the merits of the movement itself. Increasingly, fundamentalists were regarded not only as anti-intellectual dullards by a secular culture, but also as sectarian malcontents as well. When fundamentalists argued against the rationalism of scientism, they were branded as "anti-science" and "anti-rational." When fundamentalists argued against secular humanism, they were branded as "anti-humane."

Fundamentalism, for all practical purposes, became orthodoxy in exile. While it is true that they were ecclesiastical and secular separatists, it is equally true that they were driven away by both the secular culture and the mainline churches in which they once resided. And having been driven from the world, they in turn often seemed to feel little, if any, moral responsibility to minister to it.

Amidst the period of fundamentalist exile, there were those within its own community which sometimes exploited the latent neuroticism fostered by this historical experience. Playing on the rejection of fundamentalism by the secular culture were those who would appeal to the self-doubt of the exiled community by blatantly and irrationally and irresponsibly lashing out against the secular culture at large. As the secular culture sought to stabilize the post-war international political order in efforts to maximize possibilities for peace, some fundamentalist leaders lashed out at the League of Nations and the United Nations as if they were the anti-Christ. As Western governments sought to address the evils of racial, social and economic injustice both at home and in their colonial empires, some fundamentalist leaders equated these efforts with the world-wide communist conspiracy. In short: if anything was happening in the world, it was ipso facto therefore of the world. And since the world had rejected the classical Judeo-Christian heritage, anything of the world was of anti-Christ.

Regrettably, fundamentalists had so far removed themselves from the contemporary world that they were oftentimes as incapable of understanding it as the secular world was incapable of understanding them. At the same time, the outlandish antics of an extremist wing in fundamentalism often served to gain disproportionate media attention – thereby confirming the secular culture in its rejection of what it increasingly understood Christian theism to represent, and at the same time comforting the rejected and exiled minority who reveled in any attention they could interject into what they perceived to be a hostile world.

During this period of exile, however, a gradual re-gathering and regrouping of the fundamentalist dispersion has been taking place and gaining momentum. Generally referred to as "evangelical Protestantism," it has parented what are now the largest – and in some cases the most respected – Protestant seminaries in the United States. The largest journal of religious opinion is now one which represents evangelical persuasion. And the largest Protestant philanthropic agencies in the nation are now clearly evangelical in disposition. In its "regrouping," evangelicalism has found to its own surprise that there were others "hidden" in the mainline denominations which, though not joining the fundamentalists, in separation from their parent ecclesiastical bodies, remained sympathetic to classical Protestant orthodoxy through the years of fundamentalist-modernist controversy.

This evangelical renaissance has made itself manifest at the same time as secular culture finds itself in disarray. The decade of the 70s began with the "Age of Aquarius" at the top of the hit-parade, and *The Greening of America* at the top of the best-seller list. It ended in a time of social, economic, and political turmoil as difficult as any ever experienced in the two-hundred-year history of the Republic.

This juxtaposition of events has caused both evangelicals and the secular culture to reexamine what has happened to each during the preceding two generations. To the evangelicals, it has strengthened their resolve and helped heal their neurotic temperament – while at the same time tempting them with a spirit of triumphalism. To the secular culture, it has become a time of self-examination and re-assessment – a looking backward as to what has gone wrong with America.

Accompanying the apparent revived strength of evangelicalism has been an equally apparent revival of conservative politics in the country. And in some cases, the two have been "merged" together with the appearance of groups such as the Religious Roundtable and the Moral Majority. Does the emergence of religious fundamentalism from exile necessarily signify an emergence of *political* fundamentalism as well? Do groups such as Moral Majority speak for evangelicalism? The emergence of the combined political/religious right holds significance largely because of the broader emergence of evangelicalism in general. The resurgence of the political/religious right in particular would hold little significance otherwise insofar as such groups have always been a part of the American political scene.

Thus, the question before us is whether the *religious* right and the *political* right are necessarily synonymous, and if so, what the consequences of this might be for the American political scene. If it has taken me a long time to get to the main point of my presentation, it has been because I have wanted to make it abundantly clear that I have sought to understand the philosophic battle which is being waged for the mind of Western culture. And further, I sympathize with the heritage of the evangelical movement because I, as an evangelical Christian, have been part of it.

Nevertheless, I am deeply distressed individually by those who would seek to attach the religious and metaphysical convictions of the *religious* right to the causes of the *political* right as simplistically as has been proposed by the leaders of the combined political/religious right. And I am distressed not simply as an evangelical Christian, but also as a Republican officeholder who regards himself as a conservative on many of the issues of the day.

While I appreciate the contributions which the political/religious right is making in terms of encouraging Christians to involve themselves in the political process, while I appreciate the contributions which the political/religious right is making in getting people to understand the relationship between metaphysical value-commitments and applied public policies, while I understand that the political/religious left has long practiced the same trade with impunity, and while I recognize that the secular press has sometimes blatantly misunderstood both the intent and the actions of the political/religious right, there are at least six areas of disagreement which I would list personally in responding to it.

First, while agreeing with the political/religious right's critique of the metaphysical foundations of Western culture, I nevertheless find myself in disagreement with the prudential applications of that critique at the practical level. While the secular culture misunderstood the Christian opposition to scientism – be it scientific rationalism, Darwinian evolutionism, or scientific humanism – as being "anti-rational" and "anti-scientific," the political/religious right regretfully often commits the same error in reverse. In other words, just as surely as the secularist suggests that those who reject scientific humanism are inhumane, so, too, the political/religious right suggests that those concerned with humane social and political values are scientific humanists. Just as surely as the secularist suggests that those who reject scientific evolutionism are anti-scientific, so too, the religious right suggests that those concerned with interpretation of evidentiary biological and geological science in the context of evolutionary methodologies are ipso facto "anti-God" or "anti-creationist" in terms of a theory of origins. Just as surely as the secularist suggests that those who reject scientific rationalism as an all-inclusive epistemological foundation for knowledge are "anti-intellectual" and medieval religionists, so, too, the political/religious right suggests that those committed to scientific methodologies within their disciplines are "scientific rationalists" who have been co-opted by the spirit of "secular humanism."

Now, I readily concede that scientism, secularism, humanism, rationalism, and evolutionism of the sort described by the political/religious right exist. And I concede that they are antithetically juxtaposed to classical Christian theism. And I concede that classical Christian theism provides the moral and metaphysical foundations of democratic government. But the political/religious right draws its lines with such broad strokes that it encourages the Christian community to assess the secular culture just as abusively and dishonestly as the secular culture has often assessed its own. Insofar as it does this, it is mistaken at best, and dishonest at worst.

The religious right reminds us that classical Marxism has its roots in scientific rationalism, evolutionism, and humanism. From this it concludes that those who acknowledge the obligations of governments to address questions of economic justice are either part of the secularist conspiracy, or have been duped thereby. Using the same logic, I suggest that the Prophet Isaiah would recoil at being called a humanist dupe, that the Prophet Amos would be outraged at being called a scientific rationalist, or that the author of the creation accounts, Moses, would be dismayed to find himself labeled as an evolutionist.

The religious right reminds us that some of the eighteenth century utopians dreamed of a united Western Europe – and thereby asserts that the United Nations and the Common Market are potentially the embodiment of the secularist anti-Christ. At the same time, they find little to fear in Western-oriented military alliances such as NATO, SEATO, CENTO, and the Rio Pact.

Insofar as the religious right attaches itself to the reductionist rhetoric of the political/religious right, it frustrates rather than facilitates honest conversation between evangelicals and the secular community. Further, the inconsistency and excesses of the political/religious right only serves to re-enforce secular disdain and distrust of the Christian world-view.

Secondly, by simplistically connecting its metaphysical critique of contemporary culture to a selected set of political issues, the political/religious right threatens to trivialize the Gospel. The fundamental message of the religious right is that God exists, that He has shown Himself to us through the Scriptures and through His Son, Jesus Christ, that mankind is offered reconciliation to God through His Son, that we are called to live in obedience to His Son, and that in the end we shall be judged by God for our response to His call. *That* is the real message of evangelical Christian faith, not the question of the disposition of the Panama Canal!

Third, as an evangelical Christian of conservative political persuasion, I would nonetheless insist that one cannot simplistically connect theological conservatism with political conservatism in the fashion of the political/religious right. While it is true that secular humanism views man as infinitely malleable, denies that man lives in fallen revolt against God, and is therefore constantly seeking to remake man by remaking his environment, and that all this relates to the "statist" proclivities of the political left, it is also true that *because* man is fallen, *because* he is selfish, *because* he is egocentric, government is necessary to institute justice. If Revelations 13 warns us against government as anti-Christ, Romans 13 just as surely reminds us of the necessity of government as an instrument of justice in a fallen world. Just as surely as the fact that man is fallen and not capable of perfection, and therefore Christians recognize that the state cannot make man perfect through social engineering, every social order is fallen and in need for reform. In this sense, a Christian is always seeking to reform society in the name of justice just as surely as he seeks to warn against statist solutions to the human condition.

Christians do not always agree as to how their faith is to be honestly applied to the problems of the political realm. And to simplistically suggest that one group of Christians is "moral" while the other is not demonstrates an ignorance of the complexities surrounding the political world. I am reminded of the debates in seventeenth century England during the period of the Cromwellian Revolution in which two great Puritan defenders of the Revolution disagreed over the question of political censorship. Richard Baxter, the chaplain to Cromwell, argued that since men were fallen, political censorship was necessary to insure that truth would be protected from falsehood. At the same time, the great poet and essayist Milton argued that since men were fallen, those who controlled the press would be sorely tempted to abuse the power of censorship to distort truth itself. Because he believed in the power of truth to prevail over falsehood, he argued against censorship. Now *both* Baxter and Milton were articulate defenders of what would today be called evangelical Protestantism. Yet they disagreed fundamentally on one of the key questions of the day. Neither could be considered less Christian than the other. While I would argue that one was mistaken, and the other not mistaken, I find it morally pretentious to suggest that one was moral, and the other immoral, in his approach to the question.

Fourth, as an evangelical Christian I am concerned about the danger of *using God* rather than by being *used of God* when mixing religion with politics. Given my understanding of the fall of man, I would suggest that the Christian community remind itself that although justified through the atonement of the Saviour Christ Jesus, we are not yet sanctified. In other words, when we seek to apply the Word of God to matters political, it is doubly important that we be cognizant of the temptation to mask our self-interest under religious pretense rather than having our self-interest unmasked by the transcendent justice of

God. The teaching of Christ is plain: we must elevate our concern for our neighbors' interest to a level of intensity with which we seek to protect our own.

Not only are Christian people fallen, they are finite. And Christian commitment does not endow the believer with perfect wisdom on matters political. Indeed, one of the chief sins against which the Scriptures warn is the sin of pride. And it is important that Christians remember the teachings of the ancient prophets when they called upon Israel not only to seek justice, but to walk humbly before their God while doing so!

Fifth, I believe that the political/religious right is both claiming and receiving greater credit in the general public than is due their influence. The fact that the media has so easily equated the political/religious right with evangelicalism demonstrates its own lack of understanding of the diversity within the evangelical community itself. While there are roughly up to some 60 million evangelicals in the United States if we use the term loosely to describe those who would regard themselves as Christian theists in Protestant circles – the political/religious right probably does not speak for the inner-city black evangelical who attends a storefront church, does not speak for the confessional evangelicals in denominations such as the Missouri Synod Lutheran Church, nor even for the Southern Baptist Church which generally takes much more moderate denominational stands than the religious right. If we focus on the National Association of Evangelicals and its affiliated churches we find a constituency which represents only some 10% of the claimed evangelical constituency per se.

In fact, contemporary scholarship is finding that the fundamentalist/evangelical community is *not* – nor was it ever – as politically conservative as has generally been popularly assumed. The writings of David Moberg at the Marquette University, of Timothy Smith at Johns Hopkins University, and George Marsden at Calvin College have indicated that evangelicals have historically been much more diverse in the nature of the political involvement than is generally understood.

If anything, contemporary evangelicalism has begun to moderate its political posture – despite the general trend to the political right in the country at large. Survey data gathered from the University of Chicago's "National Opinion Research Center" over the last seven years indicate that there has been a national shift toward "conservative" political thinking in the nation at large. But interestingly – and perhaps surprisingly – the growth in conservatism has been largely a shift of thinking by the unchurched, while within evangelical and religious circles of the right there has been a moderating of political commitments. In other words, groups like Moral Majority and the Religious Roundtable are getting the press, when secular conservatives such as Barry Goldwater's more traditional conservatism should in fact be getting the credit.

Sixth, and finally, while I applaud the efforts of the political/religious right to generate greater public understanding of the fact that political choices are *moral* choices, and while I applaud their efforts to get people with moral sensitivity to involve themselves in the political process, and while I share their metaphysical critique of the moral foundations of our secular age, I nonetheless am concerned that they have not yet fully thought out a carefully articulated understanding of the relationship between righteousness and justice. Surely the Christian believes that as a nation is faithful to God's righteousness, it reaps spiritual rewards which outweigh the perceived benefits of rebellion against God – or to put it in biblical language, the wages of sin. And while a truly righteous nation will also be a truly just nation, it must also be remembered that the realm of righteousness speaks to the question of moral motivation and will whereas justice per se deals with the external relationships between competing individuals and interest.

Spiritual righteousness provides a moral foundation for justice. But spirituality per se cannot be commanded by the state. In other words, the political/religious right sometimes fails to distinguish between prophetic critique of society, and the political manipulation of society. For the political order to base its decisions on attempts to enforce spiritual righteousness as opposed to universal norms of justice is to subject society to sectarian creed. And evangelicals, of all groups, ought to understand that the civil liberties under which they themselves proclaim the full counsel of God stand threatened whenever one group of people seeks to impose its vision of righteousness – as opposed to justice – on the political order. Insofar as evangelical Christians honor the traditions of civil liberty, they serve to protect their own well-being in a fallen world which rejects the call of God.

Further, evangelicals ought not to forget that the norms of justice are universal – and that appeals for moral political decision-making can be legitimately made on the basis of moral conscience shared by all mankind. It is such an appeal which is acknowledged by the Declaration of Independence when it calls civil society to honor those truths which are self-evident to all people. Ironically and tragically, it has sometimes been the people of God who have been last to acknowledge the norms of justice. Hence, the danger of moral pretense raises its ugly head; and when Christians seek to address the political order in the name of the God of justice, they must be particularly careful not to use His name in vain. To whom much is given, much is also required.

General Approach

A First-term Congressman Looks at Faith and Politics

What are your priorities as a newly elected congressman?

Priorities are defined to a large extent by your district. Michigan has been ravaged by unemployment and economic dislocation, so obviously one of the priorities I have is the whole economic climate of my state. When we talk about economic growth, which has been phenomenal in this country in the last couple of years, my concern is for my congressional district to share in it. The Grand Rapids area is much more balanced economically than most of Michigan, so it has not suffered as seriously, and its long-range outlook is good. But its infrastructure is threatened. That is a transcending concern.

Also, I've been heavily involved in education issues, coming from a family of educators and having been a professor. I'm former chairman of the education committee in the Michigan State Senate, so I was involved in a number of bills trying to strengthen accountability in primary and secondary education, and in higher education as well. I did succeed in getting on the Education and Labor Committee in the U.S. House of Representatives. My second committee is Science and Technology. That committee deals with natural resource and environmental issues which I've been leading at the state level too.

Have you been involved with the question of values in education?

Values are at the heart of everything, and to say you could have value-free education or "neutral" politics is mistaken. The whole difficulty rests in our culture, where, because of our diversity and our constitutional separation of church and state, we have become almost in-

Reprinted from *Christianity Today*, March 15, 1985, by permission.

capable as a public of engaging in rational, thoughtful discussion of the issues. So the rhetoric tends to escape meaningful dialogue.

Many times people use the separational language to mask an agnostic or relativistic view. A countervailing moralism from both Left and Right simplistically baptizes certain interests with a moral appeal. The question of values in education is really difficult, because as we become increasingly pluralistic as a society, and as we have moved away from Judeo-Christian foundations that were the assumed values of American public education, then it is hard to have any purpose or coherence in public education. But you can't simply blame the educational enterprise. It's a broader fact of our culture and our society.

What is your assessment of the Conservative Opportunity Society, in which many conservative Republican members of Congress are involved?

I tend not to get involved in ideological special-interest groups with the party, particularly during the first few months when you want to take care not to get branded one way or the other. I'll try to get the lay of the map and keep up cordial relations with all at this point.

You've had some previous experience in Washington.

That's right. I was administrative assistant to former Congressman John Anderson years back, and then director of the Republican House conference staff. So at least I knew my way around the building.

Do you have a position on the President's prayer amendment, which he has mentioned in several recent speeches?

I have very serious concerns about the whole concept of spoken prayer in public schools, and I think there is tremendous public confusion out there on the issue. I think it's a symbolic issue, and that symbolism tends to obfuscate the problems.

My son attends a junior high school in Grand Rapids. Some 250 kids – including Christians, Jews, Muslims, and Buddhists – attend that school. Spoken prayers may mean a state-written prayer that is religiously neutral. It will not be a prayer in Jesus' name. People assume it will be a Judeo-Christian prayer, but it won't. It will be a prayer offered in the name of George Washington, Thomas Jefferson, and Abraham Lincoln, and maybe throw in Martin Luther King. Or it's going to be a Christian prayer on Monday, a Jewish prayer on Tuesday, a Hindu prayer on Wednesday. What would we really be teaching our children? I understand the President's concern and the public's frustration. Polling in my district shows overwhelming support for it. But I think we could also show overwhelming confusion as to what is at issue.

Would you explain how being the son of Carl Henry influenced your decision to go into politics?

My father was one of the evangelical leaders years ago, who bewailed the attrition of evangelical influence in the public sector, so I was raised in an environment where this kind of thing was discussed. One of the first books he wrote was *The Uneasy Conscience of Modern Fundamentalism*. I think he would define that book as a populist tract.

It is important to understand that our calling as Christians doesn't stop at certain areas of life. On the other hand, I'd be the first one to caution against the suggestion that people of Christian conviction have some kind of inherent infallibility in matters political. If anything is needed now, particularly in the evangelical community, it's a call for caution and also for humility – a recognition that one of the fundamental Christian virtues is humility.

As we seek justice and mercy, as we seek Christian accountability or Christian values in society, we need to be sure that we are not doing some of the same things others are doing – masking greed under the banner of the Cross. I think the real danger at this point in the evangelical community is not the mistaken notion that Christians ought not to be involved – we're coming through that. Now the danger lies in how we're being involved and whether we're listening and following, as it were, the promptings of the Spirit, or simply manipulating religious symbols.

Was the Religious Right involved in your campaign in Michigan?

No. In my primary, the local Moral Majority chapter sent out a letter opposing me, in support of someone who was making overt appeals to their issues. Some of that is due to tremendous amounts of misunderstanding. There are people out there speaking for the broad evangelical Protestant community who in fact are pretty far removed from it. My district would be somewhat different as well because of the strong presence of confessional Protestantism, with the Christian

Reformed Church, the Reformed Church in America, and Lutheran denominations. And, too, the Catholic church has a very strong relationship to evangelical Protestant churches in my part of the state, and for that reason it tempers much of what I would call the sectarian fringes of evangelical Protestantism.

What is your sense of President Reagan and his impact on the country?

It has been profound. It sounds almost corny to say, but there has been a rebirth of American spirit. You can't deny it. It's been good and helpful. We're through the morose period of self-flagellation. Reagan has an ability to bring people together, and will try more forcefully to bring in the minorities who feel they've been passed by these last few years. It's important that he do that, and I think he understands that and is genuinely concerned about it.

On his economic policies, by and large, I've been strongly supportive. I have also agreed with much of his program of military modernization, although not the full extent of it. And I think there's going to be some drawing in of the reins this year. I tend to be somewhat more moderate than he is on issues such as environmental policy and on some of the social questions.

What about abortion?

I support the right to life, so there is no difference between us on that.

On Paying Our Political Dues

ON POLITICAL MORALITY:

It's not possible to be too moral because morality brings discipline especially to those who invoke it. At the same time there has been much moralistic prattle in the public arena. Both the Right and the Left engage in various types of moralism. The Right emphasizes traditional values while the Left focuses on social do-goodism. Republicans often use evangelical-like language in speechmaking. President Jimmy

Paul Henry on "Paying Our Political Dues," *Eternity*, July/August 1988. Obtained from the Paul B. Henry Collection in the Heritage Hall Archives of the Hekman Library at Calvin College.

Carter was a classic example of one who used a sloganistic moralism by referring to Americans as a "decent" people.

Every political decision is a moral choice between good or evil or mixtures of both. It is appropriate to bring a Christian conscience to bear on public conduct. The Bible speaks of the moral rule of the state as promoting nonsectarian justice. Goodness and meekness as opposed to discord and jealousy are common grace fruits. Public and private morality are related in the Bible. Public virtue is based on justice as seen in Romans 13.

ON JUSTICE AND MORALITY:
In America we argue over the meanings of these words. Most political questions are ultimately questions of the allocation of resources; some people win and others lose in this process. There is a great need for evangelical seminaries to teach political ethics. Usually there is little thoughtfulness in training for moral political thinking and decision-making. Christians may be forced to make such decisions superficially. Another principle is "prudence" or the discernment of what politics is.

ON POLITICAL RHETORIC:
Compromise must also be considered. We still suffer from the previous generation's non-involvement in politics. We don't appreciate that the subtleties of decision-making may show moral maturity as well as moral failure. Christians learn through their experiences in politics. They should be involved in public affairs all the time and not just at election time. We need Christians to work out their political decisions into principles. When Christ says to put the concern for others equal with self-concern, this is a Christian test.

We should beware of those seeking to exploit the Christian label in non-Christian ways for this is using Christ's name in vain. There is a need for less shallow Christian rhetoric and more content. Some issues that evangelicals should be concerned about include problems of global infant mortality, the arms race and world hunger.

ON POLITICAL ACTIVISM:
Each ETERNITY reader has some knowledge to contribute to the public discourse. For example, something so essential as hauling trash is an environmental problem needing a solution. Farmers can share their insights on agriculture to lessen Third World hunger.

Only five percent of the American population ever gets active in politics in any way. So Christians can be influential. We must mature as a community. The number of people who share evangelical convictions of a Christian worldview in orthodox confessional terms and who are comfortable discussing it in Eternity's pages is larger than many think but they shy away, due to the others, from both the religious Right the religious Left, who manipulate Christianity.

Not every evangelical Christian has the same views on politics but they can be salt in contributing to the public good. As a congressman, I saw needs in my Grand Rapids district and I got onto the education and labor and science and technologies committees as appropriate for dealing with the needs of my home district. In order to address the needs of the infrastructure we must be willing to pay our dues and refine our political skills.

Getting Involved in Politics

When I ran for the state legislature in 1976, I had to collect signatures on nominating petitions to qualify for a spot on the ballot. I approached a Christian businessman who ran the local gas station and asked him if he'd lend me his name. "Sure, Paul" he said, "but if you win, don't come back to me again two years from now for help with your re-election. By then you'll be just like the rest of 'em!"

That encounter reminds me of the deep suspicion many Christian laypersons have about the political process in general – and politicians in particular. Indeed, after my election to the legislature, it was hard even for me to get used to being call a "politician." After all, I was still substantially the same person I had always been – husband, father of three children, neighbor, layperson in my local church, and hopelessly unskilled in household maintenance chores. But now I was also regarded even by my friends as a "politician," destined to become "like the rest of 'em" within two short years!

Christians are not alone, of course, in their suspicion of the political process and those active in it. What we must remember is that all forms of power can be used for good or for evil. Politics is not alone in that

Reprinted from *JustLife/88: A 1988 Election Study Guide for Justice, Life, and Peace*, by permission.

regard. Avoiding political engagement and political commitments in the effort to avoid misusing power only forsakes opportunities to effect the rightful use of power. There is no neutral ground. We cannot escape our moral responsibility in the social order through simple withdrawal, separation, or "otherworldliness."

Some folks mistakenly assume that the separation of church and state implies a separation of religious values from politics. In fact, the separation of church and state provides constitutional protection against the state's intrusion into the life of religious communities. It also protects against the state's establishing sectarian religious institutions through legal fiat. But it is neither a prescription against nor a prohibition of the expression of religious or moral values through the democratic process.

All politics, in fact, involves moral decision-making. Whether someone is considered "liberal" or "conservative," moral assumptions are inevitably involved in judging the "rightness" or "wrongness" of a social condition. We also make moral judgments concerning our proposed political remedies for that condition.

Furthermore, we cannot arbitrarily separate the spiritual from the temporal aspects of the human condition. We simply cannot read the Old Testament prophets, comprehend the social implications of the Ten Commandments, or attest to the life and teachings of Jesus Christ without regard to the fact that the Christian message speaks to the entire human condition. The Christian message addresses all the consequences of humanity's rebellion against the Creator-Redeemer God. It is not limited to the spiritual alienation of a fallen human race; it also speaks to that alienation's consequences for social behavior.

Just as surely as the Fall affects every dimension of the human condition, so the redemption afforded to us through Jesus Christ speaks to the entirety of the human condition.

We are called to seek justice (Micah 6:8), to let our lights shine (Matt. 5:16), to be the salt of the earth (Matt. 5:13). Involvement in the political process is one of many ways in which the Christian community can be faithful to the redemptive power of the gospel. Political involvement means seeking justice in and through the public, institutional structures.

At the same time, we must remember the prophetic injunction to walk humbly with our God (Micah 6:8). Just as surely as the Scriptures make plain that we are to seek justice, we cannot simply reduce the Christian message to some sort of religious party platform from which incontrovertible political specifics can be drawn. The Bible and the teachings of the Christian community point to broad principles which we dare not neglect in our Christian witness to society. But we must guard against the temptation to exploit those principles on behalf of particular applications when other equally plausible affirmations of Christian conscience can be drawn from them. We must avoid the temptation to manipulate or exploit Christian conscience on behalf of hidden agendas, thereby using God rather than being used by God.

One cannot simply deduce political particulars from the transcendent truths of God's revelation in Jesus Christ and the Scriptures. To suggest, as some do, that a true Christian is "obviously a conservative" or "obviously a liberal" misses the point entirely. For is it not true that insofar as all human institutions are fallen and flawed, they always stand in need of reform? And is it not equally true that the fundamental evils of social and political injustices stem from our rebellion against God, something which no law or dictate of government can address at its root cause?

Our democratic institutions afford us the opportunity to effect change and promote wholeness within our society and between the nations. To forsake this opportunity is to bear responsibility for the consequences of our inaction, as well as to leave the public sector solely in the hands of those who may not be sensitive to Christian values.

But in assuming our political responsibilities — both constitutional and religious in character — we must avoid the danger of simplistically wedding the label of Christian to our own special interests. We must acknowledge our own finitude. We must be mindful of the principles of civility, tolerance, and civil rights, which God ordains to be enjoyed by all. We dare not abuse the norms of justice in the pursuit of justice, lest the means employed undermine the ends pursued.

Above all, Christian conduct in the public order ought to be marked by sensitivity toward those outside the Christian community who may disagree with us at the most fundamental level, as well as sensitivity to those within the Christian community who may disagree with us at the practical level. Remember the words of St. Paul: "The fruit of the Spirit is love, joy, peace, patience, kindness, goodness, faithfulness, gentleness, and self-control" (Gal. 5:22-23). We must never forget that Christian virtue does not stop at the water's edge of the political process.

April 1989

Dear:

This is in reference to your recent phone call to my district office, during which you requested that I respond to three questions about a Christian's civic responsibility.

In response to your first question, I would answer that I serve my community first of all by representing their views and concerns to the Congress in Washington. To do this it is important that I stay in contact with my constituents by meeting with them, holding town meetings, and communicating with them on a regular basis through letters and newsletters. I need to know their concerns and positions on the various issues I vote on in the Congress. Secondly, as a U. S. Representative I must spend time assisting my constituents and our community when there are problems with the federal government – whether that be a lost Social Security check, the non-receipt of an IRS tax refund, or assistance in obtaining a federal grant.

In response to your second question, I believe I serve God by responding to the issues of today with a perspective that acknowledges Christ as Lord of all aspects of life. To do this I must recognize my own shortcomings and shortsightedness, and seek His will as a humble servant. The major issues of today are not always as black and white as many perceive them to be – and so quite often it is not a matter of choosing between "right and wrong", but of choosing the "lesser of two evils" or the "greater of two competing goods." I serve God, by serving those He has called me to lead, by providing a positive role-model in the community, and by seeking to bring my Christian perspective on life to bear on the issues upon which I vote.

And finally, in response to your third question, I believe that it is vital for people of all ages to be actively involved in the community. But it is especially important that young people, such as yourself, learn at an early age to participate in community affairs. Ways you can get involved include, writing letters to your legislators on issues of particular concern to you, volunteering at a senior citizens home, getting involved in a recycling effort, collecting food and distributing it to the needy, or praying for our nation's leaders.

Thank you for contacting me, and it is my hope that my answers to your questions will be of assistance to you. Please do not hesitate to contact me again, should you have a concern about any federal matter.

With best regards, I am
Sincerely yours,

Prison Reform

U.S. Prisons in Crisis

The United States faces a full-blown crisis in its prisons. Increased funding for law enforcement, together with public demands to "get tough" on criminals once they have been caught, has resulted in a dramatic increase in the nation's prison population. As a result, prisons have become overcrowded to the point of creating intolerable conditions.

My own state of Michigan presently has two thousand more prisoners than its "rated capacity." In Michigan, "rated capacity" includes over a thousand prisoners in a prison that is over one-hundred years-old and that – until only recently – was in such disrepair that the urinals in the 8-foot square cells wouldn't flush. Present sentencing patterns in the state indicate that if something is not done, we will be four thousand over the rated capacity by 1990. And the legislature is presently considering a new "mandatory minimum" sentencing bill which, if enacted, would add yet another two thousand prisoners to the system.

Such overcrowding is not just a problem in Michigan. In other states as well, it has created such inhumane and uncivil conditions that the inmates themselves have turned to the courts for relief against "cruel and unusual punishment," and the courts have taken over jurisdiction and control of prisons in sixteen states. In twelve other states, litigation to that effect is pending.

Why don't we simply build more prisons to respond to this crisis? First, prisons are *extremely* expensive. A new 500-bed prison, with its expensive security system, kitchens, and educational and industrial programming, would cost roughly $50 million. That comes to $100,000 per bed – and given the fact that most states borrow the

Reprinted from *The Banner* (September 15, 1980), by permission.

money for prison expansion, the true cost, including the interest on bonded indebtedness, will come closer to $200,000 per bed! This does not include the annual operational costs of a prison, which comes to almost $7,000 per prisoner per year.

While the cost of building and operating prisons is staggering, that is not the only factor that has frustrated policymakers. Increasingly, fundamental questions are being raised about the effectiveness of prisons in dealing with crime. While incarcerating criminals in a prison temporarily removes them from society, well-intentioned and motivated "rehabilitational" programming in prisons seemingly does little to protect society against a criminal relapsing into criminal behavior. Hence, some argue strongly against building new prisons. They believe that alternative forms of punishment and rehabilitation (of non-violent criminals in particular) will not only be more cost-effective, but more humane as well.

Those arguing for prison alternatives do so on several grounds. The late C. S. Lewis, for example, believed that the emphasis on "rehabilitation" in our correctional system leads to unfair sentencing. One would be sentenced not for the crime committed, but upon some arbitrary assessment as to how long it would take to "rehabilitate" him or her. The seemingly benign emphasis on rehabilitation, instead of retribution and restitution, stems in part from a humanistic world view that rejects the concepts of sin and retribution and instead focuses on the need to "re-socialize" the criminal offender.

Thus, much of the recent effort to reform criminal justice focuses on establishing a balance between rehabilitation, retribution (ensuring that the sentence fits the crime), and restitution (compensating both the victim and the community at large).

Others have questioned the dehumanizing aspects of institutional incarceration. To place a criminal offender in an artificial world composed only of other criminal offenders and expect that person to emerge from that abnormal environment as a healthy and whole person is certainly a questionable strategy. We have increasingly recognized the dehumanizing effects of placing the mentally ill, and children with special educational needs, in institutional environments. The prison is even more dehumanizing because there is a natural antipathy between the incarcerated offender and the guards and turnkeys.

Prisoners are isolated from their families and often, upon release, have no home to which to return. To expect them to "re-enter" society in a constructive manner stretches credulity. Prisoners are lonely and forgotten – there is no organized political pressure or social advocacy to ensure that they are treated humanely and justly. Charles Colson, Director of Prison Fellowship Ministry, reports that, in one institution, prisoners cut off their thumbs as a means of protesting their plight. The biblical injunctions to "remember" and "visit" the prisoner come readily to mind.

What we must remember is that most prisoners will return to our communities. Therefore, the emphasis has been, not on constructing new jails and prisons, but on developing either "alternatives to incarceration" or incarceration in conjunction with prerelease into community correction centers. It must be emphasized at this point that roughly half of all incarcerated criminals are serving time for nonviolent and nonassaultive crimes. Given the costs of building and operating prisons, and given the failure of prisons to rehabilitate the criminal, one can readily see why such alternatives are being considered so seriously.

Just as surely as there is a reluctance to build new prisons, there is a difficult political problem in developing alternative correctional programming. The general population often fails to distinguish between the violent and assaultive criminal and the non-violent and nonassaultive one. The Christian community often fails to recognize that the rehabilitative programming of prisons is modeled on an intellectual tradition which, by and large, rejects traditional Judeo-Christian concerns of fitting punishment to the crime (i.e., retribution and restitution). No organized constituency is demanding reform, and political fortune normally does not smile upon those public officials who seek to address the issues other than in an inflammatory and emotional appeal to public fears over crime.

Thus, prison reform is at an impasse. On the one hand, there is a reluctance to build new prisons to accommodate the ever-increasing prisoner population. Outdated, overcrowded facilities, offering ineffective programming at high cost, are common. On the other hand, there is a political reluctance to consider alternatives – even when such alternatives are, in some ways, more clearly rooted in the Judeo-Christian understanding of punishment.

I must confess that I had never in my life visited a jail or a prison prior to the time I was elected to the legislature. Aware of the potentially explosive prison situation that our nation faces, I had asked to be assigned to the Corrections Committee, knowing full well that it was not a particularly prestigious or powerful committee. Since that time, I have been profoundly moved over the plight of those locked and forgotten behind prison walls. I am not a "do-gooder" or "limousine liberal" when it comes to questions of law and order and public safety. But I am morally outraged at what passes for a correctional system in our nation. If we cannot become indignant at prison conditions, let us at least become indignant at the immense waste of such an expensive system, which is so ineffective.

Just as the way in which we punish our children says a great deal about us as parents, so too the way in which we punish our criminal offenders says a great deal about us as a nation. We want the best for our children. At the same time, we forget that one of God's standards for measuring Christian compassion and responsibility is the degree to which we respond to the needs of the lonely and forgotten. When the cold, gray steel doors of a prison cell slam shut, all too often there is no echo. Only silence. As difficult as it may be for us, may God give us the grace to minister to the needs of the people behind those bars.

Aid to the Nicaraguan Contras

April 30, 1985

Dear:

In my previous letter to you regarding the "contra funding" issue I indicated that I was "undecided" at that point in time as to how I would vote, but that I would continue to study the issue and would let you know how I voted. As you may know, I voted in support of the President's request for continued funding, and I want to explain some of my reasons for doing so.

Essentially the contra funding issue revolves around two questions: (1) What is the nature of the present Sandinista government? and (2) What ought our foreign policy response be in relation to that government? Weighing the evidence as dispassionately as I could, I concluded that this is indeed a Marxist government which is seeking to align itself with the Soviet Union. Further, it is a Marxist government which has repeatedly stated that its revolution is "without borders." Conflicting evidence abounds as to the degree to which this government has already funneled support for violent and revolutionary activity in other Latin American countries. In my campaign, I repeatedly stated that I did not believe it was in our national interest (or that of our Latin American neighbors) to allow another Cuba-type situation to develop in the region.

Having made that determination, I then had to answer the question as to what our policy response should be. You will recall that during my campaign, I also stated that I did not want to see the United States get involved in another Vietnam-type situation. What should be made clear, particularly because the local press did not explain this well, is that by the time the House of Representatives was called upon to vote

A typical constituent response letter after Paul's 1985 vote in support of a $27 million humanitarian aid package. Obtained from the Paul B. Henry Collection in the Heritage Hall Archives of the Hekman Library at Calvin College.

on the issue, all three proposals before the House were limited to funding for purely humanitarian purposes. There were, of course, important subtleties of difference between each of the proposals, but none allowed military use of the funds being debated.

Before the vote, the President also made written commitments to those of us who had questioned him the hardest, that:

(1) Regular monitoring and reporting mechanisms would be initiated to insure that the funds would be used only for humanitarian purposes;

(2) The U.S. will enter into direct negotiations with the Sandinista government towards a cease fire and a church-mediated dialogue between the Sandinistas and the contras.

(3) The Administration will seek to use non-military means of countering the Sandinista's threat to the region, including economic sanctions and support for the Contadora process.

Given the substantial degree of concurrence between the various options before the Congress, and given the very substantial and constructive movement which the Administration made during negotiations with the Congress on this matter, I felt that I could support the Administration's request.

Again, thank you for sharing your concerns with me. I want you to know that I took your concerns seriously as I tried to address this very complex issue, and I would welcome further communication from you on it.

Sincerely yours,

June 28, 1985

Dear:

I wish to acknowledge your communication of opposition to my vote to provide aid to the "contra" forces in Nicaragua. Quite frankly, I am tremendously moved by the depth of conscience and the degree of literacy which most of the mail and other comment opposing my vote has demonstrated. Certainly I do not impugn in any way the motives or intentions of those who oppose the Administration's policy in Central America.

A follow-up letter to the same constituent whose first communication prompted Paul's previous reply. Obtained from the Paul B. Henry Collection in the Heritage Hall Archives of the Hekman Library at Calvin College.

But once again, I personally must come back to my own conclusion on weighing the evidence that the present regime in Nicaragua is determined to establish a classic Marxist state, and that it has employed tremendous deception in the process of doing so. I would not dare to attempt to defend the history of our nation's past policies in Nicaragua, nor to deny some of the real gains in literacy, preventive health care, et al, that have occurred under the Sandinista regime. But I cannot separate these short term gains from the long term prospects of allowing Nicaragua to fall victim to a Marxist government which has on numerous occasions stated its intention to export similar revolution to neighboring states. In the long run, this is desirable neither for the best interest of the Nicaraguan people, the remainder of Central America, or our own national interest.

I do not deny that there have been and remain some very troubling aspects of our policy in Central America. I only suggest that the choices themselves are "fallen," and that continued pressure on the Sandinista regime is preferable to pretending that there is no fundamental problem with that regime and allowing a Marxist government to consolidate power without challenge.

I have had discussions with respected policy analysts on both sides of the question, and have made a deliberate effort to listen to those outside of the Administration as well as those voices from within the Administration. I pledge to you that I will continue to keep an open mind on this issue, and to learn from you and others on this matter.

Thank you again for taking the time to communicate with me, despite our evident disagreement on this matter.

With best wishes, I am

Sincerely yours,

Military and Humanitarian Aid

Mr. Chairman, as we engage in the final moments of debate over the President's request for military aid to the Contra resistance in Nicaragua, let each of us refrain from such exaggeration and rhetorical excess that we would seek to mislead those yet uncommitted on the issue, and inadvertently fall into the trap of engaging in the same polarized

From the *Congressional Record* of March 20, 1986.

extremism which has all too often characterized the politics of our Latin American friends who themselves now search for the political center.

To those uncommitted on the issue, let me note first of all that the divisions between both sides of this issue are not as great as our own rhetoric would have us believe. If we compare the President's statement of Sunday last with the response on behalf of the Democratic Party offered by Senator Sasser, we note that both acknowledge the present regime in Nicaragua to be Marxist in character, that both acknowledge the export of revolution and terrorism from that country, and that both acknowledge the appropriateness of discussing aid to the Nicaraguan resistance. What does distinguish the two positions is the issue of waiting up to 6 months before releasing such assistance, in order to allow yet one more opportunity for a negotiated settlement both within Nicaragua and between Nicaragua and its neighbors. And now even this difference has apparently been resolved.

Mr. Chairman, during the recent task force visit to Central America, of which I was a part, the nine Members of Congress met with Nicaraguan Vice President Sergio Ramirez Mercado. I asked him during that meeting why Nicaragua was the only Central American government unwilling to sign the Contadora treaty proposal. His direct response was, and I quote verbatim, "We won't get anywhere if we debate this issue. I prefer simple answers to simple questions."

Why, then, should we release these funds as immediately as possible? First, to add military pressure to the efforts to secure a negotiated settlement in the face of such intransigence. Second, to add risk viability to those who courageously resist the regime, be it militarily or from within the civil resistance.

But there is yet an even more important consequence and significance to our vote on this matter today. In Central America, we have the tale of two cities, two nations, which have experienced two very different types of revolutions. And the differing character of each of these revolutions has profound impact on the current struggle between those committed to and those opposed to the dream of freedom for the Latin American peoples.

These two revolutions are as strikingly different as the English Revolution of the seventeenth century, and the French Revolution of the eighteenth century. In the one – as in El Salvador – the necessity of mediating social change through democratic political institutions is recognized as central to the ultimate character of its final result. In the other – as in Nicaragua – the end is elevated above the means. And the "liberators" have subsequently become the new "oppressors."

Mr. Chairman, our constituents are not particularly sensitive to the critical nature of this distinction. Nor for that matter have we been as sensitive as we ought in acknowledging its importance. But our Latin American friends have been – and they look to us for a sign as to where we stand on the issue. The Nicaraguan resistance looks to us in desperate hope of revolution betrayed. And its neighbors wonder whether it is worth the while to stand firm against those who, while using the language of democracy, use tyrannical means to reach their ends.

The assistance to the resistance within Nicaragua is not only a matter of supporting the forces for democratic change within that country, but a signal of profound diplomatic significance sent throughout the region. And it has direct implications for the democratic revolution in El Salvador, which needs an opportunity to consolidate its gains against subversion from abroad.

Finally, Mr. Chairman, it is we, the American people, who are being tested. Can we continue to be passive in the face of Communist subversion in the region? Can we permit our own ignorance of world affairs, occupation with profoundly important domestic concerns, to allow the Soviet block to operate with relative impunity and without cost in destabilizing the fledging steps of infant democracies in the region?

As we close our debate, Mr. Chairman, regardless of the outcome of this vote, let us speak honorably and respectfully of those with whom we disagree on the choice before us. And as such, let us seek to move forward together in the continued quest to honor the ideals of freedom both in our own land and abroad.

March 27, 1986

Dear:

Please forgive my tardiness in responding to your recent communication of opposition to the President's request for funds for the "contra" forces in Nicaragua. As you might expect, I have received a great deal of mail on this issue, and so I have had to resort to a "form"

Another "form letter" response to constituents opposing U.S. aid to the contras. Obtained from the Paul B. Henry Collection in the Heritage Hall Archives of the Hekman Library at Calvin College.

response. But I have personally read each letter I have received on both sides of this issue, and sincerely appreciate the deeply felt and well articulated concerns which have been expressed to me. And, as many of you with whom I have corresponded in the past on this issue know, I do not approach this matter as presenting a simple black and white type of choice. The issues surrounding this matter are complex and difficult, in my opinion, and force us to choose between alternatives none of which are attractive or desirable.

On several occasions I have opposed the President on matters of importance to him. When I have felt him to be wrong, I have said so and voted accordingly. Despite the unfortunate rhetoric which has surrounded this debate, I do believe that in this instance he is correct in insisting on certain points fundamental to the issue:

(1) the Sandinista government is increasingly aligned with Soviet-styled Communism, and is repressing political freedoms in its own country;

(2) that it is training, supplying, and deploying subversion throughout Latin America; and

(3) the fortunes of fragile democracies in the region, as well as our own national interest, necessitates the use of military pressure to force a negotiated accord.

The question of negotiations over regional security is obviously central to this entire debate. In that regard, I particularly want to share with you the conversation I had with Vice President Ramirez of Nicaragua during my brief visit to the region. He explicitly *refused* to discuss the Contadora treaty proposal when I raised the issue of a negotiated settlement. Two days after I left the country, he subsequently called a conference of the international press to "invoke" the Contadora process.

Because it is impossible to reply extensively to each and every communication I have received on this important issue, I will be preparing a special newsletter to elaborate more fully on the situation in Central America as I see it. Hopefully, it will address many of the points and concerns which you have expressed to me. In the interim, I am enclosing a copy of my remarks during the debate in the House of Representatives which I hope you will give some time to consider, and which will give you at least some further indication of my thinking on this issue.

With best wishes, I am

Sincerely yours,

June 25, 1986

The Hon. George P. Schultz
Secretary of State
2201 C Street, N.W.
Washington, D.C. 20520

Dear Mr. Secretary:

As you know we finished a rather contentious debate in the House of Representatives late yesterday evening in regard to the funding of the "Contra" forces fighting against the Sandinista government. I have, as you know, generally supported the Administration's requests for continued financial assistance to the Contra forces—not because the Contra movement enjoys my unqualified support, but because of deep concerns over the consequences of a firmly entrenched Marxist regime in the Central American region, and out of concern for neighboring Central American republics which must contend with Marxist-sponsored terrorism funneled, in part, through Nicaragua.

Clearly the Sandinista government is not composed of angels, as some of the Administration's critics would have us believe. But neither are the Contras saints! The enclosed inquiry from a concerned constituent who has spent great effort in understanding the Central American dilemma and who has remained cordial with me, despite his personal opposition for my support of Administration policies in the region, is enclosed for your attention and review.

We face a dilemma in Central America not all that different from that we faced in Vietnam two decades ago. While we know what it is we are *against*, it is not yet clear what it is we are *supporting*. And unless this issue is resolved promptly, I can assure you that many of us who have stood by you on this issue thus far will have to reexamine our position.

I am asking for your *personal* response to this letter. It is indicative of a broad range of problems endemic to our policy in Central America in support of the Contra movement. I am further sending copies of this letter to Representatives Michel and Lott as notice to them of my very deep concerns over this matter, and reasserting that I request your *personal* involvement in this issue, out of minimal regard for the sup-

In this letter to U.S. Secretary of State George Schultz, Paul enclosed a copy of a letter a constituent submitted in strong opposition to U.S. Nicaraguan policy. Obtained from the Paul B. Henry Collection in the Heritage Hall Archives of the Hekman Library at Calvin College.

port I have lent you thus far, amidst substantial and well informed criticism of our policies in the region from my constituents.

With deep respect and best wishes, I am

Sincerely yours,

August 1, 1986

Dear:

Please forgive the delay in responding to your note of July 12, 1986 – but things are very hectic as we approach the end of session rush. Let me respond briefly to each of the questions in the interview with the Bishop of Nicaragua:

(1) Yes, I agree, the revolution was necessary. In fact, the United States helped engineer the revolution, and during the first year of its life, actually gave more economic assistance to the new government than any other nation.

During this time, *before* there was any organized or unorganized opposition in existence, there was a major militarization of the society. American Peace Corps volunteers were expelled. U.S. aid was going to the purchase of Soviet arms. And even the Nicaraguan government *admits* that during this time, it was funding and arming guerillas in El Salvador. It was Jimmy Carter who changed our policy toward Nicaragua – not Ronald Reagan – in light of these problems.

(2) Has the Sandinista party served the majority? Read the column in today's *Wall Street Journal* (enclosed). Surely, the civil war accounts for much of the economic malaise of the regime—but equally important are the economic policies of collectivization. I refer you again to Shirley Christian's book, *Nicaragua: Revolution in the Family*.

(3) Religious persecution? You bet – and for your Bishop to deny it represents tremendous error. You can be arrested in Nicaragua today for distributing the Gospel tract "4 Things God Wants You to Know." Pat Darien, former Assistant Secretary of State for Human Rights under the Carter Administration, has just issued a new report saying the situation is much worse than it ever was under Somoza! The Interna-

---

A detailed response to a pointed letter from a personal friend and constituent who obviously disagreed with Paul's position on *contra* aid. Obtained from the Paul B. Henry Collection in the Heritage Hall Archives of the Hekman Library at Calvin College.

tional Commission on Human Rights, which helped bring about the downfall of Somoza, says the same thing.

Incidentally, Cardinal Obando Y Bravo has never supported the Contras. He has, as he should, brought Christian critique to the violence on both sides. He has to use the foreign press, because there is no uncensored domestic press. Please see the enclosed in this regard.

(4) Are the Sandinistas Communists? No – not all of them. But those who have the power are. The "72 Hour Document," so named because it was a secret statement among the Commandantes published three days after the Revolution, makes this very clear. The only way one can challenge that these people are Communist is to declare the document a forgery, which even the leaders of the revolution do not do.

The myth that exists in liberal circles is that we drove a democratic socialist revolution to the hard left. The fact is that we had a broadly based social/democratic revolution that was taken over by the hard left.

(5) Why hostility between the two countries? Because we have a Marxist regime in a location of strategic geopolitical importance to the United States which is actively funding and equipping revolutionary terrorism in fragile emerging democracies throughout Central America. Remember, Nicaragua is the *only* Central American country not signing the Contadora treaty.

I could go on and on. And perhaps I'm sounding too harsh. But I know that you have trusted my moral instincts on this matter at least, even if strongly disagreeing with the practical decisions I have made on the wisdom of supporting the Contras, given the dilemma we face.

I do understand that the position of the church ought to be against violence on all sides. With that I agree. And I think Cardinal Obando Y Bravo's carefully balanced letter indicates the path he has taken in this regard, as well. But what is the role of the state, as opposed to the church, in this matter? Read Daniel, Chapter 6, and tell me if Darius did the right thing!

Again, I hope I'm not coming on too strong! You know how deeply I love you and (your wife), and how indebted I am to both of you for your friendship and your continuing support. But I guess I am so frustrated with the great amount of one-sided information on this question, I just felt comfortable letting a bit of my frustration show to you!

Keep praying for wisdom – for both of us!

With warm regards, I am

Sincerely yours,

A New Approach to Nicaragua Needed

Mr. Speaker; no issue so bitterly divides the Congress as that pertaining to United States foreign policy in regard to Nicaragua. No matter what position we take on the question of funding the Contra forces, we are pilloried by intense opposition from our constituents. If we choose to support administration policy, we are accused of insensitivity to the atrocities of war. If we choose to oppose administration policy, we are accused of naivete as to the Marxist-Leninist bent of the current Nicaraguan Government, and the grave implications of that reality for our national interest and that of the Central American region itself.

One of the mystifying aspects of our debate over what to do about the Sandinista regime has been the distinctly differing way in which the issue itself has been addressed within the Congress itself and the public at large. Within the Congress, there is virtually universal agreement that the current Sandinista regime is firmly aligned with the Marxist-Leninist bloc of countries, and that our policies must be guided accordingly. While we have exhibited disagreement over what the particular character of these policies ought to be, we seemingly agree on the fundamental assessment of what it is we are dealing with.

Our constituents, on the other hand, still seem to be divided on the question of the nature of the Sandinista regime itself. Differing assessments as to the nature of the regime yield differing criteria as to what is an appropriate American response.

This set of differing assessments has subsequently befuddled much of our internal debate over American foreign policy toward Central America in general and Nicaragua in particular. And as a consequence, we have allowed ourselves to fall into the trap of reducing our options in Central America to that of either supporting or not supporting the Contra forces, rather than exploring new alternatives which potentially hold greater promise for successfully upholding our national interest in the region.

In the months which have passed since the Congress last addressed this issue, the question of our policy toward Nicaragua has become even more obscured through revelations and unanswered questions pertaining to the Iran arms sales. Whether we like it or not, the issue of promoting constitutionalism and the rule of law abroad, have become

From the *Congressional Record* of March 3, 1987.

entwined with that of protecting constitutionalism and the rule of law at home. An already contentious issue has become yet more contentious. And a great responsibility rests upon us in Congress to resolve the political and policy impasse with which we are faced.

As one who supported administration policy, let me reiterate the reasons for that support, and summarize what I believe to be legitimate goals of that policy:

First, clearly, the administration is correct in its insistence that the Sandinista government is a Communist-aligned regime. Not unlike the Russian revolution of 1917, the hopes of the Nicaraguan people who overthrew years of corrupt and oppressive government in the name of democracy found their own 1979 revolution betrayed. The liberators quickly became the new oppressors. And as many will convincingly argue, the repressions of the current Sandinista government exceed those of the former Somoza regime.

Second, the administration is equally correct in noting the Leninist and expansionist nature of the Sandinista government. Indeed, it was President Carter who first formally objected to the militarization of the Nicaraguan society and economy, and its use as a base for exporting revolution throughout the region.

Third, the administration's policy vis-a-vis Nicaragua has not been a total failure. Indeed, if nothing else, it has first, drawn a line against further communist encroachment in the region; second, established bipartisan recognition of the threat posed by the Sandinista government; and third, consumed the Nicaraguan Government with the need to consolidate its own revolution, so it could not expend its resources wholly to the export of revolution throughout the region without cost.

Having said this, let me suggest that there are, nonetheless, weaknesses in current policy which must be admitted and addressed if we are to move forward from this point.

First, while administration policy has achieved its short-term goal of forestalling the export of Communist-insurgent revolution in the region, it holds little hope of overturning the Government of Nicaragua. The reasons for this are several. In seeking to consolidate itself against counterrevolutionary activity, the Sandinista regime has become increasingly repressive to the point of being an armed garrison, which could likely be overturned only with substantial and direct military intervention – a policy which the administration itself has publicly repudiated on numerous occasions.

Second, the counterrevolutionary Contra elements have failed to unify around a vision of hope which bears moral and political authenticity to the Nicaraguan masses. I do not dispute the disillusionment of the Nicaraguan people with their present government. But neither do I believe the Contras have gained the moral initiative whereby to inspire an uprising of their own people. Further, the continuing Somoza connections among the Contra leadership, in particular, and their undisciplined conduct in battle belie whatever promises they make. While a short-term strategy of allying ourselves with these elements to check Communist oppression may have been an acceptable political expedient, it is hardly the basis for a long-range American foreign policy with which the American people wish to be identified.

Third, we have reached the point in the contemporary Central American setting where an excessive reliance on military solutions is counterproductive to the process of democratization in the region. Militarizing our allies in Central America does not foster the movement to civilian government and public institutions which is the stipulated goal of our policy in the region.

Fourth, and finally, our own domestic political concerns over the Iran arms transfer demand constitutional accountability. And because this issue is inevitably intertwined with our current foreign policy toward the Central American region, a reassessment of current policy is inescapable, whether we have favored that policy or not.

Necessity mandates a change in policy. But such necessity must not be allowed to serve as an excuse to abandon a proactive policy which recognizes legitimate national interests in the region. During the last several years Congress has allowed itself to fall into the trap of supporting present policy, or abandoning present policy with nothing to put in its stead. Given the imminence of change in policy, it is incumbent upon us all to work together on both sides of the aisle in the pursuit of a proactive, constructive, bipartisan policy in the region which vigorously upholds our national interest.

What would be the benchmarks of such a policy?

First, it must come to an explicit agreement and convergence of views as to the nature of the present Sandinista regime. Quite frankly, I think we are already there. But we have allowed our political disagreements on specific policy to overwhelm the necessity of a strong, bipartisan statement which speaks not only to the American public, but also to the world community of nations which has interpreted our disagreement over specifics as disagreement on fundamentals. Such a policy should have no hesitancy in admitting the Marxist-Leninist character of the present regime.

Second, such a policy should clearly draw the line on territorial encroachments and terrorist activities by that regime. It should invoke the multilateral support, participation, and commitments of our Western Hemisphere friends, most pointedly the Central American and Contadora nations themselves, who have been insistent on this issue.

Third, such policy should speak clearly and explicitly to the degree of militarization which will be tolerated within Nicaragua, the nature and extent of armaments which will be tolerated, and the threat which such armaments pose, not simply to our own national security, but to the peace and tranquility of the region.

Fourth, such policy should not abandon consistent pressures on Nicaragua to fulfill the promises of democracy, political pluralism, and human rights which were made during the revolution. The Sandinista regime has been strong on words, but weak in performance in regard to these commitments. It should be exposed for what it is, and collectively the Western Hemisphere nations should continue to be insistent that changes occur domestically within the nation.

While there will shortly be a vote on the release of the final $40 million of the $100 million appropriated in support of the Contra forces by the 99th Congress, I would stress again that this issue is truly secondary to the broader concerns I have addressed. We must not allow ourselves to be beguiled, on either side of the issue, into reductionist rhetoric which substitutes the Contra debate for the need to formulate coherent, bipartisan, multinational policy in the region. It is time to deliberately enunciate a full-fledged policy which actively solicits and secures the support of our friends in Central America and the broader Latin American community of nations.

Why not, for example, simply invoke the proposal of the Contadora group as our own? And in exchange for declaring our national intent to enforce those proposals, secure clear commitments from the Contadora group for their diplomatic support for such a policy? And in conjunction with such an effort, why not formally accept the recent initiative of the Central American republics, and pledge our national resolve to its enforcement in exchange for their public endorsement and support of these proposals?

A bipartisan, multinational response to the Sandinista regime would not be a retreat from the purposes of present policy so much as an improvement upon it. And in that vein, I have offered these comments with the hope that our obligation to represent the national interest can rise above the partisan temptations that can threaten to leave us without any policy and exposed as politically inept and weak in the international community of nations.

In summary, Mr. Speaker, I would emphasize once again that there is no basis from which to move beyond present policy until another has been readied to put into its place. And while signals from the administration are uncertain as to its willingness to pursue such an approach, we as a Congress must move forward on our own if we are to avoid the culpability for abandoning Nicaragua and the Central American region as a consequence of repudiating the inadequacies and limitations of present policy.

Contra Aid: Bad Answer to Bad Question

One of my college professors repeatedly told his class. "To assure good answers, you must first ask good questions."

The question of continued funding for the Nicaraguan Contras has, unfortunately, been so poorly framed over the years as to ensure only bad answers. The question becomes the foreign-policy equivalent of "Have you stopped beating your wife?"

The Reagan Administration has allowed the Contra question to eclipse broader questions of American foreign-policy goals in the Central American region, and Congress has been beguiled into debating the question on those limited terms.

In so doing, both Congress and the President have been backed into a "no win" corner. If military aid is approved this week, we risk undermining the diplomatic offensive that has achieved more in six months than military aid has accomplished in six years. Such approval would give the Sandinista regime an excuse to renege on its promises of political pluralism and the restoration of democratic processes.

From *The Los Angeles Times* January 31, 1988, marking a significant change in Paul's position on *contra* aid. Obtained from the Paul B. Henry Collection in the Heritage Hall Archives of the Hekman Library at Calvin College.

On the other hand, a rejection of aid without qualification would send a signal to the Sandinistas, that Congress and the President have reached a statement on American policy toward Nicaragua. They would thus be tempted to disregard the promises made last August and expanded upon two weeks ago in Costa Rica.

Either way, the Sandinistas win, because the question has been improperly framed from the beginning. And Congress faces the dilemma of either reaffirming bad policy or rejecting it and creating the vacuum of having no policy at all.

Hopefully, the answer to this imprudent ultimatum will be yet another reprieve through an unglamorous compromise that segregates Contra support into non-lethal and lethal-aid packages, fencing off release of the latter for subsequent congressional consideration.

Such an arrangement would allow one more chance, perhaps the last, to return the Contra caboose to the back of the policy train where it belongs, and enable the Administration to forge a truly bipartisan, multidimensional and multilateral approach to the Nicaraguan issue.

Three critical dimensions of our Central American policy need to be resolved:

– An honest attempt must be made to root that policy in genuine bipartisan consensus. Bipartisanship means more than simply securing the magic number of "swing" votes needed to join the majority of Republicans, supporting the President on the issue. It means a jointly formulated policy in which there is a sense of shared ownership sufficient to engender a shared obligation to defend it domestically and aboard. Dividing Congress and the nation with "good guy-bad guy" rhetoric over charges of neo-isolationism or naivete regarding Marxist regimes can only serve to undermine this effort. Members of Congress ought not to usurp the role of secretary of state. But implementing foreign policy in the absence of reasonable political accommodation denies the stable and predictable foundation upon which foreign policy consensus must be built.

– Our Central American policy must be explicitly multidimensional. If continued democratization of Latin American societies is to be nurtured, policies addressing the problem of the drug warlords, the burgeoning Latin populations, the restructuring of Latin American debts and revitalization of Latin American economies must be given just as dramatic a focus and attention as the effort to counter Marxist subversion and presence in the region. We must rigorously examine the impact that our policies may or may not be having in inadvertently remilitarizing the very region in which we are trying to sustain the growth of fragile civilian political institutions.

– Our Central American policy must deliberately seek to strengthen multilateral participation of the region's nations. A sense of shared ownership of that policy is no less important to those affected by it than it is to those conducting it. Last fall, while Congress was once again debating additional millions to the Contras, the State Department advised the Organization of American States that the United States could not afford to meet its financial obligations to host the annual OAS meeting. And of course, it goes without saying that a Central American policy is doomed to failure if it runs counter to the joint efforts of the Central American presidents to develop a regional solution to their problems.

As long as policy-making is determined by lurching from Contra aid request to Contra aid request, there is little in the way of meaningful discussion and agreement on the broader goals and purposes of our policy in Central America, and how and when military force might be used to achieve them. In the present context of the diplomatic initiative undertaken by the Central American presidents, the continued fixation on further funding of the Contras is even less adequate as a substitute for a broader policy. Until we begin to ask the right questions, we shall be frustrated with a policy process that yields only bad answers.

The Persian Gulf War

Mr. Speaker, this is a somber and difficult debate. Each Member of Congress had hoped that Saddam Hussein and the Government of Iraq would not lead us down this path of terrible consequence. Each of us wishes that in the waning hours of the timeframe established by United Nations Security Council Resolution 768, Saddam Hussein will yet choose to withdraw from his illegal occupation of Kuwait, and fully comply with the demands of the world community as expressed in no less than 12 resolutions adopted by the Security Council.

Each Member of Congress stands in opposition to what Saddam Hussein has done. Each Member of Congress stands firm in the belief that Saddam must leave Kuwait, and restore the principle of law in the conduct between sovereign nations. And hopefully, each Member of Congress understands that international military actions of this sort cannot be allowed to succeed without gravely affecting global stability.

Before us now is the question of what means should be used to secure the ends of our convictions. First comes the question of whether or not the President, as Commander in Chief, has the constitutional authority to strike Iraq militarily without explicit congressional assent and authorization. Is the power to 'declare' war granted to Congress under the Constitution merely a formal act of declaration distinct from the power to 'conduct' war granted to the President as Commander in Chief? It is clear that under many circumstances, the President has the constitutional right to take a military action on behalf of the national interest. But I would argue strongly that in this instance, congressional assent to do so is not only constitutionally mandated but also a political necessity.

The nature and magnitude of the military operation being contemplated and the fact that U.N. Security Council Resolution 678 gives

---

From the *Congressional Record* of January 11, 1991.

us foreknowledge of the time at which U.N. member states may exercise 'all necessary means,' including military force, certainly require Members of Congress to either explicitly authorize or deny the President the authority to act in this instance. Further, any military engagement that may be necessary will be helped, not hindered, by the demonstration of domestic political support.

For the record, then, I would like to make clear that I believe that the President is required to have congressional authority in this instance, and that such authority is part and parcel of the bipartisan Solarz-Michel resolution that is now before the House of Representatives. The intent of this resolution is to explicitly authorize the United States to use force to implement the United Nations Security Council resolution on Iraq's invasion of Kuwait.

Mr. Speaker, a second question remains: Should the Solarz-Michel resolution be passed in favor of the alternative Hamilton-Gephardt resolution, which calls for continuing economic and trade sanctions against Iraq and postponing the question of using military force?

Mr. Speaker, I very strongly support the bipartisan Solarz-Michel resolution authorizing the immediate implementation of Security Council Resolution 678. I do so not because I have any less desire to see a peaceful, diplomatic resolution to the conflict in the Persian Gulf than any other Member of Congress has, but I firmly believe that passing the Solarz-Michel resolution will provide us the last best hope for peace in the days leading up to January 15.

Mr. Speaker, I support the Solarz-Michel resolution for the following reasons:

First, to delay in this matter only gives Saddam Hussein the wrong message. Surely, he will interpret delay in the implementation of the United Nations resolution as a lack of will, and not just as a disagreement over means.

Second, all the questions about postponing military actions reappear when a proposed extension expires. The questions will be the same, and Saddam Hussein will only believe that, having postponed implementation once, we shall be willing to postpone implementation yet again.

Third, the safety of our troops demands expeditious resolution of the current crisis in the Persian Gulf. The climatic factors will change very dramatically in the next 8 weeks, and will place our military position at a disadvantage in relationship to that of the Iraqi troops.

Fourth, the morale of our troops demands an expeditious resolution of this crisis. Calling up of Reserves, in particular, has our military personnel stationed in the gulf and their families at home expecting 180-day tours of duty. If it is possible, we ought to seek to honor that expectation, given the hardships this call-up has placed on families here at home. Right now, our troops' morale is extremely high. We should not pursue any policy that could undermine that strength.

Fifth, postponing the U.N. Security Council resolution will only give Saddam Hussein more reasons to try to split the U.N. alliance that currently stands against him. Just as our own nation contains a broad spectrum of political opinions on this matter, domestic disputes are present in other nations of the alliance as well. To allow Saddam Hussein to play these disputes against one another, and to play nations now allied together against each other, portends nothing but further political fragmentation of our efforts if we do not demonstrate firm resolve today.

Sixth, and finally, Mr. Speaker, I support the resolution for the simple reason that the U.S. Congress ought not put itself at odds against the United Nations, or question the considered opinion and actions of the Security Council. For the United States to turn against the United Nations in this instance would strike a blow against the struggle to refine and strengthen international peace-keeping institutions that will be so important in the post-cold-war era.

Mr. Speaker, allow me also to use this opportunity to express my strong support and agreement with the substance of the President's policy in this crisis. This is the first major test of how the world community will handle threats to global peace and stability in the post-cold-war era. The President and the world community through the United Nations have rightly understood that to allow Saddam Hussein to succeed with his aggression would encourage him to continue his regional aggressions and hostilities, and would encourage others to attempt the same. How the world community responds in this instance sets peace-keeping patterns in a world political environment that is dramatically different from the one we have known for many years.

In conjunction with that fact, the President has rightfully understood that the U.N. peace-keeping machinery is a very important part of any expression of national interest in this serious matter. We must not forget the outstanding progress that has been achieved through the peace-keeping machinery of the United Nations and the Security Council in particular. And I wish to commend President Bush for his foresight in this matter and for working through and with the Security Council in conducting our national policy.

Mr. Speaker, I hope and pray for a diplomatic resolution to the crisis. But we cannot show any hesitancy in our determination to fulfill commitments we have made to and through the world community – to the allied nations joined with us in the Persian Gulf, to the United Nations, which joins with us in this effort, to the Kuwaiti people, or to the principles of law upon which peace between the nations ultimately rests.

Environmental Issues

A National Bottle Bill? Yes

The U.S. continues to lead the world in per-capita trash produc tion. Nearly half of our nation's landfills are expected to close in the next five years. A recent National League of Cities poll ranked solid waste disposal second only to the drug epidemic as one of the top three problems facing local municipalities. Recycling has become the prophetic and inescapable call for the Nineties.

How can the federal government best address this issue amidst the budgetary constraints that will be present for the next decade?

If we are to put an end to the "throwaway" era, we must:

- get the entire nation involved in recycling;
- help create the necessary markets to absorb the materials that will be collected;
- increase the supply of materials for those markets that have already been established.

A national deposit/refund law on beverage container modeled after the deposit laws of Michigan, Oregon, Connecticut, Iowa, Delaware, Massachusetts, Vermont, Maine, and New York, is just as critical to fostering the above as are toughened federal procurement guidelines for recycled products, curbside recycling, and consumer education.

It is argued that a national "bottle bill" only addresses a small portion of the waste stream (5% to 11%, depending on how you measure), and that we need a comprehensive solution to our nation's solid waste dilemma.

I believe (as do nearly 100 of my colleagues and some 30 national environmental, state and local government, agricultural, and public interest groups) that an immediate 5% to 11% reduction in the entire

---

Reprinted from *Waste Age* (December 1989), by permission.

nation's waste stream is significant, and that a national bottle bill can and should be a component in any comprehensive solid waste management plan.

A national deposit law would get 100% of the population involved in recycling at no cost to local, state, and federal governments. Further, it conserves materials, saves energy, generates jobs, and substantially reduces nonbiodegradable litter.

Everyone agrees that recycling is a critical tool for solid waste management in the Nineties. However, not every recycling tool guarantees the steady stream of high-quality recyclable materials needed to expand viable recycling markets. In fact, one tool may work in one area of the country and not in another. But a deposit law is one recycling tool that transcends every regional and demographic variation in the country (see Table One).

Table One

Level of Public Support In Bottle Bill States

Michigan	90%	Connecticut	79%
Oregon	91%	Massachusetts	78%
Vermont	97%	New York	80%
Maine	84%		

At the same time, "curbside" recycling is slowly becoming the wave of the future. But such programs currently serve less than 10% of the population, with most of the recovered materials coming from the commercial sector. In fact, less than 4% of Seattle's highly touted 38% recycling rate comes from its residential curbside program. Likewise, only 3% of Newark's lauded 41% recycling rate comes from curbside recycling.

While the nine bottle-bill states account for the plastic that is being recycled today, many curbside programs exclude plastics because of their high volume. Curbside recycling will be less likely in rural areas. And without some major expansions in the paper recycling industry, curbside programs will continue to be too expensive for many communities to establish – regardless of whether valuable aluminum cans are removed from the waste stream vis-a-vis a national deposit law.

According to Jere Sellers, a recycling markets specialist with Franklin Associates, it is important to distinguish the unique characteristics of each component in the waste stream. For example, the market for newspaper (demand-limited) does not currently have the capacity to absorb all the newspapers that are being collected.

For aluminum, glass, and plastic the only barrier to recycling is the lack of more effective collection programs. Thus, most would agree that we need to develop markets for demand-limited materials and increase the amount of waste being collected for supply-limited materials.

The question is: What is the best means to this end?

A national bottle bill would provide a windfall for the supply-limited recycling of plastic, aluminum, and glass. Deposit laws provide a guaranteed supply of high quality material. Most deposit states have return rates nearing 90%. In fact, the nine bottle-bill states currently account for nearly 100% of the plastic, an estimated 50% of the aluminum, and an estimated two-thirds of all glass containers being recycled in this country. These materials represent an estimated 25% of the "recyclable" waste stream.

Think of what the recycling rates would be for these materials if the 41 non-bottle-bill states were pulled into a deposit system?

Most curbside programs do not remove large quantities of supply-limited materials. They collect a large amount of paper, compost, asphalt, etc., much of which, as noted previously, comes from the commercial sector.

Additionally, several of the successful so-called curbside states that are mentioned in various studies are, in fact, bottle-bill states as well. And they have no intention of choosing between the two systems. Comprehensive recycling programs (curbside, drop-off centers, etc.) and deposit laws are not mutually exclusive. Look at Connecticut. Look at New York. Look at Oregon. Look at Michigan.

In fact, Michigan's deposit law will, by the end of the Nineties, be funding comprehensive recycling programs to the tune of $50 million annually through the state's unclaimed deposit fund.

Yet what many industry representatives seem to be saying is that we ought to forgo deposits and high recycling rates for plastic, glass, and aluminum containers so that haulers will reap higher revenues from the sale of the small quantities of aluminum that are retrieved via a curbside program. Where deposit laws reclaim 80% to 90% of beverage containers, the best curbside programs struggle to retain half as much.

In other words, they are saying we ought to be dependent upon throwing away some of the most valuable and recyclable materials in our waste stream so that curbside recycling might be more profitable to the hauler. Does that make sense?

On paper (pardon the pun), the revenue theory does seem to make some sense. In fact, several industry-sponsored studies have attempted to "make sense" out of this argument. However, an Anheuser-Busch study done earlier this year revealed that a combined curbside deposit/ recycling program recovers over 40% more material than a sole curbside program in the state of Vermont. Likewise, it projected that the State of New York would recover 16% more with a combined program.

As you might assume, these numbers were not highlighted or even mentioned in the text of the report. In fact, the report's premise and conclusion was that it would be more cost-effective to eliminate the bottle bills in both of the above states.

Let's look briefly at how they reached this conclusion:

- they assumed a 90% participation rate for their hypothetical statewide curbside programs;
- they made no calculation for the avoided public costs that would be reaped by removing more materials in a dual system;
- they further confuse public and private costs by equating the costs of manufacturers, brewers, wholesalers, distributors, retailers, and purchasers of containers, under a deposit system, with the capital costs of establishing a government-funded curbside program;
- they assumed that no one would place their beverage containers at the curb under a dual deposit/curbside program; and
- the report notes that strong mandatory recycling laws are in place or proposed in 11 states, but fails to point out that five of those states have deposit laws in place.

The beverage and packaging industries would lead us to believe that a deposit law would take away revenues from curbside recycling program(sic); that there is a perfect comprehensive solid waste solution out there waiting to present itself to local government; that beverage containers are an insignificant portion of the litter and waste streams; that homes and stores will become roach-infested; and that deposit laws are an intrusion into our free enterprise system.

But, they neglect to recognize that the results in deposit-law states have been nothing short of astounding in terms of reducing litter, encouraging broader conservation and recycling efforts, saving energy and natural resources, relieving over-burdened landfills, creating jobs, and generating support for national legislation. Ask the public and public officials in each of these states.

Contrasting from what is coming down the legislative pike in the form of packaging bans and taxes, a national bottle bill would establish a nonregulatory, self-sustaining recycling system.

In fact, for those of us old enough to remember, most companies in the beverage industry operated under a deposit system years ago. But then came the onslaught of the convenient "throwaway," and it is still with us as we enter the Nineties.

With the enactment of the "National Beverage Container Reuse Recycling Act," however, we can responsibly end the era of the throwaway. A national bottle bill would enable the nation to achieve nearly a fourth of the EPA's 25% recycling goal at no cost to the taxpayer and with no government bureaucracy.

Republicans support it, Democrats support it, conservatives support it, liberals support it, moderates support it, environmentalists support it, farmers support it, local and state governments support it, nine states have it – and, most important, the public supports it.

Stewardship of the Garden

Environmentalism has been associated with the liberal political agenda, and you are generally not known for liberal political views.

It's a conservative ethic, not a liberal ethic. I have fairly consistently taken the posture that as a conservative, I have something to say about environmental conservation. There is also an analogy with fiscal issues. When you exploit the environment, you are simply building up the debt that is passed on to the next generation. If you want to look at it in terms of cost efficiency, it is much cheaper to protect the environment from harm than it is to retroactively reclaim it from exploitation.

You have said that environmental issues should be part of the "moral agenda" facing this nation. What do you mean by that?

When I was a child, we used to get injunctions around the table to "eat all your food because people in China and India are starving." The problem in the world today is not food shortage, but food distribution. We ought to apply the same standards of stewardship to the environment and not waste it in such a way that it is denied to others in the next generation. In the modern economic order, we've become highly productive, but we have in some cases become equally wasteful.

Reprinted from *Christianity Today*, April 23, 1990, by permission.

From a purely secular point of view, it is our wastefulness that will ultimately catch up with us.

However, I am reluctant to say that all resources are finite, because I think such terminology loses sight of the possibility of human creativity and new technologies, all of which are gifts of God.

From a Christian perspective, in the beginning in the order of creation, man – as the pinnacle of God's creation – was charged with stewardship of the garden. One of the effects of the Fall was that all aspects of the created order came under the Curse. But in the redemptive order, as early as the Mosaic code, there were injunctions to use and care for the land under the biblical concepts of stewardship.

How have Christians and particularly, evangelicals been responding to the issue? Have they gotten behind your legislation?

Yes, they have, but I don't think this is an issue that is uniquely Christian. If you are dealing with the Clean Air Act or clean water or acid rain, I don't think Christians are different than others in terms of their concern. Nor do I think there are "Christian solutions" relative to the issues.

However, I think there is a special contribution Christians can make. There is a fringe of the environmental movement that is militantly secular humanist. Certainly we ought not to condemn the environmental movement because of it. There is a very important mission for evangelical Christians to speak forth and correct that kind of evolutionist, humanist environmental mentality.

How do you overcome the opposition of the beverage industry to the National Bottle Bill?

It's a classic example of special interest versus diffused interest. A very small group of people who are adversely affected [by the bill] are opposing the overwhelming majority and the public good. Where there was a referendum in Washington State, the beverage industry spent more money opposing the bill than it would have cost to completely change their plants to engage in recycling. Every poll taken shows overwhelming public support for a bottle bill. The problem is mobilizing that support and showing legislators that they would be rewarded for responding to the issue.

Religious and Moral Issues

Religious Repression in the Soviet Union

Mr. Speaker, today I have joined with Congressman Chris Smith and a number of other Members in introducing a legislative resolution calling for the release of imprisoned Soviet Christians. Next year marks the millennial celebration of the Russian Orthodox Church – and nothing would be more fitting by way of recognizing this even than a change of policy by the Soviet Government in recognizing the religious rights of the peoples of the Soviet Union.

There has been much hope raised by Secretary Gorbachev's promise of openness and reform in the Soviet Union. Last summer, Konstantin Kharchev, chairman of the Council on Religious Affairs, promised officials of our Government that religious dissidents would be freed from jails, prisons, labor camps, and psychiatric institutions by the end of November 1987. This promise was broken – and the continued imprisonment of Soviet citizens on religious grounds continues.

Last week, I delivered to the Soviet Embassy the following letter, signed by some 258 of our colleagues there in the House of Representatives, outlining some 17 broad categories of the types of religious oppression and repression which Soviet citizens face – be they Christian, Jew, or Moslem. It is not just the promise of glasnost, which is important, but the practices of the Soviet government relative to that promise which we must remember in the relationship between our governments.

Following is the letter delivered to Secretary Gorbachev on behalf of those of the 258 Members of the House of Representatives who have joined in addressing this issue:

From the *Congressional Record* of December 8, 1987.

Congressional Human Rights Caucus
Washington, DC, December 4, 1987

His Excellency Mikhail S. Gorbachev,
General Secretary of the Communist Party,
Embassy of the U.S.S.R., 1225 16th Street N.W., Washington, DC.

Dear General Secretary Gorbachev:

We join in welcoming you to the United States in conjunction with your forthcoming discussions with President Reagan as you work towards reaching agreement on a proposal to reduce intermediate nuclear missiles. While we share in the desire to control the proliferation of these terrible instruments of destruction, we must also share with you our deep concerns regarding human and religious rights violations which exist within your nation.

While the reduction of nuclear missiles would be a positive step in improving relations between our two nations, it must be remembered that the very presence of these weapons is a symptom of our differences – not the root cause. The core cause of our differences and tensions between our governments is that of respect for human rights.

Our tradition recognizes human rights as divinely endowed, and thus transcending the powers of the state. Thus, we regard the question of honoring *religious rights* of citizens as the heart of the human rights question. Your tradition recognizes human rights as "granted by the government," and thus not having autonomy from the government which grants them. From this distinction are generated the differences between our governments in practices honoring human rights.

Respectfully, we note that your government was a party to the Helsinki Accords of 1975, Article 18, which reads as follows: "Everyone has the right to. . . manifest his religion or belief in teaching, practice, worship, and observance."

We, therefore, felt compelled to share with you our concerns for those institutional practices within your country which are in noncompliance with the Helsinki Accords. We believe these are objective standards by which progress in this area can be measured.

Specifically, the following violations to which we respectfully draw your attention in seeking redress, have been made known to us from citizens living with the U.S.S.R. They are as follows:

1. Interference in the religious governance of religious organizations and institutions.
2. Prohibitions against informal worship activities of small gatherings of believers and adherents.
3. The denial to religious organizations of the right to possess real property, building properties, or instruments of worship.
4. The prohibition of recognizing religious organizations as legal personhoods, which prevents pursual of legal redress in courts of law and administrative agencies.
5. The imprisonment of individuals for practices of religious belief.
6. The incarceration of individuals in mental and psychiatric institutions for practices of religious belief.
7. The forced closing of religious institutions.
8. Prohibitions against the general religious education of minors.
9. Prohibitions against the religious activities of minors.
10. Restrictions on institutions for theological education of Orthodox, Roman Catholic, Protestant, Jewish, and other religious bodies.
11. Prohibitions against and limitations on the importation and distribution of religious materials.
12. Prohibitions against and limitations on the importation of and free circulation of religious materials within the nation.
13. Discrimination against religious adherents and their immediate families in general educational opportunities.
14. Discrimination against religious adherents and their immediate families in employment opportunities.
15. Discrimination against religious adherents and their immediate families in securing housing opportunities.
16. Prohibitions against ordained clergy and acknowledged religious leaders in visiting the sick in hospitals, psychiatric institutions, or jails and prisons.
17. Prohibitions against voluntaristic and charitable activities of religious organizations within the nation.

We welcome the recent promises of your government in regard to the forthcoming release of religious prisoners. We also look forward to the millennial observation of the birth of the Russian Orthodox Church. We trust that such commemoration will be accompanied by renewed recognition of the obstacles religious communities have experienced within the Soviet Union in recent years.

While efforts to negotiate an arms settlement represent a commendable act, once again we remind you that the question of human rights, and religious rights in particular, is at the heart of the conflict between our governments. In keeping with the Helsinki Accords, we implore you to address these human rights violations.

Respectfully yours,

Civil Rights Law

I must take issue with your editorial of March 29 supporting the passage of the Civil Rights Restoration Act, and questioning my efforts to secure "religious rights" protections under that act. First, a bit of background is necessary to focus the issue.

In 1984, the U.S. Supreme Court ruled in *Grove City College vs. Bell* that the means by which the federal government had been enforcing the Title IX statute barring sex discrimination at educational institutions (and by extension, three other civil rights pertaining to age, race, and handicap) was not statutorily established. There was never any fundamental disagreement in Congress for the need to "fix" the law to reestablish the enforcement mechanism, although the legislation was delayed for nearly four years over a debate on the abortion question. This was resolved by making the bill "abortion-neutral"—nothing in the act may be construed as either requiring or prohibiting recipients of federal funds to provide abortion services or benefits.

This same Grove City decision had a second, less-noticed effect by treating "indirect" and "direct" federal assistance the same. For example, in the case of Grove City College, the institution had never received any form of direct federal aid for its buildings or operations. However, because some of its students were recipients of federally subsidized loans, the college was deemed to be subject to the civil rights laws, as if it had received the aid directly. Although the Supreme Court has, in one subsequent decision, put some limits on the extent to which indirect beneficiaries of federal programs are deemed subject to laws based on receipt of federal funds, the limits are still, certainly, unclear, particularly in areas such as education and social services.

The Grand Rapids Press, April 4, 1988. Obtained from the Paul B. Henry Collection in the Heritage Hall Archives of the Hekman Library at Calvin College.

Historically, religious educational institutions have been given exemptions to Title IX provisions pertaining to non-discrimination on the basis of sex if the institution could show that the practices involved violated the "religious tenets" of the educational institution and if the institution was "controlled by" a religious organization. Administrative problems have ensued for some years in regard to what to do with religious educational institutions which are equally religious in character as those which are denominationally "controlled," but are in fact governed by lay boards. Such examples would be the University of Notre Dame, my alma mater of Wheaton College (Illinois), as well as our own Grand Rapids Baptist College.

When the "fix" to the Grove City decision, as contained in the Civil Rights Restoration Act, is combined with the expansive scope of the definition of "recipient," the civil rights laws and regulations issued thereunder potentially reach many, many religious organizations for the first time. The expanded scope applies not only to Title IX provisions pertaining to sex, but also places an enforcement layer across recent and controversial court decisions defining the term "handicap," without disturbing those underlying definitions. Thus not only are many more religiously affiliated educational, charitable, and social service programs brought under the statute, but the requirements under those statutes themselves are substantially different than only a few years ago.

The potential conflicts between the Civil Rights Act so amended and freedom of religious expression are obviously many in number. Is a student to be denied financial aid because he or she seeks to attend a college with a religious tradition that does not ordain women to the ministry? Can a religiously affiliated educational or social agency make employment decisions based on such behavioral characteristics as use of alcohol or drugs? The answers to these questions are, in fact, not clarified in the act. There were a number of attempts by various members of Congress to say what was "meant" in these areas, but it would be far preferable to write a clear statute so as not to leave these issues unresolved.

You are absolutely correct in noting that there have been those who have scared up rather outlandish scenarios as to the imminent consequences of the passage of this legislation. And I appreciate the fact that you noted my outspoken opposition to these sorts of scare tactics. To advertise "possibilities" under the law as imminent "probabilities" is clearly misleading. But the fact is that there are serious possibilities in terms of intrusions into religious liberties which were not adequately considered or addressed.

You could also have noted that the attempt to address the issue was diminished by the fact that some arguing most vigorously for the defense of "religious fights" have pretty shoddy records when it comes to protecting other civil rights. That likely hurts the cause as well—but it does not diminish the importance of addressing the issue. And contrary to your editorial, religious organizations representing the majority of the American religious community have expressed their support for addressing this issue.

I should point out as well that when the Education and Labor Committee last considered the Civil Rights Restoration Act, it adopted a "religious tenets" amendment by a vote of 18-11. Nonetheless we were prevented from even considering such an amendment when the bill reached the House of Representatives this year. To force our religiously affiliated institutions to secularize their practices as a condition of serving their constituencies and our nation is not good public policy. And I shall continue my interest in rectifying the problems inadvertently created by this legislation.

NEA Funding

Mr. Speaker, I support the Regula motion, and I hope we will support the previous question. I think perhaps it would be helpful if we put today's debate in the perspective of the debate last month.

The very people who are now seeking to legislate in an appropriations bill objected to the efforts of the chairman, Mr. Yates, and the ranking member, Mr. Regula, to put new restrictions on the NEA, to hold it more accountable for the grant process, to hold the NEA Administrator directly accountable.

It was the gentleman from California who objected and said we are going to legislate in an appropriations bill. Now he comes to us and says, 'Well, this isn't censorship, but I have got all kinds of legislation I want to pursue.'

The same gentleman last month said, 'I am not for censorship. I am just against all public arts funding.'

From the *Congressional Record* of September 13, 1989, where Paul presents a rather vigorous criticism of the tactics of NEA opponents. "Supporting the previous question" means blocking dilatory tactics by some members of Congress that would effectively end all government funding for the NEA, regardless of the new guidelines for awarding grants.

Now he comes and says, 'I am for all this kind of restriction on procedure.'

I have to be very honest, the history of this shows such inconsistency that it lends me to question, quite frankly, the ethics involved in the process of debating a matter of ethics.

Now I want the record to show that in my case I was among those who communicated with the NEA my personal and strong objections to the funding of the Serrano project.

And I happen to believe that there are distinctions in censorship in terms of the Bill of Rights and making reasonable distinctions in terms of the use of public funds.

I believe the chairman does, and I believe Mr. Regula does. That is why they tried to bring it in their bill. That is why they brought this issue forth again in their instructions to the conferees. I believe in those distinctions.

I was offended by the Serrano exhibit.

I am offended personally, I have to say, by the Mapplethorpe exhibit.

I want to speak very personally and perhaps – I hope – not offensively to other Members in this body. I am an evangelical Christian. I have every reason to be particularly enraged. But my Lord said let your aye be aye and your nay be nay. I am opposed to the duplicity that I think has surrounded this entire debate beginning last month.

I will not be collared into being a complicit partner in what I view personally to be moral duplicity in terms of how the issue has been brought to this House. I will not squander my reputation as one concerned with Judeo-Christian ethics on a procedure which I think is built on fabrication and falsehood.

Let us put an end to political phariseeism and vote for the previous question. Let us put a vote against political pornography and vote for the previous question. And above all, let us stand by the gentleman from Illinois [Mr. Yates] and the gentleman from Ohio [Mr. Regula], who have taken the slings and arrows for every Member of this body, who have suffered distorted attacks and misrepresentation as to what their position has been on this issue all along.

Let us uphold our chairman and ranking member. I urge a vote for the previous question.

Fetal Tissue Research

Madam Speaker, I rise as a strong and consistent supporter of the right-to-life position. I believe personally that abortion on demand as provided for and protected under the conditions of Roe versus Wade, is one of the great moral outrages of contemporary American law and it is within that moral and legal framework, in addition to personal conviction which I rise in support of the National Institutes of Health authorization conference committee report.

Madam Speaker, I believe the leadership of the right-to-life community has made a major political and ethical misjudgment in attacking this legislation because it would allow for the Federal Government to renew its past practice of providing funds for fetal research. Surely the entire area of biomedical research raises a host of morally troubling and complex questions. But to focus on this question of tissue research, choosing this particular concern amidst broader questions related to biomedical research and ethics, has trivialized the question. And I am afraid it may have the effect of weakening the overall right to life argument.

What about in vitro research in which many fertilized ova are discarded in favor of the one ovum which will live? What about DNA research and human genome research? Yes, there are major ethical issues of import associated with fetal tissue research—but they must be discussed and debated on a much higher plain and a more comprehensive framework than that which has been posed thus far in the current question before us.

While serious questions can and must be raised in regard to overviewing these forms of research, it is nonetheless important to note that the purpose and effect of such research is directed toward restoring the wholeness and fullness of life, not destroying it.

Madam Speaker, of all the people phoning my office and writing to me expressing their concerns about this, most of them have taken advantage, for themselves or for their children, of measles inoculation, polio vaccine, and most of them, I am sure, would take advantage of subsequent medical breakthroughs that this research promises.

Madam Speaker, as a right-to-life supporter, I urge cautious support for this legislation.

I would like to make one other point for my right-to-life friends.

From the *Congressional Record* of May 28, 1992.

For the first time in 20 years since Roe versus Wade, we are finally to the point where the Court, we hope, we pray from my side of this question, will reopen this question and cause the American public to reexamine the entire issue of abortion on demand, which I find morally reprehensible. For right to life to attach itself to this issue as we approach this national debate is, I fear, destructive to the cause and the interests which I have sought to represent as a Member of Congress, and I would urge those who feel this way with me to have the courage to speak up in this afternoon's vote.

Partisan Politics

Partisanship

Who are we? What are we? And why are we gathered here today? First of all, we are Republicans. We bear the name proudly – and we are firm in our commitments to the basic philosophy of the Republican Party. While we acknowledge that freedom and liberty can sometimes be strengthened through the powers of government, we likewise recognize the fact that political, religious, social, and economic freedoms have historically been won against government, not derived from government. We understand that the quintessential characteristic of *constitutional* government is *limited* government. Thus, we are skeptical of any political philosophy which advocates that government's legitimate role is inherently and implicitly expansionist, or that government should be the provider of all things to all people.

We understand that when government grows too big and too remote, it also becomes too complex to be *understood* by the people and therefore can not be held *accountable* by the people. Big government – even when its intentions are benign – is unwittingly a threat to individual freedom. Living with big government is like making love to a hippopotamus – even though both parties may mean well, it is inherently a risky business!

Further, we are committed to economic freedom. We share the Republican conviction that a free, open, and market-based economy is preferable to a state controlled economy. While we acknowledge that economic freedom – as all other freedoms – can be abused and therefore is properly subject to some degree of regulation, our starting point

A speech delivered to a retreat of moderate Republicans in Michigan in late March, 1984. Obtained from the Paul B. Henry Collection in the Heritage Hall Archives of the Hekman Library at Calvin College.

is always on the side of freedom. We believe that economic freedom best promotes economic vitality and the generation of new wealth which will ultimately be enjoyed by all members of society. We believe that ultimately a free market place most efficiently distributes the new wealth which economic freedom engenders. But above all, we believe in economic freedom because it is in and of itself a key ingredient of political freedom and an open society.

The fundamental premise of the Republican Party is the premise of freedom and individual liberty. It is a Party which believes that a government big enough to give a person everything he or she wants is also big enough to take away everything he or she has.

At the same time, this gathering has been dubbed a conference of "moderate" Republicans. What is a "moderate" Republican? And what are the questions we seek to raise at this conference? Let me reaffirm that "moderate" Republicans are no less committed to the basic tenets of Republicanism than any other "kind" of Republican. They are not necessarily more or less "liberal" or "conservative" than other Republicans. They share equally in their commitments to the Republican Party's institutional, political, and philosophic goals.

What distinguishes "moderate" Republicans is not their political ideology or underlying philosophical convictions, but rather their determination to integrate basic Republican philosophy and conviction with the constantly rotating kaleidoscope of social, economic, scientific, and political environments. In that sense, "moderate" Republicans can be characterized as encouraging continual new thinking and rethinking of basic principles as they apply in new settings.

It is *because* we enjoy an open economy that the means of our livelihood as American citizens is under constant change. Moderate Republicans seek to examine those changes and articulate the implications of those changes in the context of Republican philosophy.

It is *because* we are a free and open society that the role of women in the United States today is radically different than that of even a generation ago. Moderate Republicans are concerned with articulating the basic values of their Party with the changed conditions to which they must apply.

It is *because* we are a free and open society that blacks, Hispanics, and ethnic groups more diverse than our Founding Fathers could have imagined share the benefits of living together in this great country. Moderate Republicans are concerned with integrating the concerns of these peoples into the fundamental values of their Party.

Moderate Republicans are not "deviant" from the mainstream thinking of their Party. Rather, they have chosen a unique advocacy role within their Party. They share the convictions of their Party – that is why they join with it institutionally and politically. But they also seek to be at the cutting edge of applying the principles of their Party to the contemporary social, economic, and political environment.

Let no individual, therefore, misunderstand the purpose of this conference. In no way does it represent a factional dispute with the leadership of our Party at the national level or the state level. In no way does it represent a breech between those of our Party who are here and those who are not here.

We are here today in the effort to examine effective alternative strategies of applying Republican principles to contemporary problems. Our discussions are in the open – there is no "Solidarity House" enforcer telling us what we must say and making us pretend to believe that which is against our individual conscience. Our discussions will likely indicate a range of diversity and opinion which mirrors the Republican Party itself. A diversity which is allowed *because* the Republican Party is the party of freedom and a party of individualism.

The Republican Party remains the minority party in America today. It is a minority party not because its principles are *mistaken*, but because they are too often *misunderstood*. Thus, this conference can play an important role in fostering communication and dialogue with those who would question our willingness as a Party to address their concerns.

But as we reach out to those outside of our Party who have misunderstood us, let us display equal sensitivity to those inside our Party who have likewise sometimes misunderstood us. If, in the name of moderation, we become as extreme as those who sometimes repudiate our efforts, we become guilty of the very thing for which we criticize others. Such conduct would not only be duplicitous, but also politically self-destructive. It would frustrate accomplishing the very goal we have set for ourselves here today.

Let us avoid discussion of political personalities, and focus instead on the practical steps we can take as a Party to articulate a political vision which responds sensitively to the needs and interests of all the peoples of our country. The principles of our Party – combined with patience, prudence, and hard work – are fully capable of propelling us into the role of the political majority.

The House "Bank" Scandal

March 24, 1992

Dear

I want to acknowledge your communication of displeasure as to the situation with my own checking account at the "bank" at the House of Representatives. Let me state clearly that I *do* acknowledge my personal responsibility for each and every check I sign, and my obligation to keep my own banking records in order.

Let me also remind you that I have consistently been among those favoring open disclosure of *all* the accounts and all the problems associated with the bank operated by the House Sergeant at Arms.

What I do think is important, however, is for the public to understand the *many* dimensions to the problems which have been discovered regarding this situation, including:

(1) Deposits made into accounts by Members were not uniformly posted to accounts on a timely basis. Hence, we are going to find – when *all* the records are made public – that many of the "overdrafts" by Members were not overdrafts at all, but banking errors.

(2) I cannot say with surety at this point in time how many of my own twenty account discrepancies are attributable to this problem. I do know for a fact that the maximum number of discrepancies on my account was twenty, the maximum potential fund deficiency being $413 for a period of five or six days.

(3) Because deposits were not posted or credited to accounts on a timely basis, they would sometimes appear on monthly statements received two months from the actual time of deposit. That, in turn, would encourage mistakes of "double crediting" of deposits into one's own personal bank ledger.

(4) Once one's bank ledger was off – for whatever reason – a proper balance could never be regained because the monthly statements never showed an overdraft on accounts. My own monthly statements never showed an account imbalance or deficiency.

I certainly don't want to make excuses for whatever ineptitude or mistakes I made with my own account at the House bank. But I do think it important that the public, to which each of us is accountable,

A constituent response letter explaining Paul's view of the House "bank" scandal. Obtained from the Paul B. Henry Collection in the Heritage Hall Archives of the Hekman Library at Calvin College.

understand the distinction between those who had "figured out" how the "system worked", and exploited it to personal advantage, from those others who made these sorts of mistakes in part because of the unorthodox practices at the House bank.

I do understand and appreciate the public anger over this entire mess. The practices engaged in by the House bank symbolize those very sorts of perks and abuses in the Congress which suggest that Representatives enjoy special positions of privilege which are inappropriate to the title of being a "public servant".

Again, I do want to make clear that I am not trying to absolve myself for those instances in which I was in error. I also want to remind you that I was among the original cosponsors of disclosing all records pertaining to this entire mess, because I believe the public has a right to full disclosure. I also believe that the public can be trusted to make fair judgments as to whether or not their individual Representative to the Congress "kited" the system, or whether in fact, they were bushwhacked by it. Over the next several weeks, the information you need to make these judgments and evaluations will become available to you because some of us fought for full disclosure of this mess.

For any embarrassment I have caused any of my constituents as to the problems of my own account, I clearly apologize. I only ask that those who feel strongly about this matter make the effort to sort all the issues through, because I do not believe it fair to lump all 355 Members of Congress into the same pot when analyzing this problem.

With best wishes, I remain

Congressional Organizational Reforms

Mr. Speaker, as I reflect on the situation of the House, I am reminded of the television ad where the frail lady calls out: 'Help me! I've fallen, and I can't get up.'

The differences between our parties is that we have different remedies as to how we can best get back on our feet. Your Democratic majority believes that a partial restructuring of the administrative functions of the House is adequate to the challenge of the day. Our Republican minority believes that the problems of this institution reach much deeper.

From the *Congressional Record* of April 9, 1992.

We are all tired and wearied by the onslaught of public criticism and the internal fratricide of these last months. In my heart, I want to lay down my arms and call for peace. But peace at any price, Mr. Speaker, will not do.

For 38 years, your party has controlled this institution. You own it. You run it. And you bear responsibility for it. You've had power over this body far longer than Fidel Castro has run Cuba. And under the watch of your party, power has grown arrogant. The institution has become overly bureaucratized. Governance has become fragmented. And now you come to the minority, asking us to share in granting absolution for the practices which have put the Congress in a political free fall.

Three years ago, we faced a similar crisis in confidence in this institution. And your Democratic leadership said 'I'm sorry, it won't happen again.' Once again, Mr. Speaker, the House is in a state of political crisis. And the Democratic leadership says: 'I'm sorry, it won't happen again.'

The reforms you propose are fine as far as they go. The problem is, they simply do not go very far. To simply say to the American people, once again, 'I'm sorry, it won't happen again, now that we have an 'administrator for nonlegislative affairs' watching over us,' does not reach deep enough into the practices for which we now suffer the political indictment of the American people.

The Democrat proposal is worthy of David Copperfield. It is a master of illusion. You have turned your back on those of us who sought to bargain with you in good faith in the effort to really restructure what is wrong with this House. And let me warn you that when you go home for your Easter recess, there will be no 'hallelujahs' being shouted in our hometowns over this attempt at masking what is fundamentally wrong with this House. And there will be no political resurrection from the grave of political ignominy which now holds us all in its grasp.

Next November, you will wish you had listened to those of us in the minority who wished to use this opportunity to put the House back in order. And next January, I predict there will be somebody else sitting in the Speaker's chair – somebody who understands that politics as usual is no longer enough.

Hands and Feet To Faith

Mark O. Hatfield

In 1990 the prestigious *National Journal* described Paul Henry as a congressional "rising star." This was certainly true of my friend and colleague in terms of national government service at that time, though in my considered opinion his stellar qualities were already shining long before he reached the halls of Congress.

My first introduction to Paul Henry came in 1976 when I made a visit to Grand Rapids, Michigan, to speak to a group of students and faculty at Calvin College. While there I observed Paul Henry, a very thoughtful and energetic young professor who also was one of the more popular professors at the college. His popularity was largely due to his innate ability to evoke from his students constructive and thoughtful dialogue on almost any issue or topic – controversial or not. This rare gift of bringing people together in productive dialogue continued to serve him well as he moved from the college campus into the political arena, first in Michigan, then in Congress.

It is imperative for a student of Paul Henry's life to understand first and foremost that he was a man whose faith in God was at the core of his being. It defined who he was and what he stood for. He viewed his whole life as a walk with Christ, which drew people to him for fellowship and leadership.

Paul's own philosophy and practice of politics was a measure of just how much this was so: in the way he interacted with those with whom he had both agreements and disagreements; in the way he consistently voted according to his convictions rather than according to any popular sentiments. Paul Henry always approached every issue with measured thoughtfulness, a keen intellect, and a compassionate kindness that was exceptional. Kindness and reserve were hallmarks of the character of Paul Henry; they were especially notable in times when he was engaged in difficult legislation which incited a great deal of contention. This noted reasonableness and ability to appeal to the generous sensibilities of both sides of an issue time and again brought about reconciliation and progress towards the solution of problems. As his good friend and colleague Congressman Fred Upton said in eulogy, "When Paul spoke on issues on this floor people on both sides of the center aisle listened, and his arguments in support of or against an issue were substantive. They were based on the merits, not on the politics."

It was an inclusive approach to government that enabled Paul to deflect the numerous labels that so often blind a legislator to a thoughtful and substantive approach to an issue. The notion that government is not a clubhouse sheltering a variety of elite factions, but rather a single canopy under which all sides are active and all sides are welcome was at the heart of Paul Henry's concept of how our government was meant to operate. Government was not a pursuit of power in the view of Congressman Henry, but rather a pursuit of virtue. Political service was like teaching or ministry in that it was ultimately about helping others. This is certainly what Paul did throughout his lifetime.

It was this guiding principle of serving others that at times caused Paul to buck party lines and vote for the benefit of his constituents, as was clearly the case when he voted against the MX missile project, even though heavily pressured by both President Reagan *and* former President Gerald Ford to vote in favor. Being fiscally and socially responsible to those who had sent him to Congress was far more important to the mind of Paul Henry than a comfortable position as a party dependable. If he felt that a certain program was not in the best interests of the American people, Paul Henry could always be counted on to reflect this conviction in his vote. Conversely, if there were programs that benefited people, he was a powerful ally in seeing those programs enacted. I had the opportunity to work closely with Paul on a recycling measure known as the bottle bill and witnessed first hand his effective advocacy for an issue he believed in.

It was a signature of Paul's character that he was first and foremost responsible to God; he knew that a part of this responsibility included loving and caring for others. For Paul Henry public service was more than an opportunity to distinguish himself and further a career. It was an opportunity to give of himself for the benefit of others, an opportunity to speak against the squandering of national resources at the expense of hard-working taxpayers, and the privilege of bringing a biblical worldview to substantial moral dilemmas. It was his foundation in

Scripture that provided the basis of his concern for others, the example of his risen Savior that guided the life he was to live. It is on account of this spiritual foundation that Paul put hands and feet to his faith and strove to help people. Whether with the Peace Corps in Africa pouring his energies out for the benefit of impoverished peoples, or in the classroom guiding young minds toward higher principals, or in the halls of Congress defending those principles, Paul Henry demonstrated that a living faith is full of action.

Congressman Henry and I shared a common interest concerning a number of issues. We shared a commitment to Jesus Christ and his kingdom. As former educators, we shared a life-long commitment to education, especially for increased emphasis on math and science education. He was an eloquent spokesman for the future generations of this country, reminding us of the need to invest wisely in them, to set a noble example for them, so that they could be proud to carry our cherished way of life onward and pass it down to their own children.

A noble example is what Paul Henry lived consistently; a noble example is what Paul Henry left for us all to follow. We would be wise to learn from the heritage he has left us: that a fusion between the teachings of Christ and the activities of our lives will perpetuate a legacy that our children will be proud to continue. It is far too easy to take a cynical approach to our government and sneer about such things as justice and integrity, to take a broad brush and paint the entire process as shallow and insincere. But to do this is an affront to the memory of Paul Henry. He proved himself a sincere citizen, an inclusive yet grounded educator, a loving and respected family man, as well as a thoughtful and just legislator whose whole character was marked by integrity. Paul Henry fought to wrestle justice from abstract concepts and unattainable ideals and to bring justice into the lives of every individual as a concrete reality. To observe the life of Paul Henry should instill in all of us the reassurance that God is still at work in all walks of life, that He cares to place able leaders at the forefront of mighty governments, that He can and does place those who obey Him in key positions to affect the world. Though God may have taken Paul from before our eyes, God has established Paul's memory as a testimony for our instruction.

Often in our fad-driven, instant-access culture, there are persons who burst onto the scene in a blaze but whose impact is short-lived. In contrast, Paul Henry's bright star shone with brilliance in his lifetime and, I believe, is still shedding its beam of influence, for those of us who were privileged to walk with Paul Henry will never be the same. His life, though too brief by man's standards, was a life of influence. As one congressman reflected on Paul Henry's life: "I think sometimes if we had a few more Paul Henrys around here we would shout at each other a lot less and we would work together a lot more." Would that this lesson might be taken to heart in the halls of our schools, in Congress, in our workplaces, and in our homes.

Servant Leader in a Political World

Paul C. Hillegonds

We live in a political world. I describe politics as the process undertaken whenever two or more people are trying to transform conflicting ideas into a consensus. In the family, at our places of worship, at work, and at play, we engage in a political process.

Paul Henry understood this very well. For him the question was not whether faith-centered people should become involved in politics. He was called to be involved – and constantly struggled with how best he could fulfill that calling. As a policy maker he cared deeply about achieving a just consensus in a political environment that, by its very nature, is more gray than black and white.

Paul rarely talked with legislative colleagues about his religious convictions. But he always tried to live them.

We were friends, yet he never spoke to me at length about his personal relationship with God. He didn't have to. I always felt that the example of servant leadership demonstrated by Jesus was central to Paul's understanding of public service.

For Jesus leadership meant serving God and loving his fellow women and men. He did not lead by creating a political party, starting a mega-synagogue, or organizing a resistance movement against the Romans. He didn't follow the dictates of political and religious power brokers or popular public opinion. Before his hometown synagogue he proclaimed that he was on earth to tend to the poor, the sick, the unclean – and so upset his friends and neighbors that they drove him out of town.

And Jesus acted on his teachings, befriending the tax collector Levi, healing a slave of a Roman oppressor, defying the laws of the religious establishment by curing a man on the Sabbath, and offering God's saving grace to a woman whose Samaritan ethnic heritage and personal life were scorned by upright Jewish people. Most radical of all, he asked his followers to love their enemies unconditionally, expecting nothing in return, and then submitted himself to a humiliating, painful death, asking God to forgive his persecutors.

But Jesus did not go to the cross before struggling prayerfully with his Father during a sleepless night in the Garden of Gethsemane. In a very human way he agonized over the questions that we all must confront in a political world: When should we compromise, and when do we need to stand on our convictions?

Paul Henry served as a Republican county chairman and in partisan legislative leadership positions. But for him partisan politics was an organizational means of achieving public policy goals and not an end unto itself. In his campaigns for elected office and in his endeavors to achieve legislative goals, I never saw him try to win at any cost. Paul was competitive and wanted to succeed, but, respecting his colleagues and constituents, respecting himself, and respecting the political process, Paul believed that maintaining civility and personal integrity was more important than winning.

His approach would sometimes get him into trouble with political leaders, friends, and constituents. In Paul's first couple of terms in the state legislature, he took unpopular stands for an income tax increase, wetlands protection legislation, and aid to the city of Detroit. Later, in Congress, he differed with his party at home and in Washington, D.C. by speaking out against a constitutional amendment punishing flag burning, deployment of the MX missile system, and U.S. aid to the Nicaraguan contras.

Paul at heart was a teacher and a healer who joyfully engaged friends and opponents in a dialogue about ideas. In an invitational, nonjudgmental manner he shared his thinking and listened to different viewpoints. Constituents and colleagues wouldn't always agree with Paul's conclusions, but we respected the values, discipline, openness, and self-effacing sense of humor he employed to study and resolve policy questions.

As colleagues we also respected Paul because he genuinely liked us and the diversity we represented. He was intelligent, highly moral and a rising political star, but he relished serving an institution and constituency whose members had a wide range of skills, values, life experience, and perspectives. No matter what our shortcomings he never spoke ill of or looked down on his colleagues. Paul saw God's different gifts in each of us.

It was Paul Henry's strong commitment to social justice that caused him to focus his legislative efforts on issues such as environmental stewardship and the treatment of those least respected among us. Not many state legislators I knew welcomed the opportunity to serve on the Corrections Committee, as Paul did in both the Michigan House and Senate. I fondly recall the fall evening when I accompanied Paul to a small church that was located in my legislative district – and in the shadow of a locally unpopular state prison facility. There Paul spoke with passion about the spiritual and educational needs of imprisoned inmates, about the important mission of Chuck Colson's Prison Ministries, and the need for those church members to offer their time and Christian love to neighbors incarcerated in that prison down the road.

Though Paul dedicated his life to servant leadership, he struggled with the rest of us, his colleagues, on matters of ego and ambition and when to compromise or stand on conviction. Yet in a wonderfully joyful way he possessed the ability, courage, and spiritual faith to reach across lines of party, geography, and philosophy and to encourage us to put aside our differences in pursuit of the common public good.

It has been almost twenty years since we served together in the Michigan House, but I shall never forget the legislative session that Paul was asked to open with the traditional invocation. It had been a rancorous time in the House, with Republicans and Democrats deeply divided over a controversial issue. The session that day promised to be no different. Paul stepped to the rostrum, asked us to bow our heads, and shared a prayer that essentially said:

> God our Father, we know that you are not a Democrat, but help to remind some of us that you are not a Republican either. Give us guidance and bring us together to do what is right and just for the people of our state.

That prayer was the essence of Paul's servant leadership – and the spirit of public service he inspired in those of us who were privileged to be his friends and colleagues.

Daring To Be A Daniel

Gary L. Visscher

I first met Paul Henry when I signed up for his Introduction to Political Science course as a freshman student at Calvin College. I didn't know much about him at the time, only that he was reputed to be a good professor for that required core course: He had a reputation for being interesting even if one wasn't too sure about political science.

I ended up majoring in political science. I took several additional courses from Paul. Later on I worked for Paul for about a decade, when he served in the Michigan State Senate and then in the United States Congress. Though he treated me then as an advisor rather than a student, in fact I was always learning from him – about the science and art of politics, and about a Christian's perspective on political actions and decisions.

I would fill this essay on my remembrances of being a student under Paul with anecdotes from those political science classes twenty-five-plus years ago, but I would have to make them up. My memories of specific events from those classes have mostly faded, except for a few embarrassing episodes that are better not preserved on paper. But general impressions remain, impressions reinforced by my later daily work for and with Paul.

He was, as one would expect from someone with his intelligence, able to think on his feet, comfortable with people, and a very good classroom teacher. He was one of those professors who had an infectious enthusiasm for learning generally, as well as for his subject area, political science, in particular. He was always well informed on current political controversies and issues. I often saw him in the Calvin College library going through stacks of newspapers. I think he would have loved having the Internet available.

His specialty, though, was political philosophy. He sometimes said that the opportunity to study and teach political philosophy is what drew him to academia; he had less interest in doing the kind of empirical research that is the mainstay of academic political science work. Paul often reminded those of us students who were more drawn to reading about current events than to reading the writings of long dead political philosophers that "ideas have consequences." As his book, *Politics for Evangelicals*, reflects, for Paul political philosophy was fundamental to understanding political institutions and attitudes.

It was expected that professors at Calvin College would relate their Christian faith to their field of study and teaching. Still, Paul stood out in his ability to do so, in part, I think, because he had such a broad understanding not only of politics but also of Christian history and teachings. His understanding of theology and church history was no doubt due in some part to the influence of his father, Dr. Carl Henry. Later, when I worked for Paul in Washington, D.C., I sometimes accompanied him on visits to his parents, who then were also living in that area. Those visits were a real treat for me, not least because conversation over coffee was as likely to be a discussion about some aspect of theology or ethics by two of the finest Christian minds I have ever met as it was about the weather.

Paul, I think, was an example of what it means to be "thoroughly Christian." His faith shaped not only his intellectual and ethical assumptions but also how he treated people. His faith was obvious without being pushy or showy. If, as sociologist Peter Berger said, "a sense of humor is a signal of the transcendent," it was fitting that Paul had an ever-present sense of humor. He enjoyed the ironies of life and the foibles of politics and politicians (including, later, himself). He was fun to be around, whether he was engaging us in conversation about current political events or in the zany ideas he would come up with to attract attention to a small club that he organized and led for a few politics-minded students. Anyone who was around Paul for any time learned to be wary of his practical jokes.

He enjoyed and encouraged the give and take of argument and he liked to challenge students' easy answers. One of his students later recalled, "[m]any classes were spent in splendid debate between long-haired students and this conservative instructor. Many discussions ended with differences unreconciled. But like most good arguments, the topics of these debates were soon lost. What remained was a profound sense of respect and tolerance for differing perspectives and the simple acknowledgement that ideology takes a second chair to a moral and conscientious human spirit.[1]

My memories of Paul as professor would not be complete without adding a note about how fast he moved and talked. He was very busy with teaching and writing and presumably with helping his wife Karen with their young children. He was also building an increasing role in Grand Rapids community organizations and in local, state, and national politics. As one who grew up in a small Midwestern town, I don't think I had ever met anyone who talked as fast as did Paul. He would sometimes try to cover so much so fast in his lectures that it was nearly impossible for us note-taking students to keep up. The sound of his class was often that of students noticeably dropping their pens on their desks, signaling Paul that his lecturing speed had exceeded all note-taking capacity.

It was noted in conjunction with the establishment of the Paul B. Henry Institute that Paul, together with Dr. Richard Mouw, then a professor of philosophy at Calvin College, organized an annual Conference on Christianity and Politics. Those conferences were important in a number of ways. Certainly they helped raise the visibility of, and define a new level of political and social activism in, the evangelical community. They also allowed students, such as me, to meet and hear from evangelical Christians with a wide range of differing perspectives on the relationship between Christianity and politics.

I remember as well that those conferences included not only academics and theologians, but also practitioners in government and politics. Amidst the theological and philosophical discussions about how Christians have viewed or should view "the state," it was helpful to hear the personal and practical struggles of those in government and politics seeking to be Christian in their work.

Indeed, Paul was always encouraging us not only to study politics but also to be involved in politics. During the years that I was a student, Paul was almost constantly involved in some political campaign, not only partisan races but often local, nonpartisan campaigns on a ballot proposal or school board member. As an energetic and intelligent student of politics who understood the fine points of campaign techniques, his services on such campaigns were much in demand. But I remember more (because a few of us would sometimes go with him) his willingness to hand out literature early in the morning at factories or on weekends at shopping malls, and to help send out mailings. The importance of political involvement at that level has stayed with me. He showed by example that effective politics involves a lot of not very glamorous hard work.

Paul also encouraged students' involvement in political work in other ways. He created an "Interim in Washington" in which he took ten to fifteen students to Washington, D.C., to work in congressional and other political offices during Calvin College's interim period in January. It was, I believe, the first internship program in Calvin's political science department. Although I don't recall hearing him complain, setting up the program must have included a lot of hassles. While today various organizations exist to facilitate internship programs in Washington, D.C., those organizations apparently did not exist in the early- and mid-1970s when Paul took students there. I remember that Paul used his own contacts as a former congressional staff person to find offices that would let us work for a month. He also found us lodging. Fortunately for me, Paul was always very frugal. He found us a somewhat dilapidated senior citizens' hotel near the Capitol that had some extra rooms that they rented to us for five dollars a night.

Paul encouraged my interest and curiosity about how the political world worked into a career that has focused around government and politics. I was far from alone in benefiting from Paul's interest, encouragement, advice, and direction. His interest in his students did not wane after they and he left college. He would always take great pleasure when former students would visit him when he was in Congress, especially if they were involved in some form of political activism and came to lobby him. He always expressed encouragement for their work and pride in their accomplishments.

Paul emphasized that politics is a form of Christian service. But he also emphasized that political choices are complex and often involve unknown and unintended consequences. Furthermore, "while God's standards are absolute and unchanging, we as individuals are never able to know or apply them with perfection."[2] The moral ambiguity attendant to political choices, Paul said, means that "Christians... must begin by recognizing that political choices are immensely complex and clouded. And they must recognize that the motives behind political action are generally mixed. Hence, politics is not a simple battle between good and evil, or virtuous men and evil men."[3] Paul noted that as Christians we often admit the moral ambiguity of political choices in the abstract, but then fail to acknowledge the impact of sin on our own political assumptions and ideologies.

Paul also emphasized the "legitimacy of politics" – that politics inherently involves the promotion of interests and self interest: "Conflict stemming from self-interest" lies "at the heart of politics."[4] "All politics involves compromising the conflicts of interest within a society. Political institutions and traditions are nothing more than the channels through which the conflicts are routed and the rules by which the conflicts are fought."[5]

At the same time, politics is also about creating a more fair and just society: "[P]olitics is something more than simply the struggle for personal advantage. It is the attempt of the entire society to organize and manipulate personal demands in such a way that the consensus which is reached will, insofar as possible, be fair to each member of that society. In other words, politics is intimately involved in man's search for justice."[6]

But Paul's understanding of the nature of politics and the moral ambiguity of political choices made him unwilling to claim that his or anyone's politics were "Christian politics." He was sometimes criticized for being too cautious about advocating a Christian approach to politics, often by those who felt he was either too liberal or too conservative. Others in the evangelical community were advocating that Christians should have a distinctive political agenda or a distinct political movement. Paul was emphasizing the moral ambiguity of political choices and warning that for Christians, like everyone else, "political ambitions never totally transcend [one's own] selfishness."[7]

I have come to appreciate Paul's emphasis on politics as *both* the struggle among interests in society *and* the search for justice as I have worked in the political arena. It allows for interest-group politics and partisan conflict; they are not an unnecessary or deviant part of politics. To the contrary, such conflict of interests is what politics is. This, of course, is not to say that the checks and balances on interest-group politics, such as campaign finance laws, should not be refined and strengthened. But politics is also concerned with more: "it is… essential that politics not lose sight of the concept of justice. For if we deny the existence of an abstract and transcendental notion of the political good, then the processes of politics can be reduced to nothing more than brute force asserting its will over a weaker party."[8] It is very easy, when one is in the throes of political conflict, to imagine that the "end justifies the means," whether that means seeking advantage by destroying one's opponent or being less than honest, if that serves one's purpose. Yet, as Paul pointed out, justice involves both the means and the ends of politics. Politics, at least at the national level, has undoubtedly become coarser and less manageable since Paul was teaching. It seems to me that his emphasis on *why* political issues should not be treated as a simple battle between good and evil is more needed than ever. Furthermore, understanding that politics is always both the struggle of self-interests and the search for justice also avoids the tendency to compartmentalize Christianity by treating some issues (and presumably not others) as "moral issues."

Although he taught political science for many years, I suspect that the lesson on politics that Paul taught more than any other was one that he often used when he was invited to lead adult Sunday School or church education classes, though he also used it in other contexts, such as his 1989 speech on "Morality vs. Moralism" included in this volume. The lesson was from Daniel 6, where the story is told of how King Darius, at the urging of all of his advisors and administrators except one, signed a decree that "...whosoever shall ask a petition of any god or man for thirty days, save [of the king], shall be cast into the den of lions." Daniel, nonetheless, prayed to the God of Israel with his window wide open for all to see. His rivals in the government, whose motive in urging the king to sign the decree was to catch Daniel in disobedience to it, reported Daniel to the king. Despite his anguish at doing so, the king followed the decree that he had made and sent Daniel to the lions. We know, but King Darius did not, that God would send his angel to protect Daniel. In the morning, after he had found Daniel still alive, the king had Daniel removed from the lions' den and his rivals thrown in.

Paul taught this story to emphasize the nature of politics and political choices. For Darius the choice was having Daniel thrown to the lions or undermining the fundamental tenet of his kingdom – the law of the Medes and Persians that "may never be changed." Paul asked, "What would you have done, had you been Darius? Politics involves making choices between imperfect solutions reflecting a fallen world. Those who speak in terms of black and white, rather than admitting of the shades of grey in the political endeavor, are most to be feared."[9]

There is of course another aspect of the story. Daniel himself, as one of the top administrators in the greatest earthly kingdom of his day, was no doubt well acquainted with the compromises and moral ambiguity of politics. But Daniel also knew that a greater and higher authority than the king existed. It was fitting that at Paul's funeral then-House Republican Leader, Bob Michel, referred to this same story that Paul used so often, to talk about Paul:

> If I were asked to sum up Paul's impacts on those of us who knew him, I would recall a favorite phrase of my father: "Dare to be a Daniel." By that he meant that we should have the courage of Daniel in the lions' den, retaining our convictions at difficult times, trusting in Providence, doing what is right, especially when it is the unpopular thing to do. Paul Henry dared to be a Daniel.

Reinhold Niebuhr wrote of the Christian's perspective on politics:

> Nothing is quite so difficult, yet so genuinely Christian, as to remember that in all political struggles there are no saints but only sinners fighting each other, and to remember at the same time that history from man's, rather than God's, perspective is constituted of significant distinctions between types and degrees of sin... If the tension between Christian realism and faith in love as the law of life is not to be broken the Christian must become immersed in the claims and counterclaims, the tension, conflict and the risk of overt hostilities which characterize all attempts at justice, while refusing to regard any relative justice so achieved as exhausting his obligations. He must, as a Christian, participate responsibly in the struggle for justice, constantly making significant moral and political decisions amidst and upon perplexing issues and hazardous ventures. He must even make them 'with might' and not half-heartedly. But the Christian faith gives him no warrant to lift himself above the world's perplexities and to seek or to claim absolute validity for the stand he takes. It does, instead, encourage him to the charity which is born of humility and contrition.[10]

As a professor and as an elected public official Paul engaged the political arena "with might" yet also with charity and humility. Add to that he was a warm and wise person. I was indeed blessed to know him as a teacher and as a friend.

NOTES

1. "Paul Henry Led With Conscience," by Mark Lagerwey, *Cadillac Evening News*, August 3, 1993.

2. Paul B. Henry, *Politics for Evangelicals* (Valley Forge, Pennsylvania: Judson Press, 1974), 72.

3. Ibid., 78.

4. Ibid., 67.

5. Ibid., 69.

6. Ibid., 80.

7. Ibid., 70.

8. Ibid., 80.

9. "Morality vs. Moralism: In Defense of Politics," *Vital Speeches of the Day*, LV:10 (March 1, 1989), 296.

10. From "Reinhold Niebuhr on Politics," excerpted in *Reinhold Niebuhr, Theologian of Public Life*, ed. Larry Rasmussen (Philadelphia: Fortress Press, 1991), p. 130

Section III:
Christian Politics:
No Easy Answers

Section III
No Easy Answers

This final section consists of "Reflections on Evangelical Christianity and Political Action," and "Morality vs. Moralism." Both selections originated as talks Paul gave in 1989, the former at Messiah College in Grantham, Pennsylvania, and the latter at Pepperdine University in Malibu, California. Together these articles are probably his most developed thinking on Christian action in politics.

"Reflections" is a talk presented to a largely Anabaptist audience. Appropriately, Paul begins his talk with a defense of Christian engagement in politics, a stance much at odds with his audience's view. He presents a succinct history of Christian engagement in American politics. In the process he points out his disagreements with Anabaptist and Fundamentalist assumptions about what redeemed human beings ought to do (or not do) in politics.

"Morality vs. Moralism" repeats two essential points that run through nearly all of Paul's work: the dual nature of humanity and the legitimacy of politics. First, humans always will be simultaneously capable of great good and great evil. Faith cannot change that fact; neither can legislation. There always will be irreconcilable claims about what justice demands, even by sanctified Christians. Second, politics is a legitimate, imperfect, and necessary process. Politics involves temporarily resolving conflicts between competing, never-ending, and constantly changing social forces. Its solutions will always be ad hoc, provisional, and unsatisfactory to purists. And politics will always be necessary. These are the reasons why Christians need to be involved in politics and why many Christian groups never quite accept the legitimacy of politics.

This section closes with essays by three of Paul's colleagues in the U.S. House, two Republicans and a Democrat. Republican Speaker of the House, Dennis Hastert, knew Paul first at Wheaton College in the

1960s and became reacquainted with him two decades later as a congressional colleague. Fred Upton, a moderate Republican from southwestern Michigan, served more than six years with Paul in the House where he represented a neighboring and similar district. Hastert and Upton offer personal rememberances of Paul's character and personality. David Price, a Democratic colleague and friend, shared much of Paul's academic and political background and evaluates Paul's thoughts and actions in terms similar to those that Paul himself would use. Together, these House members present a clear picture of Paul on the national political stage.

Reflections on Evangelical Christianity and Political Action

The question, "What has Athens to do with Jerusalem?" or, "How does the church relate to matters of state?" is as old as the history of the church. It is also a large question which we cannot fully answer tonight. But as one who shares the fundamentals of evangelical and orthodox Christian faith with you, perhaps I can offer some helpful perspectives on it.

The Root Question

The question you are asking is not how does or should the church relate to politics, nor how the Christian faith interacts with the political order. You are starting with a more basic question, namely, should Christians be involved in politics at all? To people of your Anabaptist tradition, this is a less foolish question than it would seem to people outside the household of faith in general and outside your tradition in particular. What I shall try to do is to relate the question to different tangents in the contemporary evangelical church.

The Anabaptist tradition rests, as I understand it, first of all on a fundamental issue of where the state comes from and why we have the state. Anabaptism recognizes that the order of the state is qualitatively different from other forms of social endeavor. It recognizes that the state is rooted in the authority which is exercised through the sword. Most Evangelicals are more comfortable engaging the state through political action than are Anabaptists. But one important thing in your own tradition is that Anabaptism clearly understands the unique character of the state. This means that there is a difference between political ethics and social ethics. We have to remind many of our Evangeli-

Reprinted by permission from *Brethren in Christ History and Life* 12:3 (December 1989).

cal brethren outside your tradition that in the rediscovery of a social ethic, we have not necessarily developed a political ethic.

The use of power as instrumental to politics as opposed to other kinds of social human interaction has been seen as the fundamental problem in your tradition. The issue then becomes for Anabaptists to determine whether or not the institution of the state is truly a creation ordinance (that is, it is ordained in the structures of creation), or whether the state is a sustaining ordinance (one that in the common grace of God keeps mankind from falling into absolute and total anarchy). As I understand the Anabaptist tradition, it is a tradition which says that the state is a sustaining ordinance of God; for those who have come to the fullness of fellowship with God through Jesus Christ, this sustaining ordinance of the state, rooted in law and backed by the sword, is of no import. The spiritual community of the church has no need of the state. Once we are of Jerusalem, the ordinances of the state are not necessary in our community.

This attitude has sometimes led to a kind of withdrawal, to the belief that we are in the church and the evil, perhaps the necessary evil, or the sword is not germane to our community. But sometimes this tradition has also led to a kind of spiritual triumphalism. Some sectarian movements in the Anabaptist-Mennonite traditions have become very triumphal in the sense that in the name of Christ we bring you to the Kingdom of God in our community. The fallen orders of law and the state are diminished in their importance relative to the triumphal manifestation of grace in the Christian community.

The Anabaptist tradition is really much more than just a pacifist tradition. Many people outside of the tradition think of it first of all in terms of its pacifism and many have dismissed it on that ground alone. But the Anabaptist tradition is much more than mere conscientious objection to being forced to utilize the sword in the name of the state, or to utilize the sword on behalf of one's own interest. I want to explain, in a round about way, what I mean.

I am a Baptist who is essentially Calvinist in theology. This position allowed me to sneak onto the faculty of Calvin College (which is, to put it in light terms, a very orthodox Calvinist institution committed to classical Calvinism). Now, classical Calvinism is really the antithesis of the Anabaptist-Mennonite tradition in terms of politics. In my classes at Calvin almost all of my students rejected pacifism. In class, I would give very dramatic arguments explaining the distinctions between the classical concepts of just war and non-just war. Then I would outline a Hitler-type situation where it is relatively easy to say who wore the white hats and who didn't wear the white hats. I would talk about the pattern of aggression, the racial extermination of the Jews, etc., and conclude by asking whether anyone would say, in the face of this institutionalized form of evil, that taking up the sword in the name of justice is un-Christian in terms of the just war criteria I had spelled out. I usually had one or two students who objected to the use of force, but normally the overwhelming response of students was to subscribe to the so-called just war concept.

Then I would set up another scenario. I would explain that given the nature of modern warfare, with the introduction of nuclear weaponry and the certainty that in any exchange of nuclear weapons innocent victims will be killed on both sides, intrigue and espionage have become increasingly important and necessary. I would add that in this age of equality, women would also be subject to conscription. Then I would look at the most attractive girl in the class and I would say, "If your government asked you, would you sleep with someone for the sake of your country?" There would be horror and great embarrassment that I would even ask the question. "Well of course not, Professor Henry." Then I would respond, "You have just told me you would kill for your country. Which is worse – killing for your country or sleeping with someone for it?"

Now I am not trying to be funny. I am trying to indicate the profound strengths of your tradition, although ultimately I disagree with it. Anabaptists would have no problem saying no to both my hypothetical scenarios. I also want to show you the sometime triviality of an equally strong tradition (in this case the Calvinist evangelical tradition) when it does not recognize the way in which we have almost without thinking said it is right to kill for the state. So really the question of politics is a much harder question for those outside your tradition. You should be aware of the power of your tradition. But fundamentally, the basic issue is whether or not the community of the redeemed stand in need of the state. And the underlying issue is whether the state is a creation ordinance or a sustaining ordinance.

The Early Twentieth-Century Evangelical Exodus from Politics

I need to tell you something about the broad withdrawal of our Evangelical community from the political arena in the twentieth century.

One factor in this withdrawal has been the influence of the Anabaptist-Mennonite model which is certainly a healthy segment of Evangelical tradition. A second factor has been the Fundamentalist reaction to the social gospel. (Now in many cases, these overlap but they are not the same thing. Particularly, many Anabaptist groups who had strong ethnic ties weren't dragged into this liberal-fundamentalist debate, thus you didn't have the fissure in your church bodies in the same way that the so-called main line churches experienced them.) So, Fundamentalism is another dimension of the political passivity or withdrawal of the Evangelical community from politics broadly understood.

Much of the Fundamentalist agenda of the early twentieth century was created in opposition to the "Social Gospel" movement. These "social gospelers" spoke of an immanentalized Jesus and they had no room for their transcendent Christ. They were theological liberals and what they finally arrived at was a kind of Kiwanis Club gospel – one that spoke generally of the social improvement of our civilization and culture. In reaction to this, the Fundamentalists said that these liberals had missed the point of what the true Christian fundamentals really were. In order to make their point doubly sure, and to be sure no [one] would mistake them for being liberals themselves, Fundamentalists also simply stopped talking about anything social. It became a kind of institutional reaction to the social gospel. This reaction is the second factor that has contributed to political passiveness within the Evangelical community.

The third factor was the development of dispensationalist theology. (Now remember that while most dispensationalists would be Evangelicals or Fundamentalists, not all Evangelicals or Fundamentalists would be dispensationalists.) At the heart of dispensationalist theology is the idea that we are, in a very literal sense, living in the last days. For dispensationalists, the imminent return of Christ means not simply that the return of Christ is imminent at any moment but that it is literally, with some sense of predictability, imminent. If you believe this way, there are obviously better things to do than trying to engage in a twenty-year struggle to build a moral majority in America – or whatever other political project you might otherwise favor. You don't have twenty years. You literally have no time for politics at all.

A fourth item that has contributed to Evangelical political passiveness – more limited in scope, but still very influential – is some rather unique historical factors that have affected conservative protestantism in this country. Among them, and very significant, is the impact of the civil war on a very large segment of our evangelical and fundamental churches. I was at a conference of the Churches of Christ at Pepperdine College[1] about a month ago. Members of the conference also were talking about political engagement and disengagement within their tradition. One of the major factors forcing the disengagement of their churches from the political arena was the impact of the civil war, at which time they split from the Disciples of Christ. Both sides claimed the same God and exegeted the same Scriptures. The result, however, has been that, being on the losing side of that war, they have ever since been predisposed to the separation of the church and state.

Sometimes I think we forget how historically relativized we are in the way we look at these things. This is not to say that truth is relative, but that all our opinions are relative because we are fallen and finite. Thus you get a different temperament in the southern Evangelical tradition. This is not just stylistic it is also theological.

So you have the Anabaptist tradition and the Fundamentalist withdrawal and counter reaction to the Social Gospel, you have the dispensationalist element, you have historical experience – all pointing away from political involvement.

The Contemporary Re-entrance of Evangelicals into Politics

The Evangelical community in this country is sizable, and suddenly in the last few years there has been a resurgent political interest in all those Evangelicals out there. In the face of the evils all about us – whether it be abortions, or television, or the tremendous problems resulting from gaps between wealth and poverty around the world, or the arms race, or environmental ecological catastrophe (the list could be extended) – a Christian's conscience wells up and says that we should do something. There is political clout in all those Evangelicals.

In the last thirty to forty years, a clear pattern of Evangelical re-involvement in politics has become evident. But, after being so apolitical for all those years, having been withdrawn from politics and ceasing even largely from discussing politics, we are still very immature in our political understanding.

Let me give a personal example of how things have changed. When I graduated from Wheaton College in 1963, there was not one Evangelical institution in the United States of America that had a professor with a Ph.D. in political science on its faculty. You might have had a historian or a retired missionary teaching government, but there were no political scientists – no one who really understood government as an academic discipline and who sought to relate Christian ethics to the disciplines of government. Now almost all Evangelical colleges have faculty with doctorates in political science. Systematic reflection on the discipline of politics is a very recent development in the Evangelical community, even in the Evangelical academic community.

What we need, among other things, is to study the heritage of the Christian community and the development and history of Christian social and political ethics. We need to study how the church is historic. Earlier in this century Evangelicals had become as ahistorical as they were apolitical. We had lost touch with the wellsprings of our traditions. I think that is one of the reasons why any polling of practical day-to-day political attitudes in your community would be rather surprising in the face of the traditional confessions of your community. It is because you have been cut off from your own origins, because there really hasn't been a systematic facing of the issue.

Another reason for avoiding this kind of reflection was the Fundamentalist movement and its reaction to the challenge of humanism in liberal theology. The result has been that most of the popular theology written in our tradition up until very recently was apologetic theology. It was not theology that grappled with the deeper issues of how systematically to relate Christian truth to the world around us. That is not to diminish the value or importance of apologetic theology. But it was theology that was almost entirely based on the challenge of the natural sciences and remained strikingly silent on the social question. We have not allowed ourselves to be haunted by ethics in the same way that we have been obsessed with dogma.

For example, look at the absolute dearth of treatises questioning, or at least struggling with, some of the problems of the missionary movement. Although my grandparents were missionaries and my mother was born on the mission field, it is important for me as a social scientist to ask about the extent to which western missions were affected by imperialism. That is not to say that God didn't use the mission movement. Historically, I think it is one of the greatest examples of ethics evangelism in practice in the history of the church. Nonetheless, we have not examined the degree to which the modern missionary movement became needlessly entangled with imperial causes and Western culture.

There is nothing wrong with self-interest as such, but being unaware of self-interest as an aspect of our behavior can be highly problematic for Christians. I believe self-interest is biblical. The Christian standard is not to deny self-interest, but to raise your neighbor's interest to a degree of intensity equal to your own. Love your neighbor as yourself. But self-interest alone is really what Marx said religion was – rationalization for self-interest – and to that extent the Marxist critique is too often descriptively true, though not necessarily normatively true.

In recent years, however, there has been an awakening in rethinking these questions. One book in particular that is often cited (and I mention it with some humility because it is my dad's) is Carl F. H. Henry's *The Uneasy Conscience of Fundamentalism*. This book came out in the late forties and attacked the Fundamentalist movement for its social silence. It is often cited as a beginning book of political ethics for Evangelicals. But I would point out that if you read that book carefully, you will find that it doesn't talk about political ethics at all. It talks about social engagement. It never develops a political strategy or a Christian political ethic. Anabaptists could read it and say "Amen," and hyper-Calvinists could read it and say "Amen," because it never went beyond social engagement. That is not to criticize my dad, and he may be right and I may be wrong, because as I said earlier, we can have social engagement and not be political.

Another very important book was Dave Moberg's *The Great Reversal.* Moberg was then at Bethel College in St. Paul; now he is at Marquette University in Wisconsin. In this book he traced the dynamic aggressiveness of the Evangelical community (including your community) in the nineteenth century when it vocally challenged the evils of slavery and spoke out for female suffrage – the women's right to vote. Clearly your community was among those in the vanguard of the abolitionist movement, and Moberg pointed out that all of these Evangelical traditions had once been active and confronting with regard to politics, but suddenly they stopped being so and sometimes they even became regressive.

This regressive kind of thinking was very common in the fifties across the breadth of the Evangelical community. Our critics of the civil rights movement in the sixties used to ask in our church publications, "What are they going to use their freedom for?" It wasn't an issue of whether Black people had a God-given right to freedom, or a constitutional right if it wasn't God-given. The question we asked was, "What will they use their freedom for?" What happened to the abolitionist in us, or the suffragist in us? So you have Moberg who challenged us, who pointed out where we were, but he didn't really move us further.

There was one other book that had a profound effect, and it is from your tradition – John Howard Yoder's *The Politics of Jesus*. This was a clear and articulate call to the Christian community to develop its thinking with regard to politics. But again, notice that while Yoder looks carefully at many questions in our society, he stops short of a political ethic, and very dramatically so. That is not to say that Christian faith is irrelevant to the issue of world peace. Clearly he is not saying this. He is not saying that the Christian faith is irrelevant to the political questions of the day. Clearly John Howard Yoder would not say that. But what he does say is that the discovery and the manifestation of the new community in Christ has a salting and transforming effect on society. Yoder's is a very able presentation, but it is not political. He doesn't really advocate political strategy. But at least the questions are being raised and very profoundly.

More recently, interest-group advocacy has begun to spill out all over the political spectrum, including into the Evangelical community. Jerry Falwell's Moral Majority efforts, which are somewhat on the wane now, is a classic example. Suddenly, a number of Evangelicals (and perhaps more Fundamentalists than Evangelicals) are speaking up. Another voice seeking to speak up and develop a political strategy is JustLife, an organization with which Ronald Sider is very active. Developing different agencies and utilizing different methodologies is the Association for Public Justice – a group fairly popular in some of the Reformed circles in which I circulate. Any number of these groups are coming forth.

A Critique of Political Separatism

Let me suggest some problems within your tradition which you are going to have to face if you really want to hold to the classical Anabaptist mold. The first is that non-involvement in terms of direct political engagement has immoral consequences. You do not rescue yourself from moral complicity by withdrawal. The danger is that you will substitute a sin of omission for the sin of commission that you are trying to avoid. I mean to put it into very simple terms: if you do not get engaged in the political arena, people who don't subscribe to your values will. You are creating a void that others are going to fill and you are responsible for that void.

Part of the problem here is the New Testament model. Some parts of the New Testament are used to justify non-political forms of social engagement as if they were opposed to politics. I would say that the separatistic vision – the Christian world view which sees the transformation of society taking place through a transformation of the Christian community which then spills out into the world at large – is valid. But this is not the only model. I don't think it is valid exegesis to read the Bible in that way. You have to understand that during the entire New Testament period the nature of citizenship was very different from what it is today. Citizenship was passive for virtually all the population in the Roman Empire, as it is in any traditional society. That is the cultural condition in which the New Testament was written. Citizens were powerless. We, on the other hand, live in a qualitatively different kind of social and political order. In the democratic and post-democratic eras, we live with the idea that citizenship means something different; it means government of the people and by the people and for the people.

Let me make an analogy here to the Christian concept of "calling." At the time of the Reformation, Calvin and Luther (and I suspect the Anabaptist tradition as well) spoke much of the calling of God. These theologians sought to see all work potentially in terms of the calling of God in reaction to the perverse Catholic thought of that time which saw non-religious work as useless. We often celebrate the fact that the Reformation allowed all of us to see our work as given to us by God – as an opportunity to serve the Kingdom of God. This was true so long as whatever you did with your abilities and talents issued in the glory of God. Such was the idea of "calling!' at the time of the Reformation.

I don't know how many times I heard about calling as a child. I struggled as I waited for "the call" – thinking everyone had calling experiences. Some of us do, but we forget that at the time when these great classics of the Reformation were written, a person's calling was self-evident from the time of birth. From the time you were conceived, your mother and father knew what you were going to be. Your calling was to perform to the glory of God the duties inherent in that station of life into which you were born. If your father and mother were shepherds, you were going to be a shepherd. It was a static society.

It is the same thing in the area of citizenship and the state. We forget that the whole nature and setting is different now in terms of ethical responsibility and moral accountability. Accountability cannot now be measured in terms of simply saying, "I have rendered obedience except in those situations when the state has demanded of me something which is contrary to the will of God for my life." We are not living in a static society. If you act as if we are, you will find yourself substituting sins of omission for the sins of commission. You will not have gained much.

But the tensions you feel are real, as you may read in Senator Mark Hatfield's book *Between a Rock and a Hard Place.* If you read it carefully, you will note that Senator Hatfield is deeply sympathetic to Anabaptist thinking.

Being a Christian Politician in the Modern Fallen World

In the Anabaptist tradition, problems begin, at least fundamentally, with the theological concept that the state is not a creation ordinance and thus is not fundamental to human existence; it is meant only as a rescue device until redemption comes to the individual. Fundamentalists, by contrast, sometimes tend to look at the state, when they do engage it, as a redemption ordinance. They try to use the state to usher in righteousness rather than simply to establish justice. Fundamentalism seeks too much from the state, Anabaptism too little.

In both cases – the Anabaptist and the Fundamentalist – what must be remembered is that just because we are redeemed does not mean that we are sanctified. It doesn't mean that when we engage the political order, somehow, just because we are justified by faith through Christ, we have totally and truly sanctimonious political opinions or that we aren't subject to the same temptations as others are to use God's name in vain by rationalizing our wishes and attaching His name to it. It doesn't mean that we are no longer fallen or no longer finite. And if the Fundamentalist exceeds this limit in one way by too much demanding a public moral majority agenda for society, the Anabaptist may well exceed this limit in another way by claiming too much purity for the separate community. Redemption does not give us instant infallibility.

We have to understand this distinction when we enter the political arena. We must accept social pluralism, but we also must not concede to value relativism. One of the problems, of course, is that many of our people confuse those two things. We do believe that there are absolute truths that are morally transcendent and that stand in judgment on our lives, on our community, on our nation, and that sometimes these truths must be spoken and spoken without compromise. But this does not mean that somehow we don't also believe in the necessity or the appropriateness of social pluralism. Keeping those distinctions very clear is important.

There are also institutional problems that we must face in our communities when we seek to develop a political ethic. Most elements of our Evangelical heritage – whether it be Anabaptist, Fundamentalist or even the broad southern range of churches with a little different historical shaping – tend to be established on a relatively congregationalist model. In your tradition, I believe you have a somewhat more traditional episcopal structure, but for all practical intents it operates very congregationally. That organizational reality has a profound impact on political involvement. Who speaks for the Evangelical church? It is very clear who speaks for the Catholic Church – the pope in council speaks for the Roman Catholic Church. Evangelicals have no such vehicle for articulating or announcing their political decisions.

In the United States we are allowed a tremendous range of freedom in expressing our political ideas. But again, this has a tremendous institutional impact on who speaks for the church and on how you organize the church. It is very different from the European situation where the individual churches or splintered religious political parties engage themselves directly in politics. These groups run on very pure ballots. They don't compromise on anything. They tend to produce virtual denominational statements and platforms. But then, of course, after the election they have to form coalition governments and they make their compromises after *rather than before the election.* The question is when the compromise takes place. That has some very practical and prudential implications about the way we go about political action.

Finally let me make some more personal remarks about my career in politics. A lot of people who wind up in politics didn't plan to do so. I suspect that many people in this room probably never dreamed they would be doing what they are doing today. It just kind of happened. Now a Christian wouldn't say it just happened – it is much more. But doors open; doors close. Opportunities are made available or they aren't. As I look back on my life, I can now see the handiwork of God in college applications that were not accepted and job applications that were turned down. But I couldn't see it at the time. These same things happen to people in public life.

I think sometimes we put public people in different cubby holes than ourselves. But they are exactly like us. Particularly because of our withdrawal from this arena we tend to be doubly prone to look at them as different. We ask, "How did you make that step?" We seem to assume that they are more prescient in their decisions than we are. We seem to assume that the issues for politicians are always clear. Often people say, "What do you do when your party wants you to do this, your constituency wants you to do this, and your conscience tells you to do this? How do you reconcile it all?" Let me be honest: I tend to reconcile them on an ad hoc basis.

I know this is not such a powerful answer that it will make the front page of the *New York Times.* But it is no different in some respects from the way in which you reconcile other little moral dilemmas in your life, but you don't think about the process because you have done it all your life. For example, most of us buy new clothes when we are tired of what we are wearing, not because we need new clothes, although we live in a world where people need clothes. What is the moral significance of that? On the other hand, God made us beings with an appreciation for aesthetics. Even Jesus allowed his body to be anointed with luxury perfumes. And I always like to say that God went first class when he ordered up the temple: he used a lot of gold, probably as much as in Fort Knox.

There are no simple answers to some of these things. And, I should point out, the direct conflicts don't occur as dramatically as many people suspect – at least not with your constituency. One tends not to get elected to positions such as my own if one holds views that are consistently diametrically opposed to the community sending one to Congress. There has to be some natural ambiance, as it were, of conviction in the community. That is not to say that it is always consistent. There are some issues in which it is impossible to be consistent. There are times in which you change your mind. During my first term in Congress I rather consistently voted to support the contras in Latin America. During my second term I did not do so. Either way, I had half the district mad at me. All you can do – the easiest thing to do – in that case is nothing more than to follow your conscience. There is no political win in some issues.

On other issues, in which I have voted against someone's sense of what was right, I have gotten people very upset when I have had to break with them on matters of conscience. I have a certain moral obligation to my party leadership because I ran on a party ticket. I have some obligation to uphold and sustain the party, otherwise I should not have used its name. On the other hand, I must represent my district and listen to my conscience. Ultimately you are who you are, and you must take all those different senses of moral obligation into consideration when you cast your vote. The answers are not always easy.

When I was here at Messiah College a couple of years ago I talked about Daniel 6. This is one of my favorite chapters in the Bible because it points out the dilemma of King Darius. When we study this chapter, we underline the fact that Daniel had the courage to pray publicly despite the order of Darius the King. We talk about the courage of Daniel without considering the agony of Darius who got tricked into making this order by evil subordinates who were seeking a case against Daniel and the king. If the king hadn't put Daniel into the lion's den, he would have had to forsake the throne and give it to evil men. Now which was the right choice? To put Daniel in the lion's den to save the empire from evil men or to save Daniel, the only truly good and just servant he had, but at the cost of turning the empire over to evil men? Neither choice was clear. Neither choice was perfect.

What I am trying to say is that we live in a fallen world with fallen people with fallen choices – particularly when you get into social and human relations. It is not like mathematics where you can say if you take two and add two to it you get four. The worst talk I ever had to give was at a local high school. They asked me to speak on the challenge of positive parenting. You see all the unpredictabilities of the situation. The teachers and the neighbors know your kids. You see good parents with horrible kids, and parents who have been disasters yet their kids turned out right. It is then that you realize anew how we all hang on the grace and providence of God which ultimately makes all things clear and whole and just, and straightens our crooked paths through this fallen world in which we live.

I think sometimes we can overly anguish about these things. We must make our decisions before God. They won't all be perfect choices, but we must make the best choices we can, given our development as Christians and as we seek continually to put our hands into the hand of God and walk through life one step at a time.

Note

1. Pepperdine University is affiliated with the Churches of Christ denomination.

Morality vs. Moralism: In Defense of Politics

When my dear friend and former professorial colleague, Professor Stephen Monsma, proposed a conference seeking to provide a forum on how Christian perspectives could inform the agenda of the new Administration, I allowed my enthusiasm to beguile me into volunteering to be a participant. I say this not in jest, but in the anguish of having wrestled with the theme of this conference for several months, knowing that I risk the danger of pharisaism in trying to open our discussion on the agenda before us.

Indeed, I do not reject the conviction that moral assumptions and moral beliefs are ultimately at the heart of public policymaking. Whether explicitly understood or only implicitly assumed, moral reasoning underlies each and every political decision rendered on public policy issues.

Nonetheless, placing a public official in a position of deciphering those moral assumptions also potentially places him or her in a position of casting moral stones against the system of which he is a part. But clearly, one cannot escape the reality of increasing public discontent over the questions of the personal "ethics" of public officials and the social "ethics" of public policy choices emanating from Washington. Ethics, per se, has become part of the "political agenda."

My first attempt at dealing with this topic was to monitor the rising public outcry against the ethical lapses and abuses of those entrusted with public office. I reviewed Brooks Jackson's recently published volume, *Honest Graft: Big Money and the American Political Process*. I read Philip Stern's new book, *The Best Congress Money Can Buy*. I considered last year's *Time* magazine article on the hundred or so Reagan

Delivered at Pepperdine University, Malibu, California, January 26, 1989. Previously published in *Vital Speeches of the Day* LV:10, March 1, 1989, and reprinted by permission.

Administration officials who were alleged to have run afoul of the law or accepted norms during their tenure in Washington. I reflected upon the moral dilemmas of "Irangate," and not yet fully resolved issues as to whether the law and the Constitution were violated at home in the effort to establish the rule of law and constitutionalism abroad. I considered the various "PAC" reform proposals before the Congress. I pondered the rationale of President Reagan's parting veto of the "Conflict of Interest" legislation passed during the waning hours of the 100th Congress. In the end, I despaired of efforts to articulate virtuous answers to these matters that would not either sound self-serving on the one hand, or evasive or simplistic on the other.

My second attempt to address the topic was much more comprehensive and overarching. Rather than focus on the *particulars* of political virtue, I sought to trace the rise and fall of Western civilization from the Golden Age of Pericles to the Plastic Age of Pragmatism. The struggle to gain the benefits of liberty under law through respect for social and political pluralism has degenerated into value relativism. Our educational institutions have failed to teach us the disciplines of moral reasoning. The transition from printed press to electronic media has moved ethical reflection, to the degree it still exists, from the right side to the left side of the brain. The modern world view which has lost its ability to admit the reality of evil is likewise unable to make distinctions about the nature of the good. After all, if nothing is categorically evil and sinful, nothing can be categorically good and righteous. In the caption of a December 5, 1988 *New Yorker* cartoon parroting a Wall Street news update: "In the ongoing saga of Western civilization, declines continue to lead advances by a wide margin."

But if the people have lost the moral vision and consensus upon which public officials must draw moral direction, how can the institutions of state be held accountable and condemned for a failure which fundamentally lies elsewhere? Indeed, does not the *totalitarian* seek to supply the unifying ideological glue through force of law in response to this moral crisis? And is it not the strength of democratic institutions that they *refuse* to do so? How could I best expose the inconsistency of a society which clamors for political virtue in the public arena, while at the same time it spurns the moral traditions that give it meaning in private life?

But alas, this Hegelian overview of the crisis of our civilization seemed a bit far removed from the mundane, day-to-day political infighting which I or any other public official faces when trying to cloak practical, ordinary, every day decisions with moral justification and value relatedness. Such grandiose schemes hardly help answer day-to-day questions – such as what type of hormones ought to be allowed in dairy cattle – to which those in political life must contend.

My third attempt to address the topic was that of a psycho-socio examination as to how an elected official, subject to the daily scrutiny of investigative reporting and public censure, "adjusts" and "adapts" to the clamor for perfection in all things. I remembered a personal anecdote involving my own first official "campaign committee." In 1974, I was appointed to a vacant seat on the Michigan State Board of Education by Governor William Milliken. It was a coveted appointment for the remaining six years of an eight-year term for what, in Michigan, is an elective position. Since this was just after the Watergate Crisis, I was among the first generation of public officials caught in the so-called "sunshine disclosure" laws of the post-Watergate reforms. Imagine my surprise, then, when I was advised by the Secretary of State that I would have to file a campaign committee spending report, despite my neither raising nor expending funds for an elective office to which I had been appointed. "No matter," the Secretary of State sternly informed me, "the law requires that you have a Committee, that it be established through a regulated banking institution, and that the reports be made public." Conforming to both the letter and the spirit of the law, I duly created my committee and filed my report. Upon the counsel of faculty friends at Calvin College, where I then taught, I named my Committee "UNUS VIR AD PIETATEM RESTITUENDAM," loosely translated as "One Man Committee to Restore Piety." I became the Committee's sole donor, served as both its Chairman and Treasurer, and duly deposited my $1.00 into the Committee's campaign coffers.

Four years later, the Committee was "discovered" by an investigative reporter for one of Detroit's major newspapers. The first question put to me by the reporter was "What are you trying to hide?" He later told me that he had spent some time trying to "untangle" the facts, convinced that something was, indeed, fishy with this entire scam! The fact is that the only legal difficulty I had with the Committee was fulfilling the legal obligation to close the Committee when I departed the State Board of Education, because I had lost the bank passbook with its $1.00 balance plus accrued interest. As silly as this example may seem, it illustrates the manner in which the trivial is sometimes elevated to intense scrutiny when practical, day-to-day activities of public officials are under investigation.

But, a presentation focusing exclusively on anecdotal accounts of political exotica also has its limitations. And thus, my third attempt at addressing the topic met the same fate as the others which preceded it.

But before showing my hand as to how I wish to directly address the topic of morality and moralism in the political arena, I want to reflect briefly as to why I rejected the first three approaches, intriguing as each might have been. The *first* – focusing on the public outcry over executive and legislative breaches of ethics – fails to address adequately the *breadth* of the problem. It unfairly separates the political endeavor from problems which are equal in magnitude and not qualitatively different than those in business, academia, or the pulpit. In the business community, for example, there is increasing anguish as to what the ground rules are for acceptable individual and corporate behavior. Harvard Business School advertises that "ethics in business" courses are an essential ingredient in its MBA program. Touche Ross recently published a major study entitled "Ethics in American Business," and concludes, incidentally, that "legislation offers the least effective way to encourage ethical behavior." The academic research community has been shaken by increasing reports of counterfeit data utilized to attract federal research dollars, and of "distinguished" scholars pirating and plagiarizing the work of others. And the scandals pertaining to various religious ministries are so legion as not to need elaboration.

"Good" politicians and public servants object strenuously to being blanketed with the same disdain which is cast on the "bad" ones, just as academics and entrepreneurs resist the same thing. But obviously, should I have chosen merely to defend those in political life in such a manner, it would have seemed altogether self-serving, posturing, and perhaps even hypocritical by those reviewing this presentation. It is important, nonetheless, to acknowledge that the problem we are addressing is not limited just to the political dimensions of our corporate and communal life as a nation. Unfortunately, academics and religious constituencies particularly are prone to do so. And I trust that as we work through our agenda during the coming two days, there will be a willingness to recognize that we can't afford to attack the problem with a "double standard" of virtue.

The *second* approach I had considered in dealing with the topic before us, you will recall, was my "Platonic-Hegelian-Metaphysical-Rise and Fall of Nations" philosophical treatise. I firmly believe that our modern civilization suffers from an inability to engage in moral reasoning. And just as "ideas have consequences," so too, "a lack of ideas has consequences." I suspect that the majority of our people are unable to distinguish between the concept of social pluralism and moral relativism, and that threatens the ability to have truly meaningful public square discussion on those "values" which are critical to and foundational to the moral assumptions of constitutional government. And how long our society – or any other – can sustain itself in a moral vacuum of this sort is a profoundly important question.

But, I consciously rejected this approach to the topic for two basic reasons. First, this problem is not "political," *per se*, at least in the sense of being amenable to resolution through governmental policy. Nothing is so frustrating to me as a public official as to hear the clergy decry the "decline of values in our society," and turn to the Congress for social salvation! The role of government – at least in a constitutional system – is not that of "making new men," but addressing the conflicts between them. Government is not responsible for the human condition, it responds to it.

Second, it bears remembering that for all the moral failures of the present age, there are also some tremendously important moral gains. In addressing the evils of the present, we tend to put a "utopian" cast on the past. We robe our history like we robe our judges. And if we are not careful, we are tempted to romanticize the past and to endow it with religious value and stature which blinds us and makes us incapable of honest comparisons – comparisons which are extremely difficult in and of themselves. How, for example, do we weight the "moral unity" of a past age against the practice of slavery or the oppression of the "weaker" sex? How many points do we assign to infanticide as opposed to abortion, to MTV as opposed to the public spectacles in the Roman arenas?

The ultimate danger, however, is allowing a sort of moral cynicism to enter in at this point which makes us caustic and hardened in clearly and prophetically identifying and decrying the evils of the present. While we must avoid simplistic cries over our current civilizational calamity, we must not drift into an historical relativism which simply concedes that "what will be, will be." But I know of no pending House or Senate bill before the Congress which resolves this question. And alas, I turned away from this approach to the question.

The *third* approach, you will recall, approached the topic from an "insider's point of view," endowed with anecdotal "if you were there, you would understand" insights to the political process. Consider the prophet Daniel's experiences in the court of Darius during the Medo-Persian Empire. Darius had the choice of relegating Daniel, the one just public servant he had, to the den of lions, or turning the empire over to the evil men who had plotted against him. What would you have done, had you been Darius? Politics involves making choices between imperfect solutions reflecting a fallen world. Those who speak in terms of black and white, rather than of admitting the shades of grey in the political endeavor, are most to be feared, I thought. But once again, I could see the one-line newsquotes back home the next morning: "Congressman Henry Repudiates Moral Standards!" Of course, the issue is not whether there are moral absolutes, but the degree to which we can confidentially apply them absolutely without falling into moral pretence. For obvious reasons, I rejected this third approach to the problem before us.

The question of political virtue and political morality involves *all* of these three approaches to questions. It involves those very particular concerns of personal conduct of those entrusted with public office – and the consequent political debates over such issues as campaign finance reform and the revolving door of moving from public to private sector positions. It involves broad questions of civilizational definition and public, social virtue – abortion, the arms race, global hunger, economic production, economic distribution. And it involves some sensitivity to the problems of those who must decide the questions, given the fact that such decisions are not necessarily choices between good and evil, but between competing goods.

If we are going to get beyond moralism and move toward genuine moral critique in our discussions during the next few days, there are two very important sets of moral assumptions which must be expounded upon and clarified. The first deals with a common understanding as to the nature of man. The second deals with common understanding as to the nature of politics.

With the inauguration of George Bush as our nation's 41st President, we have begun the third century in America's experiment in representative government. One of the reasons for the success of our experiment over the years has been the wisdom of those who drafted our basic Constitutional document, and the assessment they made of the human condition. Alexander Hamilton, in particular, expounded, in his *Federalist Papers,* on the lessons of past failures in brief and fleeting attempts at the republican form of government.

The first point he makes over and over again is that "men are not angels." There is no claim as to the innate "goodness of man," but rather an admission that man has capacity for good and evil. Government is instituted not just to allow the potential for goodness, but also to restrain his capacity for evil. It is not a government by angels for angels – but a government of men for men. Thus, the justification for the elaborate sets of checks and balances and limitations on the exercise of power in our form of government – limitations which would be even further expanded in the first ten Amendments to the Constitution.

To the extent we can learn from the past and refine those checks and balances, and to the extent we can augment our basic document with practical legislation – be it sunshine laws, conflict-of-interest legislation, or whatever – so much the better. But, the danger occurs when we romanticize the past saga of human history, or utopianize the future, in such a way as to tear down the very institutions we have developed over time in response to the lessons which history has taught us about the human condition.

And we do this whenever we assume that laws, in and of themselves, will somehow "make better men," rather than admitting to a more limited vision of laws checking the evil impulses of men. The question of politics is not the elimination of the reality of evil in the human condition which reflects itself in politics, but in seeking practical means whereby to contain it. The problem is not new. The struggle to address it is not new. And the officials who wield power are qualitatively neither better nor worse than previous generations. A bit of humility in the face of history and the human condition will do much to inject realism into the current political debate – a humility which moves us closer to genuine moral critique of the political process, and away from political moralism.

The Judeo-Christian worldview has consistently fought the modernist heresy that men are essentially shaped by their environment, and that better laws ipso facto make better men. But at the behavioral level, I have found things quite different. Preachers in the pulpit decry the "heresy" that "mankind is inherently good and perfectible." But when they enter the political arena, they are tempted to pitch the battle in terms of men vs. angels, and refuse to admit that all political actors – including themselves – are still affected by the human condition.

The ancient prophet exhorts us to seek justice, love mercy, and walk humbly with our God. Somehow, we have all been tempted to lose sight of the last of those injunctions – that of humility. The religious community is not particularly different from the secular community in the temptations to speak in political absolutes and certitude. But anyone who claims to speak in the name of God runs the risk of using God's name in vain as opposed to speaking in humility, admitting the fallenness and limitations of human nature to which our own religious teachings attest. When the religious community does this, it becomes secularized, and loses the very salt whereby it can savor the political arena to which it seeks to speak.

Second, we must not lose sight of the *legitimacy* of politics. The religious community, as well as the secular community, has tended to romanticize and optimize its assessments as to the "nature of man." It has also tended to romanticize and optimize its assessments as to what the political process itself involves.

Politics involves resolving conflicts between competing demands within society. Not just competing demands in the abstract, but competing demands as to how society's goods are going to be "allocated" – allocated in such a way that there are always "winners" and "losers." Altogether too often, religious communities fall into the trap of endorsing one set of values and demands without recognizing the legitimacy of competing sets of values and demands. Political justice involves allocations on behalf of *both* rich *and* poor, black *and* white, producer *and* consumer. Politics involves mediating the differences between competing demands – and such mediation seldom involves situations where political virtue is exclusively on just one side of the equation.

Christianity does not condemn the advocacy of interest, per se. Rather, it tells us to elevate our neighbor's interest to a degree of intensity with which we are prone to defend our own. Disdain for "interest group politics" or "special interests" reflects a lack of understanding pertaining to the inherent nature of the political process itself. To eliminate all organized political advocacy, for example, or to eliminate all PAC Committees, for example, would not change the fundamental nature of the political process. It would simply change the way in which demands are mediated.

Too often, religious groups enter the political arena with inherent disdain not only for the political process, but in opposition to the concept of politics, in itself. And once again, it reflects a yielding to the temptation to secularize the eschaton in the name of the Kingdom of God.

That is why I have titled this paper "Morality and Moralism: In Defense of Politics." For whatever transpires in our subsequent proceedings, my sincerest hope is that it takes place within the context of a Christian view of the human condition which avoids the temptation merely to invoke God's name as an "add on" to secular understandings of the human condition, and a moralistic attempt to "reform" the political order by decrying its very existence.

A Stickler

J. Dennis Hastert

My friendship with Paul started long before our terms in Congress. It goes back almost thirty years to the time when Paul and I were undergraduates together at Wheaton College in Illinois. When you go to a small school such as Wheaton you get to know each other well and those experiences are pressed into your memory. Paul was a year ahead of me in school, and he was the ROTC sergeant in my platoon. Already in college Paul was demonstrating his leadership abilities. He was a stickler for shiny shoes and clean rifles, and he was not hesitant to hand out demerits when they were necessary. He lived life like that. Paul was a stickler. He was a stickler for what was right, for what was good, for what was decent, for what was fair, and for the rights not just of his electorate, but of people all over this world: people who were downtrodden, people who needed help, and people who were too proud sometimes to reach out. When he came to Congress he was there to work for those causes. He was there to speak up for the people of Michigan's Fifth Congressional District. He was there to share everything he had.

Paul was in Wheaton's class of 1963. I was the class of 1964. And there was another fellow by the name of Dan Coats, former Senator from Indiana, who was in the class of 1965. We were kind of the Wheaton Mafia, in a sense. All three of us were in Washington, and I was the last to arrive. Paul represented Michigan, and of course I was there to represent Illinois. Being new to the world of Washington, I remember coming to him from time to time for advice. Naturally, one day, Paul and I got into a conversation about our families. I started questioning him: Is it better to leave our families back home in the district? Is it better to bring them out to Washington? These were tough questions for me as I began my Congressional career. He put his arm around me – I'm sure he still thought of me as a Wheaton undergraduate – and we had a talk about what was best for our families. We talked through the pros and cons. Because we shared similar values, his insight was invaluable. His support and friendship provided an enjoyable introduction to my first days in Congress.

Paul showed us what is good in a legislator, and he gave anyone involved in making laws a model to emulate. I remember one particular bill he pushed while in Congress. It was the national bottle bill, a waste reduction measure to establish a nationwide refund on beverage containers. The reason it still sticks in my mind is that he *made* it stick in my mind. Paul, dedicated to conserving our environment, worked and worked and worked on this bill. He would just pester you to death to sign on. He didn't give up. That's the way Paul was. He was very persistent – as well as very thoughtful – when it came to the issues he cared strongly about.

Both Paul and I, of course, were Republican members. When we were in Congress, the Democrats ran the House. Despite this, Paul still managed to be an effective legislator. Unfortunately, he never got to see the Republicans take over the House. I often think that Paul could have driven the House's education agenda. He had a lot of experience in this area. He was a former teacher as well as a past member of the Michigan Board of Education. In fact, teaching was common to both of us. Before entering politics I had taught government and history. It was quite fitting that Paul sat on the House's Committee on Education and Labor. He would have been a great example for us today.

One of Paul's role models was his father, a great theologian. He carried his influence with him always. You cannot separate a man from his religion, and Paul was no exception. Despite pressures – which can be many in Congress – he lived out his faith and convictions. Rather than back away from truth, he made it the backbone of his policy decisions. No wonder he was such a fighter. The foundation of his beliefs could not be stronger.

Paul Henry had an indelible impact on the House of Representatives. We will remember his words, his deeds, and his dedication. His voice will not go the way of so many others in the Capitol, voices that fade away after the lights go out. Paul will be around here for a long time – in his commitment to what he believed in, in the way he did his job, and in his dedication to people.

The Very Best of Friends

Fred S. Upton

In chapter four of his second letter to Timothy, Paul tells his good friend to be faithful and to learn from the way he has lived his life, saying, "I have fought the good fight, I have finished the race, I have kept the faith. Finally, there is laid up for me the crown of righteousness which the Lord will give me" (2 Timothy 4:7,8).

Paul Henry and I were the very best of friends. He was a thoughtful, honest, caring, intelligent, decent guy. He was also my mentor and confidant, a man who set a wonderful example for all of us in Congress. He never let Washington go to his head.

Congressmen Carl Pursell, Dave Camp, Paul, and I did almost everything together. We sat next to each other on the plane coming home to Michigan; we ate sometimes five or six meals a week together; we talked about legislative issues almost daily and cast literally thousands of votes together. I have to echo what House Republican Leader Bob Michel said – Paul Henry was the soul of our delegation, the soul of Congress.

His colleagues listened when Paul spoke, leading debates both in committee and on the House floor. He was a principled leader in every sense of the definition, invoking all the respect and love of his colleagues one could imagine possible. After his diagnosis, there wasn't a single day when at least a handful of members didn't stop me to inquire about his status – even freshmen.

Paul lived his faith and he never lost that faith or his wonderful sense of humor, even as he struggled in the last several months of his life.

Paul was a regular at the weekly prayer breakfast. As we shared life's struggles we developed an even stronger bond through the Bible. A favorite chapter, one that we both leaned on, was the twenty-third Psalm: "The Lord is my Shepherd, I shall not want." We'd help each other out by repeating those words to each other. In fact, sometimes we'd just smile at each other and signal or say, "two-three."

Many of you know that Paul's dad is a leading theologian. Paul had a calling too – for helping others. From his service in the Peace Corps, to his work as a congressional staffer, to professor, to elected official, Paul acted on his belief that public service is a sacred trust.

Paul never lost that perspective. As some say, once a staffer, always a staffer. No task was too small for Paul. All of his staff in the district and in D.C. reflected his deep caring and thoughtfulness for constituents and for each other. When Paul got the very rare, angry, constituent phone call it was standard practice for him to deal with it personally.

He was a tireless worker – both at home in Michigan and on Capitol Hill. In D.C. he'd work late, then come in the next morning at seven o'clock. Paul's personal touch on everything confirmed to all of us that he did his homework well.

Every weekend he spent at home in Grand Rapids with his family. Sundays, of course, were sacred. You'd see him at church in the morning, but after that, Sundays were always Karen and Paul days.

Paul was known for his ability to understand an issue and work with all sides to hammer out the winning formula that everyone knew was best. He won not with politics but with substance. He was always viewed as a rising star in Congress. The *National Journal* wrote that he was the kind of person who is well regarded even when people disagree with him.

Today there's a lot of cynicism about Congress. One of this country's leading columnists, David Broder, wrote specifically last year of Paul that he "represents the other side – the unpublicized side of politics and Congress. When people express their scorn for politicians and legislators, it tells me that we in the press have not done our job in depicting what the honorable men and women in those fields contribute through their service."

Those of us who want to make Congress better should look to the marker established by Paul. In public life one has to juggle legislative priorities as well as family responsibilities. Not everyone can honestly say he or she made a difference. Paul certainly could. He stuck by his convictions and altered the lives of many still to come. He had so many successes: work for the disabled, tax incentives to encourage savings for college, the National Institute of Health bill. And Paul was respected for his work on a national bottle bill and OSHA reform.

But as I said earlier, despite his tireless legislative efforts, Paul also kept his family priorities. I can remember a birthday or an anniversary that conflicted with a state GOP convention in Detroit. Even though Paul was the odds-on favorite to be the GOP candidate in the 1994 U.S. Senate race – Paul's priorities were right. He spent the weekend in Chicago with his wife Karen and even took in a Cubs game. And I remember one October when Paul's daughter Megan was part of the homecoming court at a Friday night football game. Paul, who had nearly a perfect voting record, missed Friday votes to fly home and surprise her, and then returned to D.C. for votes the next day. Paul had his priorities in the right place all the time.

Many members of Congress move their families to D.C. Paul kept his family home in Michigan, but he shared them with all of us, through the value he placed on them and the time he spent with them. As I've gotten to know the family better through Paul's struggle, I can see that his legacy will live on through Karen, Kara, Jordan, and Megan. Just as Paul had such a knack for the personal touch, his family, too, extends love and warmth to others. We still have Paul through them, and their touch shines like a rainbow.

Though his last illness was tough on Paul and his family, I know that he knew we all appreciated him. There were all the loving gestures: the wonderful nurses who brought him meals every day and even added a little extra ice cream when I showed up. The carrot cakes, flowers, and beautiful notes friends sent helped him as he walked "through the valley of the shadow of death" where he "fear(ed) no evil." And we know that "surely goodness and mercy shall follow (him)" now, where he "dwell(s) in the house of the Lord forever." (Psalm 23:4,6)

The *1986 Almanac of American Politics*, sometimes viewed as the Bible of Capitol Hill, summed up the potential of Paul's impressive intellect and solid electoral base after his first election like this: "The question is, to what use will a GOP of this stripe – and a junior member of minority party in the House – put it to?" The answer can again be found in the Bible, the *real* Bible, in Matthew 25:21: "Well done, good and faithful servant, well done."

Life will always seem too short, and when you really think about it, our lives do not give any of us a long time to make our mark. We do the best we can with our lives. Paul made the very best of his, and because of his life, all of us have a better chance to make the very best of ours. Because of his life, our world is truly a better place.

Giving Politics Its Due

David E. Price

Before Paul Henry's life and career were tragically cut short, he was widely recognized both as an insightful interpreter of evangelical Christianity's witness to the political order and as a gifted teacher of politics and proponent of political engagement within the evangelical community. The writings and talks gathered in this volume leave little doubt that his recognition was richly merited, even as they cause us to mourn the loss to both church and state inflicted by Henry's early death. I am honored to be asked to reflect briefly on his contribution to this realm of discourse and political action.

I served with Paul Henry in the House of Representatives from the 100th through the 102nd Congresses. Although I did not know him as well, or spend as much time with him as I would have liked, I felt a special kinship with him because of the similarity of our backgrounds and interests. We pursued similar academic courses: He came to Duke University to earn his doctorate in political science about the time I left North Carolina to pursue a similar course of study at Yale. Henry then went off to teach at Calvin College shortly before I returned to North Carolina to teach at Duke. He and I arrived at somewhat different points politically and philosophically, although not as different as our respective party labels might suggest. During the short time that I knew him, I came greatly to admire his forthrightness in thought and action, coupled with his willingness to listen and learn with great civility. He worked hard at relating his faith to the challenges of public life both in his academic career and during his time in elective office.

Henry's *Politics for Evangelicals* (1974), written soon after his arrival at Calvin College, made his convictions and insights available to a wide audience. The letters, speeches and articles from the 1970s and 1980s reprinted here, written during his years of full-time public service, extend his thought and provide some theological background. I will not attempt to offer anything approaching a comprehensive view, but I do want to comment on several characteristic emphases of Henry's that are pertinent to our ongoing struggle to relate the realms of faith and politics.

Henry repeatedly stressed that, for the Christian, simple withdrawal from the political order is not an option. Sensitive to the moral ambiguities of politics, he nonetheless insisted that withdrawal offered no escape from moral complicity: "The danger is that you will substitute a sin of omission for the sin of commission that you are trying to avoid.... You are creating a void that others are going to fill, and you are responsible for that void."[1]

Henry described himself as a "Baptist who is essentially Calvinist in theology," and he grounded his defense of political engagement in the Calvinist view of the state as an "ordinance" of creation – integral to human existence, "ordained in the structures of creation." To this he contrasted what he described as the Anabaptist view of the state as a "sustaining" ordinance – "a rescue device until redemption comes" – and the tendency of some fundamentalists to look at the state as an ordinance of "redemption" – trying "to use the state to usher in righteousness rather than simply to establish justice." "Fundamentalism seeks too much from the state," he concluded, "Anabaptism too little."[2]

This was Henry's suggestive way of dealing with what H. Richard Niebuhr termed the perennial "Christian perplexity" in relating Christianity and civilization. Niebuhr's classic work, *Christ and Culture*, sketched a "series of typical answers" given by Christian thinkers and practitioners in struggling with the paradox of God's immanence in and transcendence over creation. Niebuhr found in Calvin's thought elements of the dualistic view he attributed to Luther but ultimately categorized him as a proponent of the "conversionist" idea: Christ as the transformer of culture. "More than Luther he looks for the present permeation of all life by the gospel... [insisting] that the state is God's minister not only in a negative fashion as a restrainer of evil but positively in the promotion of welfare."[3]

This interpretation seems consistent with Henry's view. But Paul was acutely aware of the dualism that pulls evangelical Christians by virtue of the tension between their "moral absolutism" and their recognition of the compromises politics requires. "Politics involves mediating the differences between the competing demands – and such mediation seldom involves situations where political virtue is exclusively on just one side of the equation." The tension is often more than committed moralists can stand:

> Either they become political extremists seeking to impose their self-assured truths on society in the effort to establish the grand and final solution to social conflict, or they withdraw from political life because they refuse to taint themselves with compromise.[4]

Much of Henry's work is a brief for overcoming such antinomies, not by abandoning a transcendent view of morality or acceding to "value relativism," but by giving politics its dues as a divinely ordained instrument for human betterment and the pursuit of justice in a sinful world. Our Christian faith offers "insights and moral commitments" which help us go beyond, if not completely to transcend, the egoism of politics. It also offers "justification" to one who faithfully takes on the world's suffering and injustice – a reality that gave Paul Henry comfort in his own journey: "We must make our decisions before God. They won't all be perfect choices, but we must make the best choices we can, given our development as Christians... as we seek continually to put our hands into the hand of God and walk through life one step at time."[5]

Justification, however, is not sanctification. Being "justified by faith through Christ," Henry stressed, "does not mean that we are sanctified [in our political engagements]... or that we aren't subject to the same temptation as others are to use God's name in vain by rationalizing our wishes and attaching his name to it." Henry's counsel of "humility and restraint," partially based on a sense of the inherent limits of politics, was more profoundly rooted in his conviction of human sinfulness, "the fallenness and limitations of human nature to which our own religious teachings attest." Henry faulted both theological liberals and modern fundamentalists for sometimes pitching their battles in terms of "men vs. angels," forgetting that all political actors – themselves included – are "still affected by the human condition."

Henry's counsel of humility, like his call to engagement, continues to speak to our political situation, and in the context of faith, one cannot fully be understood without the other. Among American statesmen, it was Abraham Lincoln who perhaps understood this most profoundly. Recall the words of his second inaugural address, all the more remarkable for being uttered after almost four years of civil war:

> Both [sides] read the same Bible, and pray to the same God; and each invokes His aid against the other. It may seem strange that any men should dare to ask a just God's assistance in wringing their bread from the sweat of other men's faces; but let us judge not, that we be not judged. The prayers of both could not be answered – that of neither has been answered fully.

Reinhold Niebuhr once wrote that this passage "puts the relation of our moral commitments in history to our religious reservations about the partiality of our moral judgements more precisely than, I think, any statesman or theologian has put them."[7] Lincoln expressed the moral commitment against slavery in uncompromising terms, along with his determination to "finish the work we are in." But there followed the religious reservation, the recognition that ultimate judgment belonged to God alone, the refusal, even in this extreme instance, to presume an absolute identification between his own cause and God's will.

Paul Henry's political service is impressive not only by virtue of many of the causes he championed but also because of the intellectual and theological context within which he placed that service. He promoted scholarship and faithful reflection within the evangelical community in the conviction that its contribution to American political thought and practice could be greatly enhanced, and he proceeded through his own academic and political career to demonstrate the ways that might be accomplished.[8] We can still learn from him, and we are much in his debt.

NOTES

1. Paul B. Henry, "Reflections on Evangelical Christianity and Political Action," *Brethren in Christ History and Life*, 12:3 (December 1989), 275. See also *Politics for Evangelicals*, 71-72.

2. Henry, "Reflections," 268, 277.

3. H. Richard Niebuhr, *Christ and Culture* (New York: Harper and Brothers, 1951), 2, 217-18.

4. Paul B. Henry, "Morality vs. Moralism: In Defense of Politics," *Vital Speeches of the Day*, LV:10 (March 1, 1989), 297; *Politics for Evangelicals*, 70.

5. Henry, *Politics for Evangelicals*, 79; "Reflections," 281.

6. Henry, "Reflections," 277; *Politics for Evangelicals*, 79; "Morality," 297.

7. Quoted in William Lee Miller, "Lincoln's Second Inaugural: A Study in Political Ethics" (Bloomington, Ind.: The Poynter Center, 1980), 8. I am drawing here on Miller's

insightful exegesis. For a further discussion, see David E. Price, *The Congressional Experience*, 2nd ed. (Boulder, Co.: Westview Press, 2000), 215-18.

8. See Henry, "Reflections," 269-71, and *Politics for Evangelicals*, especially chapter two. For a recent brief by a sympathetic outsider, reminiscent in some ways of Henry's views, see Alan Wolfe, "The Opening of the Evangelical Mind," *The Atlantic Monthly*, 286 (October 2000), 55-76.

Conclusion

Paul Henry spent his adult life integrating Christianity and politics, a complex, demanding task. He often shared his thoughts with others, a happy fact that makes this volume possible. Paul repeatedly made two fundamental points: One, political action will never lead to a perfect society even if led by intelligent and well-meaning Christians; two, active involvement in American politics is a fully legitimate Christian activity. Weaving these two themes together in most of his writings, he developed and applied them in response to a variety of political and social events. Perhaps, with more time in life, he might have written a grand *summa* to guide those interested in the integration he came to.

Many of the personal essays included in this book give brief evaluations of Paul's thought and action. But analysis is not their major purpose, nor is it the goal of this conclusion. Rather, this concluding essay is intended as a beginning: to initiate a more informed conversation about Paul Henry's contribution to Christian political thought by highlighting five points of his thinking that put it in a larger context.

Intellectual Antecedents

The first important point to make about Paul's thought is its intellectual backdrop. Of course, merely living in the Carl F. H. Henry household steeped Paul in the knowledge and application of the Bible and evangelical theology. But Paul's writings on Christianity and politics rely on sources beyond those usually tapped by orthodox evangelicals. Many of these additional influences can be traced to his graduate years at Duke University, especially when Paul discusses the limits of Christian activity in politics.

Paul's masters thesis at Duke was "Eric Voegelin's Concept of the Gnosis," a sympathetic treatment of the thinker and his views. Voegelin was a political philosopher known most widely in America for *The New Science of Politics,* his 1952 University of Chicago Walgreen lectures. In them Voegelin argued that modern ideological movements such as communism and fascism repeated the gnostic heresy of early Christianity. Early Christian gnosticism separated a person's "spiritual" elements – claimed to be real – from his or her "material" parts – claimed to be unreal. Jesus was perfect because his spirit – his reason and motivation – was perfect. Gnostics believed humans who grasped this truth could also achieve perfection on earth and not have to wait for the eschaton.

Voegelin argued that in modern times gnosticism has become politicized. Politicized gnosticism asserts that personal and social perfection is possible. Such perfection, however, usually requires a few sages who understand the truths and who must sometimes rather ruthlessly and violently impose "perfection" on others. Both fascism and communism, according to Voegelin, are gnostic-like attempts to "immanentize the eschaton;" that is, to overcome the limitations, anxieties, and uncertainties of human experience for an enlightened vanguard to build a "heaven on earth" (wonderful theory, its implementation always goes astray). One destroys real democracy and politics in the process of imposing a "perfect" social vision.

Without mentioning Voegelin, Paul Henry applied that philosopher's critique to at least some politically conservative Christian political actions and actors. In *Morality vs. Moralism,* one of his later writings, Paul asserted that "(t)oo often, religious groups enter the political arena with inherent disdain not only for the political process, but in opposition to the concept of politics, in itself. And once again, it reflects a yielding to the temptation to secularize the eschaton in the name of the Kingdom of God."

Paul's other major thrust, his defense of the political sphere as worthy of Christian action, also relied upon thinkers whom he studied during his years at Duke. Paul's doctoral dissertation reviewed the various attitudes toward natural law held by Protestant theologians from Calvin and Luther at the Reformation through the likes of Paul Tillich and Rudolf Bultmann in the mid-twentieth century. Paul grappled with questions such as the extent to which natural law conforms to God's divine law, the breadth of common grace, the distinctions between natural law and "laws of nature," and how much weight to give general and special revelation. Paul favorably comments on theologians who assert that common grace and general revelation are quite expansive and accessible to secular thinkers.

His generous reading of grace and revelation led Paul to several important conclusions about politics. For example, it allowed him to argue for the American political system's compatibility with Christian principles without requiring America's founders to have a firm or self-consciously Christian worldview. Paul could see God's providential hand in the American founding; yet avoid claims that America is God's chosen nation, or other elements of American civil religion. And to Christian critics of the American system Paul could respond that, through God's working at the founding, the system is at least "good enough" for Christian political involvement. Thus Paul urged Christians to get involved in American politics because the system is already suitable, not because Christians bring special insight to public policy or political action.

Paul's position on grace and revelation are directly related to his view that all humans are made in God's image. Unlike many other Christian intellectuals, Paul believed that one does not reflect God's image better *merely* if one is a believer in Christ; one's reasoning ability, especially, is not necessarily improved. In fact, he argued, applying Christian thought to the political sphere might do more harm than good, because deep Christian faith often is used to excuse poor political thinking.

Relationship to Reformed Christianity

The second important consideration for anyone examining Paul's political thought is to compare his views to characteristic Reformed Christian views about religion and politics. Paul rightly claimed that his views were in that tradition, and he openly claimed allegiance to it, distinguishing his views from Anabaptist and Fundamentalist traditions in "Reflections on Evangelical Christianity and Political Action."

Paul agreed with the Reformed tradition's expansive view of creation. In this view, creation extends beyond the material world to "orders of life," which include political and social systems. This expansive view is critical to Paul's defense of politics, because politics then becomes one of many spheres that God in God's providence uses. And the use is not merely negative – to restrain evil by instituting order – but positive – to advance good by promoting justice. To those Reformed Christian critics who don't like the compromise that politics demands, Paul stayed truer than his critics did to Reformed doctrine. He admitted that compromise is part of politics. But, he quickly added, in a fallen world compromise is part of every social interaction. Why should politics be held to a higher standard?

Paul's wide berth to general revelation put his views outside the mainstream of Reformed thinking, but not entirely outside the tradition. Here his writing is at odds with some Reformed Christian thinkers who criticize America's complicated system of separated powers, federalism, and unprincipled political parties. Mixed with his skepticism about the unique power of Christian reason, Paul's views on revelation and grace allowed him to reject as unnecessary and unrealistic some of the strict Calvinist notions for political reform, such as proportional representation or Christian political parties.

There are additional aspects of Paul's thought that, though they are not shared by most Reformed Christian writers, do not disqualify him from being considered Reformed. First, Paul was skeptical of the "transformational" language common in some Reformed discussions. While he embraced the point that Christians have a special calling to be involved in political institutions and processes, he did not see much need for their transformation and often regarded such language as arrogant and reckless.

Finally, Paul's political agenda was a bit different from that of many Christians. He thought organized Christian political action too often rested at one political extreme or the other. Theologically orthodox and evangelical, and so in that way conservative, Paul argued that conservative theology should not immediately translate into conservative politics. Faithful scriptural interpretation would highlight issues such as racial reconciliation and poverty, not common on the conservative agenda. On the other hand, for Paul these "issues of the left" would not necessarily lend themselves to solutions proposed by a left that is too optimistic about changing human nature through politics.

The Nature of Politics

A third important consideration for understanding Paul's thought is his view of the essential nature of politics and government. Paul appeared to accept the pluralistic definition of politics common in traditional political science. His politics is procedural and allocative, not quite value-neutral but certainly not value-centered. Paul's favorite definition of politics was Harold Lasswell's, who described politics as the process of deciding "who gets what, how, when, and where." In a few places Paul expressed a more value-oriented view of politics, defining it as "the authoritative allocation of values and resources for all society." But Paul used the term values differently from those who want to use politics to reinforce particular social values. For him, values referred back to resource allocation. By mentioning it, Paul was merely noting that all decision-makers bring their own personal (including religious) values to bear on decisions about allocating resources. While these values would clash in some allocation decisions, such as government funding of abortion, it was not right to immediately assume Christian values should control such decisions. Rather, Christian values help improve the allocation process, but do not change the fact that resources must somehow be allocated to all claimants.

At times Paul even seemed to exclude moral questions from political discussion. In *Moralism vs. Morality*, for example, Paul implied that a necessary requirement for a question to be deemed political is that it is "amenable to resolution through governmental policy," hardly a description of many issues advanced by the extremes of right and left.

Paul was no supply-sider on economics or movement conservative on social issues, even as these two trends came to dominate his Republican Party. On economic and fiscal policy Paul was very much a "balanced budget" Republican, willing to cut spending on defense and social programs and perhaps even raise taxes to balance the government's budget. And while Paul shared social policy views of many movement conservatives, he spent the bulk of his time tending to the material concerns of his congressional district rather than the moral agenda of conservative religious leaders.

Paul applied his pluralistic definition of politics to the work of Christian elected officials. Such officials, he argued, have an obligation to represent the views of all their constituents – Christian and non-Christian, supporters and opponents. In "Moralism vs. Morality" he stated, "Christianity does not condemn the advocacy of interest per se. Rather, it tells us to take up our neighbor's interest with the same intensity that we defend our own. Disdain for 'interest-group politics' or 'special interests' reflects a lack of understanding of the inherent nature of the political process."

For Paul Henry the political task for the Christian elected official is to "perfect pluralism," to ensure one faithfully represents the needs and concerns of one's neighbors. This will sometimes mean sacrificing one's own sense of what is appropriate to advance different views strongly held by one's constituents. The closing lines of "Strategies for Political

Action" should be understood in that context: "The Christian who enters politics learns to make the needs of his neighbor his own. In doing so, his search for justice becomes an act of sacrificial love."

Paul's support for the American political system, his discomfort with moral issues, and his pluralistic view of politics are logically connected. Paul trusted that the broad outlines of history followed God's providential intent, and that these outlines included the American system of government and style of politics. Christians and non-Christians alike should promote their own ideas of justice within our pluralistic system, which is adequately structured to reconcile these competing claims. If Christians faithfully carried out their political roles and obligations, their faithfulness would be honored with a public order that provided imperfect but sufficient justice for individuals, groups, and society as a whole.

CONSISTENCY

A fourth point important for understanding Paul Henry's thought it to see it as a whole. On first impression one might easily conclude that Paul became more politically conservative over time. His earlier writings urge evangelicals to pursue a fairly specific Christian agenda, similar to that proposed at the time by the liberal wing of the Democratic Party. His later writings, on the other hand, seem to argue that it is impossible to know the Christian position on any particular issue, or even to know what issues should compose a Christian agenda.

A closer examination, however, finds that Paul was quite consistent in his basic objectives. First, the context of Paul's writings changed far more than his basic premises. The earlier writings lay out a positive agenda for politically reluctant evangelicals, urging them to combat poverty, racism, and the causes of war. These issues demanded concern about social morality, not just individual morality, and required long-term dedication to solving complex and difficult social evils. Paul's call to engagement in these early writings is mixed with criticism of evangelical individualism which allowed it to ignore and misdiagnose these social ills that Paul believed were critical to the evangelical political task.

Paul's later writings came after the explosion of evangelical political engagement that focused on abortion, an issue that reinforced the very individualistic worldview Paul had criticized so strongly. While Paul agreed with the newly active evangelicals on abortion, he was dismayed that their focus on the issue (and similar issues such as homosexuality and school prayer) reinforced an individualism that inhibited effective political engagement on important structural issues. Simultaneously, Paul was frustrated with politically moderate and progressive evangelicals, mostly in the Anabaptist tradition, who held policy positions close to Paul's own but whose theological views blocked direct political engagement. Caught in these twin frustrations, Paul emphasized that mixing Christianity and politics did not *necessarily* lead to the kind of Christian political engagement that was everywhere around; rather, faithful Christian politics would manifest itself in a variety of ways.

Also one must note the change in Paul's personal situation. At Calvin College, Paul could exercise a great deal of academic freedom. Rooted in a deep and intellectually developed faith, he could range widely and freely in his early discussions of the interplay between Christianity and politics.

In his later writings, however, Paul seems ever mindful of his public position. He knew his once-uttered thoughts would never be "off the record" nor immune from distortion. In these later writings, Paul never completely leaves his job as a representative; indeed, his position becomes engrained in his thinking. In these writings politics becomes even more pluralistic, almost completely defined by the clanging competition one finds in campaigning and lawmaking. So in his later work Paul does not fill in the details of the broad outline of Christian politics he developed earlier at Calvin, frustrating both his friends and opponents. Rather, he presents a more narrowly focused commentary on the proper role of a Christian elected representative.

TOO MUCH HUMILITY?

It is unfortunate that Paul's original works only sometimes reveal his personality. Paul Henry was an extremely enjoyable person to be around. He had a sharp and self-deprecating wit, a warm and charismatic personality, and a humility that is rare among politicians. Fortunately the essays by Paul's friends relate many instances where these characteristics shone through.

Paul's personality, especially his humility, directly affected his political thought, and is the fifth important consideration in understanding his work. One looks in vain for bold assertions about the "true end" of politics, expositions on the ideal political system, sweeping solutions to chronic problems, or overly confident assessments of politics and policy. In the place of such self-assured pronouncements are calls for humility about the ends and means of the political process. As he states in "Getting Involved in Politics:"

> We cannot simply reduce the Christian message to some sort of religious party platform from which incontrovertible political specifics can be drawn. The Bible and the teachings of the Christian community point to broad principles which we dare not neglect in our Christian witness to society. But we must guard against the temptation to exploit those principles on behalf of particular applications when other equally plausible affirmations of Christian conscience can be drawn from them. We must avoid the temptation to manipulate or exploit Christian conscience on behalf of hidden agendas, thereby using God rather than being used by God. One cannot simply deduce political particulars from the transcendent truths of God's revelation in Jesus Christ and the Scriptures.

Paul Henry's politics is a struggle open to all persons of good will. Respect for the pluralism of religious belief and unbelief is at its core. Respect for others forces Christians to reflect appropriate humility about their own knowledge and reason, a humility that should (but often does not) follow from their understandings of sin and salvation. To counter the natural tendencies of superiority to which they are not immune, Christians in public office must constantly acknowledge and critically engage their motivations and their arguments to ensure that their views are not overly elevated and the views of opponents not overly discounted. As Paul wrote:

> We must be mindful of the principles of civility, tolerance, and civil rights, which God ordains to be enjoyed by all. We dare not abuse the norms of justice in the pursuit of justice, lest the means employed undermine the ends pursued. Above all, Christian conduct in the public order ought to be marked by sensitivity toward those outside the Christian community who may disagree with us at the most fundamental level, as well as sensitivity to those within the Christian community who may disagree with us at the practical level.

Paul Henry possessed a real, and perhaps too great, humility about his ability to clearly see and communicate a comprehensive Christian vision for politics. No crusader, he was, instead, a servant of the real but ambiguous claims of justice. May all Christians seeking political justice find instruction in his life.

About the Paul B. Henry Institute

The Paul B. Henry Institute for the Study of Christianity and Politics was established in September 1997 at Calvin College in honor of the late U.S. congressman Paul Henry. Paul taught at Calvin College in Grand Rapids, Michigan, in the 1970s before beginning an auspicious career in public service. After serving on the Michigan Board of Education and the Michigan House and Senate, Henry was elected to the U.S. House of Representatives in 1984. He served there until his untimely death in 1993, at age 51, of brain cancer.

In both his academic and public life, Paul, son of evangelical theologian Carl F. H. Henry, was a leader of Christian vision and action. Known as a person of conviction, credibility and courage, his academic and political careers were characterized by a constant search for justice, providing powerful evidence that politicians may be principled and effective. The Paul Henry Institute was established by the generous contributions of Paul's friends and colleagues to continue his quest to promote serious reflection on the interplay between Christianity and public life.

The Henry Institute fosters this work by providing resources for scholarship, structuring opportunities to disseminate scholarly work, seeking avenues to communicate and promote such efforts to the larger public, and training and motivating future scholars to engage in such study. The Institute undertakes a number of activities including:

- *national conferences* on critical topics dealing with the interplay between Christian faith and political thought and action
- *collaborative research projects* with faculty and institutions within and beyond the Calvin community
- *graduate and undergraduate courses and seminars* on topics in which Institute staff has special expertise
- *summer research fellowships* for graduate and undergraduate students to promote the scholarly study of the interplay between Christianity and politics
- *an informational and data center,* serving as a national resource for scholars, journalists, and others engaged in the study of Christianity and politics
- *the annual Paul B. Henry Lecture*, featuring a Christian who has served or is serving with distinction in public life.

Corwin Smidt, Professor of Political Science, holds the Paul B. Henry Chair in Christianity and Politics, and is executive director of the Institute. Douglas Koopman, Associate Professor of Political Science, is the Institute's program director. The Henry Institute can be reached at 616/957-6870 and through e-mail at henry@calvin.edu. Its world wide web site is www.calvin.edu/henry.